VIRGINIA BEER

VIRGINIA
Beer

a guide from
COLONIAL DAYS
to
CRAFT'S
GOLDEN AGE

....

LEE GRAVES

UNIVERSITY OF VIRGINIA PRESS

Charlottesville and London

30886 8015
R

University of Virginia Press

© 2018 Lee Graves

Printed in the United States of America on acid-free paper

First published 2018

1 3 5 7 9 8 6 4 2

Library of Congress Cataloging-in-Publication Data
Names: Graves, Lee, 1948– author.
Title: Virginia beer : a guide from colonial days to craft's golden age /
Lee Graves.
Description: Charlottesville : University of Virginia Press, 2018. | Includes
bibliographical references and index.
Identifiers: LCCN 2018024173 | ISBN 9780813941714 (pbk. : alk. paper) |
ISBN 9780813941721 (ebook)
Subjects: LCSH: Beer—Virginia—History.
Classification: LCC TP573.U6 G723 2018 | DDC 641.2/309755—dc23
LC record available at https://lccn.loc.gov/2018024173

All photographs are by the author, save for the following: page 21, photo
reproduction courtesy of Chris Johnson; page 22, courtesy of Portner
Brewhouse; page 62, courtesy of Charlie Papazian; second color plate (first
page of gallery), Valentine Richmond History Center.
Map by Nat Case, INCase, LLC.

Cover art based on Blue Ridge Parkway autumn sunset over Appalachian
Mountains layers (*background;* WerksMedia) and beer texture (*top;* Pogonici)

To Marggie and Les, for their love, support, and friendship

Contents

Preface

Remember this moment: 6 P.M. sharp on Friday, September 8, 2017. That's when I stop by Bedlam Brewing, one of several businesses in an otherwise nondescript strip on Augusta Avenue in Staunton, to mentally kick up my heels and draw a line to end one of the most incredible adventures of my life.

Bedlam is the 150th brewery I've visited in Virginia. That's out of 213, with 30 in planning, according to an August 2017 announcement at the Virginia Craft Brewers Fest in Charlottesville. Five years ago, the number of breweries stood around 40, and now, while I'm settling down in a seat at the bar and looking at the offerings at Bedlam, the Old Dominion has more breweries than any other state in the Southeast. North Carolina, with heavy hitters such as Oskar Blues, Sierra Nevada, and New Belgium, not to mention Asheville's thriving array of small breweries, had been the headliner of the East Coast beer scene. Now Virginia gets at least a share of the spotlight.

New breweries are opening throughout the state every weekend. As I sit in Bedlam, Reason opens its taproom in Charlottesville tomorrow. Intermission opened in Richmond last week. Beer events crowd the calendar as well. Stone celebrates its one-year anniversary of brewing in Richmond with a Throw Down tomorrow. A huge Battle of the Beers will be waged in Virginia Beach tomorrow, just as Basic City hosts the Virginia Street Art Festival in Waynesboro.

Paint the sunset. Take a photograph of a river. They are frozen moments trying to capture fluidity, change, and dynamic energy. This is what this book aims to do—portray, convey, and give context to the shifting and evolving landscape of beer and its story in Virginia, from the colonists who landed at Jamestown—carrying with them attitudes about beer dating to the dawn of civilization—to brewers such as Bedlam's Mike McMackin, whose appreciation of the art, science, and history of his craft extends the story one generation more.

I couldn't ask for a better place and time to freeze the frame and celebrate the journey that's taken me here. McMackin is a natural publican. Details of the beers flow from him as if each were a child. The Farmhouse Ale is not a saison but a "pay beer," he says, as workers were paid in beer in the part of Belgium that is the brew's heritage. The DIPA is hopped with Centennial, Cascade, Columbus, and Simcoe varietals. The numbers say it's rated at 100 IBUs, but perceived bitterness is lower. "I get it at 85," he says. And none of the beers has a clever name or personal reference—no puns, no homages to pets, no local ties. DIPA is just DIPA. "Nothing is named, because I'm always tweaking them."

The brewery's name does have a story. Bedlam was a nineteenth-century insane asylum in London, and you can understand the connection. A former high school history teacher, McMackin left a salaried job to realize his passion for brewing. "I've been homebrewing for more than twenty years," he says. "I left a full-time, salaried job. I must be crazy." Setting up the brewery, the taproom, and the pizza oven; getting label approvals; dialing in his one-barrel system; establishing a presence in the industry's explosive growth—it's easy to understand Bedlam's motto: "Embrace the chaos."

I feel an affinity for his outlook. Tracking the history and evolution of Virginia beer; witnessing how craft beer has affected a cultural shift in society's perspective of this ancient beverage; keeping up to speed on newbies; trying the latest releases; reading about technological advances; writing about people and their stories, their creativity, their challenges and achievements—throughout my journey I've experienced a touch of chaos as well. But my personal beer trail has gone from the mountaintop setting of Dirt Farm to the urban swirl of Big Lick, from Tidewater's Wasserhund, where surfboards hang from the ceilings, to Richmond's The Veil, where the ceiling opens to welcome wild yeast. I've tasted hundreds of beers and met scores of friendly, dedicated people who believe in the spirit of community.

McMackin, a New York native, says something along those lines that heartens me, something that has been a constant among brewers since I began writing about beer in 1996. "This business is fantastic," he says. "When somebody calls somebody else needing something, nine times out of ten they're not blowing smoke. Sure it's competitive, but if they need help, you help them." That spirit of collaboration and collegiality has been a defining characteristic of brewers and true beer aficionados. I've been blessed to be a part of it.

So even though I draw the line at 6 P.M. on September 8, 2017, and click the shutter for a snapshot, the current of events will keep flowing beyond the pages of this book. New breweries will open; some older ones will close. Trends will come and go. But one thing's for sure: Beer will always be here.

Method and Madness

My method for choosing which breweries to profile in chapters 5 through 12 is simple—I had none. It would have been impossible to profile each of the 213 breweries that existed when I visited number 150. (For candor's sake, I did visit a couple more breweries before adding the final words to the manuscript—and I'll never stop exploring—but in terms of current events, that was where I had to draw the line in order to complete the work for timely publication. That said, the attentive reader will notice updates of major developments.) Some breweries were obvious choices to spotlight because of their veteran status, their size, their stature in the community, and their prominence in the larger industry. Others appealed because of their individual stories. I also tried to be evenhanded in representing each region by targeting different pockets within each area and by profiling breweries that aren't mentioned in the text or pictured in the photographs elsewhere in the book. Virginia is not a small state, and many breweries draw on local history for beer names, so capturing regional flavor became a challenge for me. I wanted to portray the state's "tastes of places" in as many ways as possible. And after visiting 150 breweries and tasting beers at each, I believe that the overall standard of brewing in Virginia is high.

Another point to keep in mind: I have tasted the beers singled out in the **Try this** recommendations at the end of each brewery profile. And though I've attempted to vary recommendations beyond the IPAs that dominate the market, hoppy styles represent the niche and the mastery of some breweries.

Finally, a confession: I am not a foodie. Six days out of seven I have a PB&J sandwich for lunch. As a result—and because I had my nose broken twice while playing football in high school—my palate is not as sophisticated as I'd like it to be or as finely calibrated as many of those in the food and beverage field. My philosophy is that beer and food can be enjoyable at any and every level of sophistication, and that subjective judgments have objective limits.

And I hope that's the way this book comes across—as something that appeals whether you're a Certified Cicerone® or someone who is just curious about beer. If you come away with a deeper appreciation of this ancient beverage, the golden age we're experiencing, and the people who love, brew, and consume beer, then Mike McMackin and I will join you in a toast to good times and great beers.

Acknowledgments

This book would not have been possible without the support and help of many individuals and organizations, but two in particular deserve special thanks—Marggie, who has edited nearly every word you'll read (not to mention countless galaxies of verbiage I have spewed in the past), and my best friend, Les Strachan, who continues to play the role he has occupied for four-plus decades, sharing good times and great beers. I credit his love of flavorful beer with igniting my passion many years ago.

I want to acknowledge the folks at University of Virginia Press, particularly my acquisitions editor, Boyd Zenner, and Mark Mones, my hands-on editor, for their help in completing the book. And I'm indebted to Jay Burnham, my cohost on the RVA Beer Show, WRIR-FM 97.3, for keeping me on my toes about all things beer in Virginia.

The research I did for my previous two books about beer in Richmond and Charlottesville informed this project, and several people who played key roles in those endeavors deserve thanks here as well. Lucia "Cinder" Stanton, former director of research at Monticello and author of several books, including *Free Some Day: The African-American Families of Monticello* and *"Those Who Labor for My Happiness": Slavery at Thomas Jefferson's Monticello*, was gracious in sharing resources for the Charlottesville book and this work. Her friendship and scholarship inspire me. Two other professional historians—Mike Gorman and Eric Mink—have been sidekicks in learning about beer's past and sharing the fruits of the current craft boom.

The Virginia Historical Society has been instrumental in shining the spotlight on beer history in Virginia. The inaugural BrewHaHa in August 2017, which I was fortunate to have a hand in, proved a great success. Several individuals—Greg Hansard, Paige Newman, Jamison Davis, and VHS President Jamie Bosket—have been helpful to me personally and to the greater cause of beer history. Other organizations and people that have played key roles include The Valentine, particularly Kelly Kerney; the Library of Virginia, particularly Carl Childs; the Richmond Public Library; the National Park Service; the Thomas Jefferson Foundation at Monticello; the Albemarle Historical Society; the Smithsonian Institution; the Library of Congress, particularly its *Chronicling Virginia* website; the National Archives; the Virginia Beer Museum, particularly David Downes; the Albert and Shirley Small Special Collections Library at the University of Virginia; and the Virginia Craft Brewers Guild, particularly Brett Vassey of the Virginia Manufacturers Association. A special nod goes to Frank Clark, master of historic foodways for the Colonial Williamsburg Foundation, for his many years of scholarship and his ongoing leadership in the realm of beer and food history. The "Ales Through the Ages" conference that Clark hosted in Williamsburg in 2016 created a groundswell of excitement among beer geeks.

On a national level, the Brewers Association, based in Boulder, Colorado, has been an invaluable resource for data about craft brewing and trends in the industry. Julia Herz (its craft beer program director), Bart Watson (its chief economist), and Charlie Papazian (its founder and past president) have been tremendous not only for their knowledge and resources but for their friendliness and accessibility.

I would be remiss if I didn't acknowledge the role that former governor Terry McAuliffe has played in spreading good will (including a bit of taxpayer money) and creating a fertile environment for the growth of the craft beer industry in Virginia. I think I've got him beat in the number of breweries visited, but we're both still adding to the score.

Finally, I owe a tremendous debt to the brewers, the brewery owners, the brewery reps, the distributors, the homebrewers, my sisters and brothers in the beer-writing community, the taproom owners, the taproom personnel, the beer lovers, and the beer readers. The beer community in Virginia is a special group; I'm honored to be a part of it.

Thanks to all!

VIRGINIA BEER

Virginia's
BREWERIES AND BREWPUBS

See appendix B (pages 287–311) for full listings (including addresses, websites, and contact information)

Inner Northern Virginia
1. Chantilly: Honor, Mustang Sally, Ono
2. Reston: Lake Anne
3. Herndon: Aslin
4. Vienna: Caboose
5. McLean: Gordon Biersch
6. Arlington: Heritage, New District
7. Falls Church: Mad Fox, Sweetwater Tavern
8. Alexandria: Hops Grill, Port City, Portner
9. Lorton: Fair Winds, Forge
10. Manassas: BadWolf, Heritage, 2Silos
11. Centreville: Sweetwater Tavern

Loudoun County
12. Bluemont: Dirt Farm
13. Round Hill: B Chord
14. Purcellville: Adroit Theory, Belly Love, Jack's Run, Old 690
15. Leesburg: Barnhouse, Black Hoof, Black Walnut, Crooked Run, Dog Money, Loudoun, MacDowell Brew Kitchen, Vanish
16. Ashburn: Lost Rhino, Old Ox
17. Sterling: Beltway, Crooked Run, Sweetwater Tavern, Twinpanzee
18. Dulles: Ocelot, Solace
19. Aldie: Quattro Goomba's

Outer Northern Virginia
20. Gainesville: Tin Cannon
21. Broad Run: Farm Brewery

22. Delaplane: Barrel Oak
23. Vint Hill: Old Bust Head
24. Warrenton: Wort Hog
25. Sperryville: Hopkins Ordinary, Pen Druid
26. Brandy Station: Old Trade
27. Culpeper: Beer Hound, Fär Göhn
28. Midland: Powers Farm
29. Lake Ridge: Water's End
30. Woodbridge: Brew Republic, Growling Bear
31. Stafford: Adventure, Wild Run
32. Colonial Beach: Colonial Beach
33. Montross: Montross
34. Fredericksburg: Adventure, Battlefield, Highmark, Maltese, Red Dragon, 6 Bears and a Goat, Spencer Devon, Strangeways
35. Spotsylvania: 1781

Richmond Region
36. Ashland: Center of the Universe
37. Glen Allen: Intermission
38. Rockville: Midnight
39. Goochland: Kindred Spirit, Lickinghole Creek
40. Powhatan: Fine Creek
41. Midlothian: Extra Billy's, Steam Bell
42. Richmond: The Answer Brewpub, Ardent, Canon and Draw, Castleburg, Champion, Final Gravity, Garden Grove, Hardywood, Isley, Legend, Rock Bottom,

Stone, Strangeways, Three Notch'd, Triple Crossing, Väsen, The Veil
43. Petersburg: Ammo, Trapezium

Eastern Virginia
44. Williamsburg: Alewerks, Anheuser-Busch, Brass Cannon, Virginia Beer Company
45. Newport News: Hilton Tavern, Tradition
46. Hampton: Bull Island, St. George
47. Fort Monroe: Oozlefinch
48. Norfolk: Bearded Bird, Benchtop, Bold Mariner, Coelacanth, O'Connor, Rip Rap, Smartmouth
49. Portsmouth: Legend, MoMac
50. Cape Charles: Cape Charles
51. Chincoteague Island: Black Narrows
52. Virginia Beach: Back Bay, Commonwealth, Deadline, Home Republic Brewpub, Pleasure House, Reaver Beach, Smartmouth, Wasserhund, Young Veterans
53. Chesapeake: Big Ugly
54. Smithfield: Wharf Hill

Central Virginia
55. Farmville: Third Street
56. Palmyra: Antioch
57. Scottsville: James River

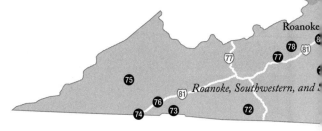

Roanoke

Roanoke, Southwestern, and S

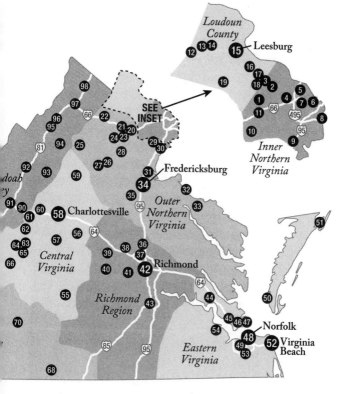

CHAPTER 1

An Ancient Beverage Endures

In one sense, the history of beer in Virginia begins on a muggy day in May 2012, when Hardywood Park Craft Brewery in Richmond hosted a gathering of brewers, elected officials, and industry representatives. The atmosphere was formal but festive, and the bready-sweet smell of beer-in-the-making seemed appropriate for the task at hand—signing a bill that would forever change the landscape of brewing in the state.

In another sense, the history of beer in the Old Dominion can be traced to May 1607, when three ships carrying 104 passengers and 39 crew members weighed anchor off a site they would name Jamestown. The cargo included beer, a staple that provided nourishment and sustenance for Englishmen accustomed to viewing water as unfit to drink.

In the broadest sense, the history of beer reaches back to the dawn of civilization. Records of brewing exist in Sumer, Egypt, and other ancient cultures. Workers were paid with rations of beer; pharaohs required beer for their journey to the afterlife; bad brewers met with harsh penalties; and myths celebrated the power of beer to sustain life.

Why does such a simple drink—traditionally composed of just water, grain, hops, and yeast—play such a fundamental role in human history? The simplicity of ingredients belies the complexity of its impact. Be it beer's function as a social lubricant, an economic engine, a nutritional necessity, a sophisticated complement to fine foods, or a tasty relaxant after a tough day, beer endures. Even in America's failed attempt to prohibit the consumption of alcoholic beverages, beer and other "ardent spirits" found their way around the law and into glasses of thirsty consumers.

"Beer is proof that God loves us and wants us to be happy." That often-cited saying is commonly attributed to Benjamin Franklin. It echoes a similar statement from over four thousand years ago: "The mouth of a perfectly contented man is filled with beer." Such sentiments resound in various forms through history. Consider the reference to beer in the *Epic of Gilgamesh,* composed around 2700 BCE, and its advice to Enkidu, a wild man, in adopting the ways of men:

> "Eat the food, Enkidu, it is the way one lives.
> Drink the beer, as is the custom of the land."
> Enkidu ate the food until he was sated,
> He drank the beer—seven jugs! and became expansive
>   and sang with joy!

Tracing the roots of this beverage of happiness and joy has led some historians to suggest that beer arose by accident shortly after humans discovered baking. Bread, made from the same grains as beer, might have been left outside, where rain would have activated the yeast and turned a sodden loaf into a slurpy delight. While wheat was better for bread, barley suited beer, and records show numerous efforts to cultivate this grain for alcoholic beverages. Babylonians drank beer through straws to keep from ingesting the porridge-like mix that brewing created. Gods and goddesses alike drank beer, often to excess, and the Sumerians created a hymn to Ninkasi, their goddess of brewing, that mixed praise of the deity with details of the brewing process.

In addition to inducing that haze of happiness, beer

had properties that made it a staple for centuries to come. It was a healthful beverage, loaded with vitamins and nutrients—hence one of its nicknames, "liquid bread." And making beer required the water to be boiled. Back when rivers and streets flowed with waste and filth, water was generally considered unfit to drink. So beer evolved as a staple to quench thirst and supplement the diet.

Such was the case when bands of English adventurers came to the New World. The first attempts to establish a permanent settlement were in the Outer Banks of North Carolina, considered "Virginia" then. The Native Americans they encountered were somewhat of an exception to the history of beer, for there are no records or indications that they developed intoxicating beverages. Tribes in other parts of North America—specifically in what is now New Mexico, Arizona, and northern Mexico—brewed a weak corn beer called *tiswin,* but the mid-Atlantic was a beer desert.

That did not deter the Englishmen. Thomas Hariot wrote in 1587 of a grain the inhabitants called *pagatowr,* which we know as maize or corn: "Wee made of the same in the countrey some mault, whereof was brued as good ale as was to be desired." Some historians eye this with skepticism, arguing that Hariot was putting a positive spin on brewing to attract and please investors.

Multiple efforts to settle in the Outer Banks failed, however. Theories about the Lost Colony of Roanoke Island, which was found abandoned in 1590 with the word "Croatan" carved into a post, still intrigue researchers. The only certainty is that another effort would be needed to establish a colony, which spurred the formation of the Virginia Company of London in 1606.

Beer would be needed to succeed, and the three ships that arrived off Jamestown on May 13, 1607, carried this necessity. It not only served the colonists but also proved helpful in establishing relations with indigenous inhabitants. Shortly after arriving, Captain John Smith, Christopher Newport, and a band of marines probed up the James River to its fall line, by the site of present-day Richmond. There, they joined the local Powhatans in a village overlooking the river for a feast that included "beere, Aquavitae [brandy], and sack [wine]." The mixture of beverages was so potent that Parahunt, son of the powerful Chief Powhatan, complained of feeling "very sick."

Actually, the beer drunk by the masses in those days was a low-alcohol version called small beer—2 to 3 percent alcohol by volume—that resulted from a technique then common among brewers. They used the same grains for repeated mashings, like using the same coffee grounds for multiple brews, so each run resulted in beer that was less potent and more suited for simple thirst-quenching. And thirst was definitely an issue in Jamestown. The settlers' fear of drinking the water, combined with the steamy, swampy conditions at the settlement, made beer disappear quickly. To complicate matters, the company had neglected to send along brewers, one of many signs that the effort was poorly planned and ill-provisioned.

The summer of 1607 tested the colonists with withering heat and humidity. Foul water and poor diet, exacerbated by lack of beer, paved the way for disease, from scurvy to beriberi. The death toll mounted—forty-eight by September, and another twenty-eight by January.

Hardship continued until 1609, when ships laden with fresh supplies met colonists already under sail to abandon Jamestown. Disaster was averted, and in the same year the colony's governor, Sir Francis Wyatt, approved an advertisement in London for two brewers to join the settlement. The Second Virginia Charter of 1609 indeed lists two such tradesmen among its ranks, John Reynold and Jame Duppa (spellings vary). The latter seems to have enjoyed a dubious reputation once at Jamestown, as shown by this complaint from one of the colony's inhabitants:

"I would you could hang that villain Duppe who by his stinking beer hath poisoned . . . the colony."

Perhaps that explains why several years later, in 1621, records show that two new brewers of French Wallonian background—Jacques de Lecheilles and Pierre Quesnee—signed up for the voyage to the New World.

Brewing and the cultivation of barley were already under way in Jamestown by 1620. So important was beer that in their session of 1623–24, the colony's fathers recommended that all arriving newcomers should bring a supply of malt to be used in brewing. As before, maize helped keep brew kettles bubbling, as Smith noted: "For drinke, some malt the Indian corne, others barley, of which they make good ale, both strong and small." An Episcopal priest, the Reverend George Thorpe, even crowed that the corn beer was "much better than British ale," but by any measure it was preferred to the water. "For as strong beer in England doth fatten and strengthen them, so water here doth wash and weaken these here," one indentured servant wrote home in 1623.

Two brew houses operated before 1625, and that number grew as the colony expanded and the wilderness receded. According to a 1907 analysis of the economy of seventeenth-century Virginia, "In some places, beer was, about the middle of the century, the most popular of all the liquors drunk in the colony, the great proportion of it being brewed at this time in the houses of the planters," and "[w]ith the progress of time, the cultivation of barley practically ceased." Six public brew houses existed in the colony some twenty years after the Virginia Company's demise in the 1620s.

Taverns supplied imported English ales, but the work of keeping mugs filled on the patchwork of plantations that sprawled westward fell to the women—and the slaves in the kitchen. Evidence of the value placed on domestic brewing is apparent in this ad in a Virginia newspaper:

"For sale: A valuable young Negro woman, very well qualified in all sorts of Housework, as Washing, Ironing, Sewing, Brewing, Baking, &c."

Pumpkins to Pea Shells

Recipes made use of whatever was at hand—spruce, persimmons, sassafras, molasses, ginger, corn, green corn stalks, mulberries, pumpkins, pea shells. Brewing at Mount Vernon made good use of such ingredients. "I find from experience there is a fine spirit to be made from persimmons, but neglected to gather them for that purpose; only got some for the purpose of making beer," farm manager Lund Washington wrote to his distant cousin George Washington in 1778. Much earlier, in the late 1750s, the latter recorded a recipe for small beer that used molasses and "bran hops." Washington, "a beer lover of the first order," also brewed strong beer and kept a ready supply of his favorite, porter.

When not consuming beer at home, Washington and others frequented taverns such as the Swan in Charlottesville, the Eagle in Richmond, and the Raleigh in Williamsburg. Not only was beer itself available to fuel talk of politics, court cases, or local news, but beer was also used in popular tavern drinks such as flip, toddy, buttered ale, and cock ale. Ale and beer also were prized for their alleged medicinal value. Whether the malady be a "weak brain," hysteria, lassitude, a lack of virility, or melancholy, these beverages were believed to contribute to the cure.

It's important to note that a distinction existed between ale and beer, terms we sometimes use interchangeably now. Hops, which provide the bitterness to balance the sweetness of malt in beer, were abundant in England, but prior to the sixteenth century brewers made what was called "ale" without using hops. If the beverage made use of hops, spices, or similar ingredients, it was "beer" and the brewer was subject to fines. Such fines failed to squelch

CORN BEER RECIPE

Soak one pint of corn, and boil it until it is soft; add to it a pint of molasses and one gallon of water; shake them well together, and set it by the fire, and in twenty-four hours the beer will be excellent. When all the beer in the jug is used, just add more molasses and water. The same corn will answer for six months, and the beer will be fit for use in twelve hours by keeping the jug where it is warm. In this way the ingredients used in making a gallon of beer will not cost over four cents, and it is better and more wholesome than cider. A little yeast greatly forwards the working of the beer.

From the *Staunton Spectator and General Advertiser,* Tuesday, July 16, 1861

experimentation with hops, which also functioned as a preservative, an important attribute in helping beer mature on transatlantic voyages.

Not all beer arrived in good shape from England. "Such trash was never before brewed," one Virginian complained to his supplier in 1729; "I offered it to my negroes, and not one would drink it." And so it was inevitable that commercial ventures would sprout as the colonies grew, with one misguided attempt surfacing near Fredericksburg.

In 1766, John Mercer attempted to reverse his financial misfortunes by starting a brewery. Mercer was an Irishman who left the Old World in 1720 and six years later settled in Marlborough, a former village northeast of Fredericksburg. A self-made lawyer and gentleman planter (and guardian of the young George Mason, who would later write the Bill of Rights), Mercer achieved significant stature among Virginia's gentry but also accumulated sizable debt through extravagant living. Observing that "our Ordinaries abound & daily increase (for drinking will continue longer than anything but eating)," he launched the brewing enterprise by building a malt house and a brew house, each one hundred feet long. He also purchased forty slaves to expedite the process.

Missteps followed. The first brewer he hired, a young Scotsman named Andrew Wales, insisted on altering the malt house. A second—a head brewer named William King—arrived and criticized Wales's plans, but ended up dying within three weeks. King's nephew, William Bailey, appeared unannounced and not only echoed his uncle's concerns but also claimed that he, Bailey, was a better

Reenactors at Colonial Williamsburg demonstrate domestic brewing practices that were common in Virginia's early days.

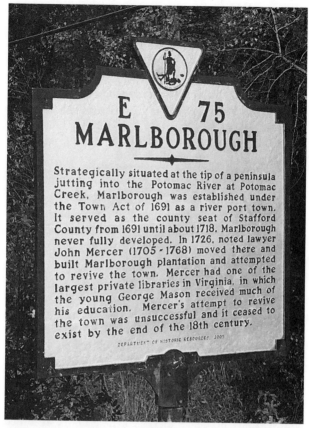

John Mercer attempted to make brewing a commercial enterprise at Marlborough in 1766, but his efforts to revive the town failed, as noted in this Virginia historical marker.

brewer than Wales. Each was allowed to brew separate batches, and Bailey failed. The beer was so bad no one would buy it. Wales's brew, however, was "the only beer I had that Season fit to drink," Mercer wrote.

In April 1766, Mercer advertised that strong beer, porter, and ale using "nothing but the genuine best MALT and HOPS" would be sold at the Marlborough Brewery.

Wales could not brew enough to pay the bills, however, much less cover his salary. Part of the problem was that barley couldn't be grown in sufficient quantity to brew the volume of beer Mercer needed to turn a profit. His plans called for ten thousand bushels; he ended up with two thousand. Other misfortunes followed, and Mercer died in 1768. Wales stayed for another year, enhancing his reputation for good beer.

One of Wales's fans was George Washington. The master of Mount Vernon ordered a cask of the brewer's beer in April 1768; subsequent purchases included fifty-four gallons of strong beer and fifty-two gallons of ale the following January. Washington's patronage continued as Wales moved from Marlborough to Alexandria, where he established the city's first commercial brewery at Point Lumley on Duke Street. Wales survived turbulent times during the Revolution—he was a Tory and was suspected of helping British soldiers and sailors escape from the Alexandria jail—to become a prominent citizen, though debt plagued his final years.

Another prewar brewery rose by the James River at Westham, about six miles upstream from Richmond. This was connected to a foundry built to make and bore cannon barrels using local coal and imported iron ore. Colonel Turner Southall, who supervised the foundry, recorded expenditures for work on a brewery, which was sold in 1780. Documents indicate that William Hay and Southall teamed up to produce "most of the beer consumed in the city of Richmond."

The foundry was destroyed and the brewery threatened when General Benedict Arnold sent soldiers upriver during his raid of Richmond in 1781. But the brewery "was saved by the intercession of the widow who owned part of it," wrote Lieutenant William Feltman of the First Pennsylvania Regiment after passing through the area in August 1781. The "very fine brewery" had escaped the ravages of "that d—d rascal Arnold."

After the smoke cleared from the Revolutionary War and the new nation emerged as a sovereign power, beer continued its role as a staple beverage and an economic force. Multiple businesses flourished, including the Union and Potomac breweries in Alexandria and the Richmond Brewery in the capital. One other factor, though, loomed large among the concerns of the Founding Fathers—the importance of beer as a drink of moderation in a time of rampant drunkenness. "I wish to see this beverage become common instead of the whiskey which kills one third of our citizens and ruins their families," Thomas Jefferson wrote.

Domestic Brewing at Monticello

Jefferson's wife, Martha, gained local renown for her domestic brewing at Monticello. During her first year in residence, she brewed sixteen batches of ale. Decades later, when the former president retired to his Virginia mountaintop after two terms in office, he took brewing to a new level. Fortune delivered to his doorstep—literally—Captain Joseph Miller, who had been a professional brewer in London but left England to claim family estates in Norfolk, Virginia. His mission faltered because the War of 1812 was under way, rendering his English background suspect even though he was born in America, and his misfortunes left him stranded in Albemarle County.

Jefferson welcomed Miller into his home and proceeded with a full-scale brewing operation at Monticello. Peter Hemings, a brother of Sally Hemings, served as his student, not only learning sophisticated brewing techniques but also experimenting with the malting of wheat and, later, corn (recall that barley, beer's main grain, was expensive and did not grow well in Virginia). Hemings proved a quick study—a man of "great intelligence and diligence," Jefferson said—and a good brewer. Hemings stood at the pinnacle of slaves' involvement in brewing, which was not confined to Monticello. Evidence points to slaves at Mount Vernon brewing beer for their own use. The cultivation of hops by slaves at both plantations is also documented. George Washington paid Boatswain, a "ditcher" at one of Washington's farms, $1.25 for six pounds of hops. That pales beside Thomas Jefferson's paying Bagwell Granger, a prominent member of Monticello's slave community, $20 for sixty pounds of hops in 1818 (an amount equivalent to $800 today). In addition, purchases of hops from "Nottoway Negroes" helped supply the brewery that existed at the College of William and Mary.

Jefferson also grew hops, built a malting house, and designed a brew house; the location of the latter has never been determined. Brewing was seasonal—one hundred gallons of ale in the fall and one hundred gallons in the spring, according to an 1821 letter. Jefferson had no recipe, he told a friend, but he insisted on flavorful beer. He specified a bushel of malt for every eight to ten gallons of strong beer and three-quarters of a pound of hops for every bushel of wheat. Jefferson criticized breweries that cut corners on their grain bills, making "their liquor meager and often vapid."

Modern drinkers would probably use words other than "meager" and "vapid" to describe the ales of those times. Cloudy, usually dark, and often with a funky tang from wild yeast, those brews had much more in common with the beers of the pharaohs than those in today's six-packs. That was about to change.

Less than a decade after Thomas Jefferson's death in 1826, the nation began experiencing an influx of German immigrants. One account estimates that some ten thousand Germans arrived in Virginia in the three decades following 1830. In Richmond alone, the German community accounted for nearly 25 percent of the total white population in the years immediately preceding the Civil War. Many immigrants didn't stop at the urban centers but pushed into western pockets, especially the Shenandoah Valley, where land was available and affordable.

Germans Bring a New Beer Style

These newcomers brought a different brewing tradition—lager beer. The word comes from "lagern," which means "to store." Before refrigeration, brewing was a seasonal task, lasting from October to March; summers were too hot for yeast to work properly. To prevent spring brews from spoiling during the summer months, Germans hauled casks to caves, where the beer was "lagered" (or so we are told by centuries of beer lore).

While the kegs sat, the yeast settled and the beer matured into a clearer, brighter beverage than ales, where the yeast did its fermentation at warmer temperatures while sitting atop the liquid. Germans also were beholden to a law passed in 1516 that restricted ingredients to barley, water, and hops (yeast, not fully understood until the nineteenth century, was added later, cementing the four pillars of brewing). Contrast that with the grab bag of ingredients that flavored colonial beer.

Lager beer caused a sensation. "It is a new beverage, of German origin, but used everywhere, by everybody . . . in immense quantities," wrote Englishman David W. Mitchell in 1862 while living in Virginia. "Nobody liked it at first, but most people who use drinking-houses get to take it in surprising quantities. Germans have sworn to taking sixty glasses in an evening without being intoxicated."

Lager breweries blossomed like edelweiss. Alexandria received its introduction to homegrown lager brewing in 1858 from Alexander Strausz and John Klein. They built a brick-vaulted beer cellar on Duke Street in the city's West End that went by various names—Shooter's Hill Brewery, Shuter's Hill Brewery, West End Brewery, and more.

In prewar Richmond, "lager has raised its head and . . . gone ahead of all other beverages," wrote Samuel Mordecai in his 1860 memoir. One enterprising individual in the vanguard of that boom was J. D. Goodman, who traded a career as a clothier for one as a brewer. In 1859, he produced Southern Rights Lager Beer, which a local newspaper declared "the first beverage of the kind ever brewed in this city." That year a Great Union Lager Beer Trial was held the day after Christmas at Richmond's New Market Hotel. For fifty cents, patrons could drink all they could hold—after all, lager was *not* intoxicating, many argued. Nor was it universally embraced. An editorial in the 1856 *Richmond Daily Dispatch* described the taste as "like a decoction of bad tobacco juice." Another prewar brewery, owned by Edward Euker, was built at Clay and Harrison streets, a location that would later house one of Richmond's most storied breweries.

As the war raged, lager spread. In 1863, a Union general in Alexandria lamented the easy access soldiers had to alcoholic beverages at various establishments: "Lager beer is the principal article they deal in—that they deal out in great abundance. It is all over the division. I do not think there is a tent in the division, but what has more or less of it."

Chimborazo Hospital in Richmond, which treated roughly seventy-five thousand sick and wounded soldiers during the Civil War, valued beer for its medicinal qualities, and a brewery on Chimborazo Hill (ostensibly Goodman's) provided a steady supply. Judith McGuire related in her wartime journal that beer saved her nephew, who was wounded and dying at Chimborazo. He could retain no food or liquid until she got him to drink some porter. "Life seemed to return to his system," she wrote, "and I never witnessed anything like the reanimation of the whole man, physical and mental. The hospitals are now supplied with this life-giving beverage."

The chaos of war provided opportunities for those able to seize them. One was Robert Portner, who had come from Rahden, Germany, to the United States in 1853 at the age of sixteen. In 1861, when Alexandria was deserted save for Union troops, Portner opened a grocery store with a partner. Beer was a best seller, so Portner and three other individuals started a brewery in an old flour warehouse at King and Fayette streets. Two other hometown breweries—Klein's Shooter's Hill and the Alexandria Ale Brewery owned by Henry S. Martin—and several "come-here" Northern breweries also benefited from the soldiers' thirst for beer.

Portner Spreads the Brewing Footprint

Portner became a bona fide brewer largely by chance. In 1865, he and his partner, Frederick Recker, bought out two fellow businessmen, and Portner offered Recker the choice of operating either the grocery store or the brewery. Recker initially opted for the brewery, but after a week he asked Portner, who knew little about making beer and less about the business of brewing, to trade roles. On such small points life often turns—few could have foreseen that fortune and prestige awaited Portner as the company grew to become the largest brewery in the South.

Alexandria escaped the war relatively unscathed. Richmond, however, lay ravaged by fire, explosions, desolation, and defeat. Many buildings remained only as charred ruins; wooden shanties sprang up where people sold everything from molasses candy to spruce beer. Here again, though, opportunities existed for investors, builders, and brewers. The 1866 city directory lists sixteen brewers and bottlers of beer—including porter, ale, lager, and other styles. Edward Euker's brewery continued at Buchanan Spring. John Deuringer opened the City Spring Brewery on Eighth Street, north of Leigh. In Petersburg, the Cockade City Brewery opened in 1865 for a three-year run.

The most impressive, though, would rise on Richmond's eastern outskirts, at Rocketts Landing. There, D. G. Yuengling Jr. and two other men—John Frederick Betz, who was D.G. Jr.'s uncle and a prominent brewer in his own right, and John A. Beyer, also a brewer—established the James River Steam Brewery. Yuengling was the eldest son of D. G. Yuengling Sr., who had started the Eagle Brewery in Pottsville, Pennsylvania, in 1829 (the name later was changed to D. G. Yuengling and Son). The youngster had apprenticed at the Pennsylvania brewery and received further training abroad. By 1866, he was ready to test his mettle away from home, and Richmond—with its river and rail transportation, its rebuilding boom, and its strong German community—beckoned.

Yuengling and his partners built their brewery on eight acres by the river, just downstream from the urban center. The facility stood five stories above ground—some eighty feet high—with vaults below ground capable of holding six thousand barrels, according to the *Richmond Whig*. Production capacity was four hundred barrels a day of lager, porter, and ale; barley seed and hops were sold as well. Schuetzen Park, as the grounds were called, became a community center for shooting contests, celebrations, and afternoons spent relaxing in the beer garden.

Though steam-powered equipment provided a leg up in some regards (as well as the brewery's name), the lack of another innovation proved fatal. The operation followed the traditional model—brewing in cooler weather and storing the beer in cellars when temperatures rose. James River, however, was built just before the spread of commercial refrigeration. Other breweries could brew year-round, did not need to cellar their beers, and could ship greater volumes over longer distances with less spoilage. "The extensive cellars of the James River Steam Brewery had become something of an anachronism even during their brief period of use," according to a 2013 report

JAMES RIVER STEAM BREWERY, RICHMOND,
D. G. YUENGLING, Jr., Proprietor.

D. G. Yuengling Jr. was one of three men who started James River Steam Brewery in Richmond in 1866.

nominating the cellars for historic designation. A global economic crisis in 1873 crippled many businesses, and by 1879 the James River Steam Brewery had run its course. A fire in 1891 destroyed the main building but spared the cellars, which were placed on the National Register of Historic Places in 2014.

The same technology that hobbled Yuengling would propel Portner. An innovator as well as a savvy businessman, Portner followed early advances in refrigeration and air-conditioning and adapted them to his plant. Rather than relying on ice or cool cellars, he devised a system in which liquid ammonia, mixed with water, circulated through pipes along walls and in ceilings to cool large spaces. He received a patent in 1880 and was cited by trade journals for his designs. With this innovation, brewing was no longer handcuffed to the weather, and Portner proceeded to establish branches and depots throughout the South, including Richmond, Charlottesville, Lynchburg, and Roanoke. Advances in pasteurization developed by Anheuser-Busch also allowed brewers to reduce spoilage and target distant markets.

Portner's earliest brewing featured ales, but the lager tradition quickly dominated with flagships such as Tivoli ("I Lov It" spelled backward) and Vienna Cabinet; the portfolio also included a "Culmbacher" beer, a bock, and other lagers. Sales boomed. In the decade from 1883, when the business was incorporated, to 1893, production grew from twenty-six thousand barrels to more than sixty thousand barrels. Construction of a plant, called Tivoli Brewery, on Saint Asaph Street in Alexandria boosted capacity to one hundred thousand barrels and made Portner's brewery the largest enterprise in the city in the early 1890s.

Success led to fortune and prestige, but Portner's health failed as his wealth grew. Extended trips back to Germany revived his spirits, and Portner moved to the Virginia countryside, building an expansive mansion on eighteen hundred acres in Manassas where his large

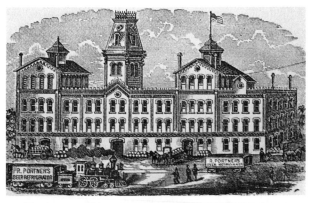

This 1884 image shows the Portner brewery in Alexandria, with the refrigerated cars used to transport Tivoli and other brands in the foreground.

family—he and his wife, Anna, had thirteen children—could stretch out.

The final years of the decade saw growth elsewhere in Virginia. Roanoke proved fertile brewing territory for Louis A. Scholz, who started the Virginia Brewing Company there in 1889. Refrigeration was installed from the first, facilitating the brewing of lagers as well as ales and porters, and the brewery included its own malting operation. Records show annual production at seven thousand barrels.

The business of brewing took a significant leap forward in Richmond in the early 1890s, thanks to two native Germans. Alfred von Nickisch Rosenegk and Peter Stumpf came to the city representing out-of-town breweries, which were plentiful. Rosenegk managed the local branch of Bergner & Engel, a prominent Philadelphia brewery; Stumpf's portfolio included Anheuser-Busch. The town also flowed with beers from Christian Moerlein of Cincinnati, Joseph Schlitz of Milwaukee, Louis Bergdoll of Philadelphia, Darley Park of Baltimore, and George Ehret's Hell Gate Brewery of New York.

The success of these "come-here" breweries prompted Rosenegk and Stumpf to embark on their own enterprises. The former broke ground first and, in partnership with brewer Emil Kersten, opened in August 1891 as Richmond Brewery on Hermitage Road (Rosenegk's name is barely visible on the current incarnation, the Todd Lofts). Stumpf followed in 1892 with a facility at Clay and Harrison streets, where Edward Euker's brewery once flourished. Stumpf's original name for the business—Richmond Brewing Company—led to confusion among patrons, so he renamed it the Peter Stumpf Brewing Company. It would change again in 1897 to Home Brewing Company upon Stumpf's retirement from the business.

The two rivals went head to head in hometown competition, to the extent that their wrangling over the award for best lager at the 1892 State Exposition ultimately resulted in a court case, which Rosenegk won. Their brands spanned a diverse spectrum: Challenge, Edelbrau, Tidal Wave, Palest Export, and a porter from Rosenegk; Weiner, XXX Brown Stout, Extra-Brew Porter, Piedmont Export, Standard Lager, and, later, the flagship Richbrau lager from the brewery Stumpf started.

Confusion about names popped up elsewhere in Virginia. In 1895, two unrelated businesses named Consumers' Brewing Company appeared, one in Virginia Beach, the other in Rosslyn near the District of Columbia. The former, which was equipped with refrigeration, is credited with producing a steam beer, a style with roots in California that was later popularized by Anchor Brewing in the early days of the craft beer renaissance. Annual production was pegged at eighteen thousand barrels.

The Rosslyn version of Consumers began through the efforts of seven men, including William McGuire, Thomas Walsh, and Dennis Connell. Production initially focused on lager beers, both light and dark, but later included porter and other ales. The plant, which officially opened on January 1, 1897, was equipped with electricity and refrigeration.

These breweries were on the down side of a national trend that peaked in 1873. That year, the nation counted 4,131 breweries, a high point unequaled until 2015. The aforementioned economic crisis of 1873 buffeted some businesses, but the real gale was yet to come, as temperance groups gathered force around the country.

Though anti-alcohol laws can be traced in America back to colonial days—Massachusetts and Georgia both had prohibition statutes—the formation of three groups in the late nineteenth century kindled the fires that would consume the nation. First, the Prohibition Party organized in 1869 and fanned the sparks of activism among women. The Woman's Christian Temperance Union, begun in 1874, really focused the calls for change, from combating drunkenness to promoting women's suffrage. Further momentum came from the Anti-Saloon League, formed in 1893 in Ohio for a single purpose—to legalize national prohibition.

Forces of Prohibition Combine

In Virginia, a decades-long effort gelled in 1901 when the state's branch of the Anti-Saloon League took shape at a meeting in Richmond's Second Baptist Church. In 1904, the leadership reins went to the Reverend James Cannon Jr., a Methodist minister from Blackstone. He quickly became a political force through adroit dealings with state legislators and other people of influence.

Brewers sensed the change afoot and played to a centuries-old strength—the image of beer as a nutritious beverage. As a 1910 Home Brewing Company ad noted, "[Beer] supplies nearly all the liquid and solid nourishment necessary to sustain life. It furnishes nutriment in the most highly assimilable form." Rosenegk echoed this view: "Purity and healthfulness are combined in our Challenge and Edelbrau brands of bottled beer. . . . The purest materials, with an absolute cleanliness results in a temperance drink of unsurpassed delight."

Brewers also had the deep pockets to fund anti-prohibition efforts, but another development worked against their cause. The outbreak of war in Europe cast German Americans, their flag-waving for the fatherland, and their beer-loving ways in a different light. "While most Richmonders stared in disbelief, the Germans in their midst reenacted the jubilant scenes of the Kaiser's mobilization," observed Klaus Wust in *The Virginia Germans*. This zeal fostered prejudice and persecution against these communities and brewers in the Old Dominion.

After at least two unsuccessful attempts, Cannon

and his followers persuaded legislators in 1914 to hold a statewide referendum that September on prohibition. A spirited debate ensued. Tempers flared; bitter words flew. Morality and temperance aligned against the loss of tax revenue and local self-governance. When the final votes were tallied, Virginians favored going "dry" by 94,251 to 63,886. Four cities—Richmond, Arlington, Norfolk, and Williamsburg—stood alone as "wet" advocates. The legislature enacted the Mapp Act, making it illegal, among other things, to manufacture, transport, sell, or keep for sale ardent spirits. The act also set November 1, 1916, as the date for Virginia to go dry, and surreal scenes of Halloween revelers partying on city streets while church bells pealed at midnight played out in Richmond and elsewhere.

The nation followed by ratifying the Eighteenth Amendment in 1919, but by then a different bell had tolled for Virginia's breweries. Portner curtailed operations in May 1916, then totally closed that October. More than one hundred workers at the Alexandria plant alone lost their jobs. Rosenegk's brewing company also closed its doors, and its founder died suddenly at his summer home in Virginia Beach in August 1917. His obituary noted his wide business interests, concluding that "it is said that perhaps his greatest interest commercially was in the brewery established by him in Richmond."

Going dry spurred creative efforts to adhere to the law in a beery way. Virginians could purchase beverages such as Alpha, certified to have neither malt nor alcohol, and Bevo, Anheuser-Busch's "strictly non-toxicating . . . delightful, wholesome, and nutritious drink."

Home Brewing Company in Richmond shifted gears in order to survive. It technically ceased to exist as a corporation, morphing into the Home Products Corporation. Though one of its early products was "Dix Brannew," a non-malt, nonalcoholic drink in the mold of Bevo and Alpha, soft drinks and water stole the limelight. Fritz Sitterding, who had taken over from Peter Stumpf when the company was reorganized in 1897, together with his colleagues arranged to lease bottling facilities to the Beaufont Company, renowned for its ginger ale and spring water. Consumers' Brewing Company in Tidewater and Virginia Brewing Company in Roanoke closed their doors in 1918; the latter turned to soda and bottled water to survive. Like many other breweries, it also made money from selling ice, a commodity already at hand.

Though folks couldn't buy beer, they continued to make it at home. In fact, homebrewing exploded in popularity, propelling a gradual increase in beer consumption during the Roaring Twenties. One University of Virginia professor recorded multiple batches of homebrew from 1919 to 1921. Like most novice zymurgists, he experienced his share of exploding bottles and overflowing fermenters, as well as producing tasty ales.

Virginia Breweries Come Back to Life

By the early 1930s, it became clear that anti-alcohol fervor had waned, and in 1933 the U.S. Constitution was again amended, this time to repeal Prohibition. Initial legislation allowed only beer of 3.2 percent alcohol by weight or less, but that was enough for breweries to reopen, if they were able. Years of disuse hamstrung many facilities, which would have required upgrades costing large sums.

Three Virginia breweries, however, found the resources to revive. Richmond's Home Brewing Company re-formed and spent $275,000 on remodeling its plant; an eighteen-year brewers' drought in the River City ended with beer deliveries on April 30, 1934. In Norfolk, the Consumers' brewery reopened on Washington Avenue, though for only a three-year period before changing its name to Southern Breweries. It was soon joined by the likes of Mohawk, Glasgow, and Century breweries.

In Roanoke, the Virginia Brewing Company reemerged,

briefly under Louis Scholz's leadership, but he died in 1936 and management went to local entrepreneur E. Cabell Tudor. Quality suffered, and relations with tavern owners became strained, according to one account, which noted that "[r]umors spread that the brewery used potato skins for starch." Another change in ownership ensued, with Olde Virginia and Virginia's Famous beers as flagship brews.

Those beers went to market in new packaging, thanks to a revolutionary innovation that debuted in Richmond in 1935, when the city made history by being the first place in the world where you could buy beer in cans. Virginia's capital served as a market for the Gottfried Krueger Brewing Company of Newark, New Jersey, to test a concept pushed by the American Can Company. Brewery officials were understandably reluctant because contact with metal generally made beer go bad. The canning folks, however, proposed a can with enamel lining similar to that used in kegs. In addition, the can would be strong enough to withstand the pressure of carbonation and the process of pasteurization.

The curtain lifted on Krueger Cream Ale in cans on January 24, 1935. A newspaper ad and instructions on the side of the can helped consumers adjust to the innovation, and the test became an instant success. By the end of 1935, thirty-six brewers in the United States and beyond were offering beer in cans.

Though that development proved a boon for brewers, other factors moved the brewing world in a direction far removed from that which existed before Prohibition. Farms closed during the Great Depression, making grain more costly. When the Second World War broke out in Europe, America supplied grain to Allies, increasing the pressure on brewers. And once the Yanks entered the war, grain rationing fed brewers' inclination to lower their grain bills—and downsize their beers' flavor—by using adjuncts such as corn and rice.

The American palate changed. Years of drinking soda instead of beer during Prohibition, followed by more years of drinking lighter brews, produced a generation that knew little more than mass-produced lagers geared to be the least offensive to the most people. Consolidations among breweries fed big beer and gave producers economies of scale that made competition brutal.

Such was the case in Roanoke. The Virginia Brewing Company had changed hands in 1954, and the new owner, S. F. Huff, increased distribution beyond Virginia to Kentucky, North Carolina, and West Virginia. He also kept the price low—twenty cents a bottle—but found his efforts undercut by retailers who charged twenty-five cents and kept the nickel. National brands sold for the same and tasted better, so the brewery suffered. In 1958, Leroy Overcash of North Carolina took over and changed the name of the business to Mountain Brewing. A new brew, Dixie, joined Old Virginia Special in the product line, but despite clever marketing (including a spot where a Southern colonel tells an aide who had spotted some Yankees to "Hush up and drink your beer"), the operation closed in 1959.

Richmond's Home Brewing Company met a similar fate a decade later. Though it expanded over the years to a capacity of one hundred thousand barrels and distributed Richbrau, its flagship beer, throughout much of the state, the brewery suffered operating losses and closed in December 1969. In a letter to stockholders, Frederick Sitterding III, the company's president, explained that national competitors had shown more interest in Richmond, and they were able to sell beer for less even though the cost of materials and supplies increased.

Nation Hits a Low Point in Brewing

The following year marked a nadir in breweries in the United States. By 1979, a decade after Home Brewing

Company's demise, the number of breweries in the country had fallen to 90, a far cry from the high of 4,131 in 1873. In his 1977 classic book, *The World Guide to Beer*, author and beer guru Michael Jackson noted that the U.S. produced more beer than any other nation—Anheuser-Busch alone produced almost as much beer as the Soviet Union—but added that biggest is not necessarily best: "A people usually anxious to proclaim the virtues of things American are uncharacteristically self-deprecating about their nation's beers, despite a great brewing tradition."

So how did we get to 2015, when the number of breweries in the country eclipsed the 1873 mark for the first time, and the diverse styles being brewed have made American craft brewers the toast of the globe? Give a tip of the hat to President Jimmy Carter, who in 1978 signed legislation legalizing home brewing. Not that the hobby needed his seal of approval, for people returning from trips abroad, where they experienced the flavorful lagers of Germany and the malty, hoppy ales of Britain, had already tried their hands at re-creating those brews in their kitchens and backyards. A student at the University of Virginia proved seminal in that regard. Charlie Papazian was introduced to homebrewing while living in Charlottesville and went on, through his books and leadership, to be instrumental in kindling and guiding a revolution in the national brewing landscape (more about this in chapter 3).

In 1972, the same year Papazian graduated from UVA, Anheuser-Busch opened a brewery in Williamsburg capable of cranking out 3.2 million barrels a year of various brands (that figure grew to 8.5 million barrels in 2012, and the plant was targeted in 2017 for an \$18 million upgrade as part of a \$2 billion company-wide capital investment program). The craft brewing movement had sprouted on the West Coast in the 1960s and 1970s, but the first efforts didn't blossom in Virginia until 1982. The Chesapeake Bay Brewing Company formed in Virginia Beach's

Lynnhaven area through the efforts of two homebrew-ing buddies—Jim Kollar, a veterinarian, and Lou Peron, an orthodontist. The first commercial craft brewery in the South, Chesapeake required $250,000 and hours of hands-on labor—including the help of both men's wives and Kollar's brother—piecing together used dairy tanks and equipment from a soda plant. Though Kollar had taken a brewing course at the University of California–Davis, they decided to hire a professional. Wolfgang Roth, a young brewmaster living in Germany, moved to Virginia Beach to take on the job of developing Chesbay Amber, Chesbay Superior Lager, and other beers. His crew in-cluded an ambitious apprentice named Allen Young, who would later emerge as one of the region's seminal brewing figures with gigs at Fordham Brewing Company, Gordon Biersch, and Brewers Supply Group. Though Chesapeake Bay's beers won critical acclaim, including a gold medal for its doppelbock at the Great American Beer Festival, the brewery struggled to find its niche in a market domi-nated by mainstream lagers, and in 1986, Kollar sold it to a group of investors. "We were way ahead of our time and on the wrong coast," Young told the *Virginian-Pilot.* "They weren't ready for us."

The following year saw another landmark development when two brothers opened Blue Ridge Brewing Company, Virginia's first brewpub, in Charlottesville. Burks and Paul Summers were grandsons of William Faulkner, who was writer-in-residence at the University of Virginia in the late 1950s. Paul had been a merchant seaman and had worked at a brewery and a restaurant in San Francisco, while Burks, known as "Bok," was the homebrewer. Plans for a restaurant with a brewery capable of producing four hun-dred barrels annually took shape on Charlottesville's West Main Street. Of the four beers that anchored the lineup, two were lagers, which was unusual at the time because most microbreweries favored quicker-fermenting ales.

"What we're doing is going back to the old way of making beer," Bok Summers said.

On the other side of the spectrum, Old Dominion Brewing Company in Ashburn was making a mark by pushing the palate envelope. Founded in 1989 by Jerry Bailey and Bud Hensgen (who later served as executive director of the Mid-Atlantic Association of Craft Brewers), Old Dominion used a recipe developed by Bob and Ellie Tupper for "a Beer Out There that nobody was making: an amber harvest ale that would be dry hopped, aged for six weeks like a lager, and bottle conditioned." Tuppers' Hop Pocket Ale won gold among American pale ales at the Great American Beer Festival—one of many medals won by the brewery—and fed a market eager for brews with a bit of bite. Old Dominion also gained a national reputation for the prowess of brewers such as Ron Barchet, who went on to cofound Victory Brewing Company in Pennsylvania, and John Mallett, who later played an instrumental role in the expansion of Bell's Brewery in Michigan. The Virginia scene also benefited from Old Dominion alumni such as Matt Hagerman and Favio Garcia of Lost Rhino, Kenny Allen and Dave Hennessey of Mustang Sally, Dean Lake of Dog Money, and Rob Mullin of Three Notch'd. Old Dominion's run in Ashburn ended in 2007, when it was sold as part of a joint venture with Fordham Brewing Company and Anheuser-Busch.

In the meantime, the wave of microbreweries was swelling. Tom Martin planted his Legend Brewing Company flag on the south bank of the James River in Richmond and tapped the first keg of Legend Brown Ale in early 1994 in grand fashion at Commercial Taphouse and Grill in the city's Fan District. Richbrau Brewing Company added to the surge with a brewpub in the city's historic Shockoe Slip. To the north, Bill Madden made kölsch a household word among beer geeks with his pioneering efforts at Capitol City Brewing Company. Steamship Brewing opened in 1995 in Norfolk but, like many in that first wave, saw demand ebb; it closed in 1998.

Other closures followed. Inconsistent quality, unsound business plans, and the realities of transitioning from a five-gallon homebrew to a multibarrel system proved the undoing of numerous enterprises. But the list of micro-breweries conjures memories of many good (and a few bad) beers and breweries that marked the 1990s. Potomac River, Mobjack Bay, James River, Rock Creek, Bardo Rodeo, Blue-N-Gold, Williamsville, Main Street, Monticello, Virginia Native—all closed their doors and drained their brew tanks, some forever, some to transition to other sites, some to reopen once circumstances improved. Several brew-on-premises (BOP) operations—where you could brew your own beer with equipment at the site—also popped up around the state in the 1990s. The Monticello Brewing Company operated in an old milk bottling facility in Charlottesville, and Shenandoah Brewing Company fired up its brew kettles in Alexandria. Both businesses would fade, but both buildings would later house breweries.

The reverse proved true with St. George Brewing Company to the east. The building in Hampton where it began offering BOP services in 1996 was destroyed in an early morning fire on Christmas Eve in 2000. It might not have seemed like a gift at the time, but the relocation allowed the brewery to blossom and gain a larger audience for its porter, nut brown ale, and other signature beers.

Craft Scene Begins to Surge

Charlottesville saw a surge in the late 1990s with the opening of South Street and Starr Hill breweries, the latter in the same building on West Main Street that housed the state's first brewpub. (Starr Hill relocated to a larger facility in nearby Crozet in 2005.) A narrow road that snakes through Nelson County and offers scenic views of the Blue

Ridge Mountains became home to three breweries—Blue Mountain, Devils Backbone, and Wild Wolf. A novel concept emerged—combine beer with tourism—and the Brew Ridge Trail was born, the first such connect-the-dots effort among Virginia breweries.

It was another initiative, though, that primed the pump for the state's gushing growth in breweries. Keep in mind that in 2010, Legend was the only brewery operating in the Richmond city limits; statewide, roughly forty breweries kept their heads above water. Growth was limited by a state law dictating that any brewery wishing to sell its beer on-site also had to sell food.

That changed in May 2012, at the gathering at Hardywood Park Craft Brewery in Richmond noted at the start of this chapter. Then-governor Bob McDonnell signed two pieces of legislation. The most influential was Senate Bill 604, which eliminated the food requirement. Breweries now had the right to sell beer—fresh beer, pints of it, growlers, crowlers, tastes, and flights—right there at the site, straight from the gleaming tanks squatting within sight of the patrons clustered around taps and tables in tasting rooms across the state.

The ceremony that day included a beer brewed specifically for the occasion—SB604 Special Bitter. The style, a quaffable extra special bitter (ESB), seemed appropriate, except there was nothing bitter about the portent of that day. Under the aegis of the Virginia Manufacturers Association, craft breweries in Virginia opened in droves and formed the Virginia Craft Brewers Guild. By the middle of 2017—a scant five years after SB604's signing—the Old Dominion would be home to more than two hundred licensed breweries; Richmond alone would boast thirty-some breweries in its metro area. West Coast stalwarts such as Stone, Deschutes, Green Flash, and Ballast Point found fertile ground in the state's mid-Atlantic location and business-friendly environment.

Virginia's surge was part of a nationwide boom that would see far-reaching changes in the business and brewing of beer. Who could have foreseen that beer authority Michael Jackson, who lamented the country's lack of creativity and diversity in his 1977 book, would celebrate Virginia beers in later works? Or that, if he had lived to 2017, he could have ordered Virginia craft beers at one of the pubs in his native England?

CHAPTER 2

Making the Most of "Taste of Place"

The city of Ingolstadt, Germany, lies on the banks of the Danube River in the heart of Bavaria. It served as the capital of its duchy for nearly fifty years in the fifteenth century and was still considered a prominent urban center when two dukes assembled regional officials there in 1516 to address a pressing concern—beer.

Their attention focused on the quality, or the lack thereof, in the Bavarian brewing industry. It was hardly a new issue. Nearly a century earlier, the city councilmen of Munich, some sixty miles south of Ingolstadt, had issued a decree stipulating the ingredients to be used in brewing beer. Even this effort had precursors in Nürnberg, Thuringia, and other areas, where brewers had strayed from barley by using millet, oats, rye, wheat, peas, beans, and other sources of fermentable sugars. And instead of hops, they tossed in juniper, caraway, salt, and even hard-boiled eggs—allegedly to improve the taste but more likely to cut costs and hide off-flavors.

So on April 23, 1516, Duke Wilhelm IV, Duke Ludwig X, and the gathered elders laid down the law: the German Purity Law, to be precise, officially known as the Reinheitsgebot. It decreed that beer should be made solely with barley, hops, and water. The role of yeast, essential to fermentation, was not understood at the time, but it was added to the decree later.

Those four ingredients still stand as the pillars of traditional brewing. Their sole use for years defined craft brewing in the United States. It wasn't until 2014 that the Brewers Association, the not-for-profit trade association that represents small and independent brewers in the country, indicated that adjuncts such as rice and corn also play traditional roles in flavorful beer.

Today's craft brewers in Virginia and elsewhere show both respect and disregard for the Reinheitsgebot. Many have built their brew houses on the four pillars. But even the most traditional have found a receptive market for beer brewed with a cornucopia of grains, spices, herbs, fruits, berries, and other ingredients. Homage to tradition goes far beyond Germany—the oatmeal and milk stouts of Britain, the fruited lambics of Belgium, the farm-friendly saisons of Wallonia, even the smoky Piwo Grodziskie of Poland—all have inspired breweries in the Old Dominion. Obscure historical recipes also have found fans in the modern era, such as Old Stitch Brown Ale, one in a series of collaborations that Alewerks Brewing Company in Williamsburg has produced with Colonial Williamsburg.

As the growth of craft brewing has spurred creativity and innovation, the spotlight on local ingredients has intensified. *Terroir*—the "taste of place"—gives brewers the chance to create a unique niche in a competitive market. As a result, Virginia has seen increased attention paid to growing hops and barley, to identifying and propagating singular yeast strains, and to accessing water that, in the words of one brewer, is "perfect."

Brewers Turn to Local Ingredients

Lost Rhino Brewing Company in Ashburn pioneered the concept of an all-Virginia beer with its release of Native Son in 2014. Labeled a table beer—a term used by Thomas Jefferson for his ales—Native Son was brewed with barley grown on the state's Northern Neck and malted at Copper Fox Distillery in Sperryville. Cascade and Columbus hops came from Sage Hill Farms in Leesburg, and yeast from Northern Virginia via Lost Rhino's fermentation expert, Jasper Akerboom. Even the water, though filtered through a charcoal-sand system, was left untreated to reflect the taste of Loudoun County. A cloudy gold with notes of honey in the nose, the ale weighed in at 6 percent ABV and drew positive reviews and an international award for its herbal flavor and dry finish.

Pioneering efforts popped up elsewhere. Lickinghole Creek Craft Brewery in Goochland County evolved from the hops-growing hobby of cofounder Sean-Thomas Pumphrey into a farm producing pumpkins, six-row barley, rye, rosemary, hops, and other ingredients for its beers. Releases of some ales, such as the Russian imperial stout Virginia Black Bear and the Enlightened Despot, drew crowds and lines to the rolling 260-acre property west of Richmond.

Other farm breweries—Bald Top in Madison, Backroom in Warren County, Wood Ridge in Nelson County, Dirt Farm in Loudoun County, Great Valley in Natural Bridge, Stable Craft near Waynesboro—have fed the hunger for unique flavors in beers, reflecting consumers' appetite for that "taste of place." Dozens of hop farms also have sprouted, initially through the efforts of growers in Nelson County such as Stan Driver and Taylor Smack of Blue Mountain Brewing Company. A 2014 meeting of hops hobbyists at the Rockfish Community Center near Nellysford resulted in the formation of the Old Dominion Hops Cooperative, a seminal group in organizing research and commercial operations in the state. Early efforts indicated that Cascade hops, one of the fundamental West Coast varieties known for its grapefruit aroma and modest bitterness, fared well in the state but lacked the bountiful yields of long-standing industry leaders in the Pacific Northwest. Virginia Tech, Virginia State University, and North Carolina State University have contributed research

Billie Clifton, founder of Backroom Brewery, tends to her Cascade hops growing in Warren County.

to co-op farmers, who numbered nearly one hundred by the end of 2016.

The industry actually has roots in the state's earliest agricultural history. Thomas Jefferson wrote in *Notes on the State of Virginia* that hops are native to Virginia. He and his wife, Martha, also recorded numerous purchases of hops from slaves, as noted in chapter 1. Other payments to slaves for hops were recorded in Williamsburg, at Mount Vernon, and elsewhere.

Even before the Jeffersons' interest, one of Virginia's gentry wrote an essay that illustrates the importance of hops. Landon Carter, son of Robert "King" Carter and a colonel in the militia before the Revolutionary War, described in great detail the process of growing, nurturing, picking, drying, and bagging hops on his plantation in Richmond County. Over the course of seventeen pages,

HOPS

Making flavorful beer requires a balancing act among the ingredients, and hops and malt sit astride a seesaw that challenges the brewer's skill. Both provide aroma and flavor, but it is the interplay of the bitterness of hops and the sweetness of malt that defines many beer styles.

Hops are believed to have originated in China. They are native to Virginia and other temperate zones in North America, Europe, and western Asia. Their Latin designation, *Humulus lupulus*, roughly means "little wolf [plant]," and they are a genus of the *Cannabaceae* family, which includes hemp and marijuana.

The bines emerge in spring from a perennial crown and grow rapidly upward in clinging spirals, producing cones (or flowers) with glands containing acids, oils, and resins. Some hops shine as bittering agents; others, for their aroma. Brewers pay close attention to the percentage of alpha and beta acids as well as humulone and cohumulone levels, all of which contribute to bitterness, aroma, and flavor. IBUs, or International Bitterness Units, give some measure of bitterness, though perceived bitterness is a better subjective guide.

Hops also are dioecious; only the female plants (those with pistillate flowers) are used in commercial cultivation for beer. Particularly in Virginia's humid climate, they are susceptible to mildews, mites, Japanese beetles, and other stressors. Harvest comes usually in late July or August.

Growers in Virginia have found that Cascade, one of the defining hops of West Coast pale ales and IPAs known for its floral and citrus aromas, fares relatively well compared with other cultivars; Cascade hops accounted for more than half of the 2016 crop. Chinook and Nugget, both powerful bittering hops, have come on strong as well.

Many brewers use freshly harvested, locally grown hops in special batches to capture a "taste of place."

he wrote about the ideal soil content ("a Rich, deep mellow, dry Soil more inclining to Sand than Clay"), preparing the soil for planting ("digg it with the Spade in October as deep as you can"), judging when to pick ("when the hops begin to change Colour, are easily pulled to Pieces, smell fragrantly . . . you may conclude them ripe"), and other concerns.

During the mid-1800s, Virginia was the top hops-producing state in the South. The 1862 annual report of the federal Commissioner of Agriculture credits the Old Dominion (listed as one of eleven "disloyal" states) with 10,597 pounds in 1840; that's out of a total of 14,470 pounds among rebel states. Over the next two decades, harvests stayed relatively stable; Virginia produced 10,015 pounds in 1860 (a later report credits the state with only 7,006 pounds during that time). By contrast, hops harvested in the twenty-three "loyal" states catapulted from 3.5 million pounds in 1850 to nearly 11 million pounds in 1860; New York alone produced 9.7 million pounds that year (more than triple its output a decade earlier).

An 1887 report prepared for the U.S. House of Representatives shows that annual hop production in Virginia had fallen to 1,559 pounds. Oddly, that's the same number given for all ten states in the South, down dramatically from 14,290 pounds in 1870. "Hops are only raised for domestic use, except in a few cases. When planted, the vines grow luxuriantly and bear well," the report stated. "Large areas of land similar to the hop lands of Kent in England and to those in the State of New York can be found in Virginia, and hop culture could be advantageously undertaken in many localities to vary the industrial production."

The Civil War had taken its toll, as would Prohibition. It wasn't until homebrewers explored cultivating hops as a backyard hobby a century later that interest blossomed and led to efforts such as the Old Dominion Hops Cooperative and the Loudoun County Hops Association. As craft breweries proliferated, locally produced hops became both available and attractive for use in specialty beers. Soaring Ridge brewery in Roanoke, for example, uses hops grown at nearby Ikenberry Orchard for Ike's Fresh Hops Smash every fall. Hardywood Park Craft Brewery in Richmond has fostered interest through its community hopping program, where each spring rhizomes are offered to enthusiasts who return the favor by bringing in the fruits—or flowers—of their labors for a collaborative Hardywood brew.

Hops Growers Face Challenges

Local efforts have relied largely on brewers using freshly harvested "wet" hops. A major challenge for farmers has been upping their game to offer dried, pelletized hops, which are the industry standard for brewers because of their consistency and stability. Lucketts Mill & Hopworks, in conjunction with its companion business Black Hops Farm, brought a drying and pelletizing facility to the Leesburg area in 2015 and offered services to growers within an hour's distance. A statewide survey showed that production jumped from more than 13,000 plants in the two previous years to nearly 23,000 plants reported in 2016, and most of the fifty-two growers who responded to the survey had commercial goals. The yield that year, according to the survey, totaled an estimated 12,357 pounds of wet hops, almost identical to the weight recorded in the pre–Civil War years.

"I think we are at a turning point," Laura Siegle said in a 2017 interview. As agricultural and natural resources agent for Virginia Cooperative Extension in Amelia County, she has been involved in hops outreach and grower support for several years. "Some growers have good, long-term outlets for fresh/wet hops and want to stick with that marketing plan. Others in certain areas are running into difficulty offloading fresh hops or have found that the brewers they

Jonathan Staples invested in hop processing machinery at Black Hops Farm near Leesburg.

are marketing to have different needs. So pelletizing may be our best route for larger-scale production in the future. Many brewers have emphasized that the only way they can buy from us in Virginia is if we have pellets."

Similar challenges face barley growers, and though the grain lacks the marquee attraction of hops, it has its place in Virginia history. Barley was expensive to import and did not grow well in colonial days, spurring brewers to rely on corn and wheat. (Thomas Jefferson doggedly sought one specific beer book for information about using "Indian" corn in brewing.) Barley production in the South remained fairly stable in the wake of the Civil War, increasing slightly from 419,895 bushels in 1860 to 573,747 in 1880. One modern Virginia farmer and brewer, Barry Wood, not only has grown several varieties of barley and other grains but also has set up a small malting operation on his Nelson County property.

The state's Northern Neck is home to another barley operation—the 1,200-acre farm run by the late Billy Dawson. Growing barley for malting and, ultimately, for use in beer and distilled spirits is something of a gamble compared with producing barley for animal feed. The quality of the grain must be higher and can yield four to six times the prices, but reaching that level of consistent quality relies on greater care and, of course, on the weather. A 2015 article on AmericanFarm.com noted that more than thirty-three thousand acres of barley were harvested the previous year for animal feed while about five hundred acres went toward malting barley.

Several cultivars fare well in Virginia's climate, but Thoroughbred, a six-row barley originally introduced as a winter feed grain, finds particular favor among the state's producers targeting the craft brewing market. Roughly two dozen growers were working on plots ranging from two to twenty acres in 2016. Wade Thomason, professor and Extension grains specialist at Virginia Tech, said that, as with hops, the state's barley growers lack the consistent yield to supply high-volume breweries such as Stone and Ballast Point. Smaller breweries, however, can highlight using local products in flavorful beers with unique appeal—as with Lost Rhino's Native Son.

Growing barley is one thing; malting is another. Turning the raw grain into brewery-ready malt requires specialized equipment and dedicated expertise. Operations such as Copper Fox Distillery have added impetus to the state's ability to fill that role. Copper Fox began after founder Rick Wasmund became fascinated by the single-malt whiskies of Scotland and interned at Bowmore Distillery in Islay, known then for being one of the few distilleries in the world to malt its own barley. He launched his own operation in Sperryville, received acclaim for his applewood-aged whisky, and then found a side market in supplying malt to craft breweries. A second location with nine buildings and increased production possibilities opened in Williamsburg in November 2016.

BARLEY

While hops provide the spice of beer, barley malt gives it soul. This cereal grain represents the common denominator in the question of which came first—bread or beer—as the catalyst for motivating hunter-gatherers to become grower-gatherers. The origin of the variety most associated with brewing beer, *Hordeum vulgare*, can be traced to the ancient Fertile Crescent in the Middle East, where wild barley still grows.

Modern barley largely falls into two groups—six-row or two-row—and two subgroups, winter and spring. The former refers to the rows of corns along the length of the ear; the latter, to growing periods. Winter barley is sown in autumn and overwinters in the ground, while spring barley is sown as quickly as possible when winter has passed. Barley grown for animal feed is far more common—and less demanding—than that grown for use in brewing or distilling. In 2014, about two dozen farmers grew malting barley in Virginia on about 500 acres, compared with 33,000 acres for animal feed.

After the grain is harvested, it goes through a malting process that requires precise periods of steeping, germinating, and kilning, with further modification possible through roasting. The goal is to maximize the availability of carbohydrates in the kernels that can be converted to sugars, which will later be fermented into alcohol (along with carbon dioxide and other compounds).

Though the German Reinheitsgebot of 1516 specifies using barley malt in beer, many brewers also use wheat

Immersing barley in water causes the grain to sprout, part of the process pictured here at Copper Fox in Sperryville.

(which can be malted) and other grains such as oats, rye, rice, and corn. Brewers find many options for producing flavorful beer by combining various grains with malts that have been modified or roasted differently. For example, an oatmeal stout would combine oats (which provide smoothness) with several types of barley malt (including a highly roasted black malt for dark color and an almost acrid, bitter flavor) and perhaps a touch of flaked wheat for head retention.

Matt Tarpey's brewing techniques at The Veil in Richmond's Scott's Addition include traditional fermentation in tanks as well as coolship wild fermentation.

Now, what about beer's two other pillars? Yeast's role has evolved from mystery to microbiology. Brewers' attention to various strains of yeast—traditional as well as unique native strains—has spawned businesses such as RVA Yeast Labs, formed in 2013 by microbiologist Jason Ridlon and chemist Malachy McKenna. The Veil brewery in Richmond built a rooftop "coolship" facility in the Belgian lambic tradition, where fresh wort is exposed to wild airborne yeast to create singular flavors in each batch. Specialists such as Akerboom at Lost Rhino have added to the "taste of place" in yeast. One 230-gallon barrel of ale at Lost Rhino was fermented with yeast from the adjoining parking lot. Another brew, Bone Dusters Amber Ale, used yeast captured from a dusting of protocetid whale fossils found near Virginia's Dismal Swamp.

Virginia's water also earns kudos from brewers, particularly those basking in the beauty of the Blue Ridge Mountains. While brewers can doctor water to suit various needs and styles of beer, Mary Wolf, head of Wild Wolf Brewing Company in Nellysford, notes that "[w]e have perfect water here. Perfect water." Low concentrations of ions and a fairly neutral pH characterize the water captured in wells serving breweries along the state Route 151 corridor, which provides a relative blank slate for brewers. At Blue Mountain Brewery in Afton, the water is "medium-hard, and that's our terroir," said co-owner Taylor Smack. In contrast, the water is much softer at its affiliated brewery, Blue Mountain Barrel House in Arrington.

Ami Riscassi, senior research scientist in the University of Virginia's Environmental Sciences Department, sees two basic factors contributing to the water quality in Nelson County. The first is that the bedrock does not readily dissolve into the water, and the ions that are dissolved have the ability to neutralize acidic water (all rainwater that percolates to the groundwater is slightly acidic in the atmosphere). The second is that the watersheds that feed the groundwater are relatively undeveloped for housing or industry.

Water was a key consideration in the decision by Miller-Coors (Coors Brewing Company at the time) to build an East Coast facility in Elkton in 1987. Bill Coors, former chairman of Adolph Coors Company, said what sold him on the Rockingham County location was a natural spring near the site. "It was a spectacular thing, and we were able to buy it at a reasonable price," he said in a 2007 *Denver Post* interview. The plant initially served to dilute highly concentrated beer shipped from its base in Colorado; a $300 million build-out in 2007 led to active brewing there.

Water quality goes hand in hand with quantity, and Stone Brewing Company, which opened its Richmond site in 2016, is one of many breweries that keep a close eye on water usage. Company-wide, Stone touts using 33 percent less water to make beer than average brewers. At the other end of the process, Stone officials worked with

YEAST

The fermentation process depends on yeast to convert sugars in the wort to carbon dioxide and alcohol—bubbles and buzz, if you will—and other compounds that give us beer. Yeast is pitched into cooled wort after it has been thoroughly oxygenated; fermentation times and temperatures vary depending on the styles of beer desired.

Yeast are single-celled living organisms (fungi) that weren't fully understood prior to the research of several

Yeast collected from the employees' parking lot is used for fermentation in a barrel at Lost Rhino brewery in Ashburn.

scientists in the mid-1800s. Before then, brewers would scoop the yeast off the top of one batch and use it to ferment the next. An early English expression for yeast was "Godisgood." French scientist Louis Pasteur is credited with decoding the mysteries of fermentation and establishing the importance of microorganisms in making—and spoiling—beer. His research showed that the fungi require oxygen to live, and if they don't get it in the air, they consume it in other compounds, such as in wort.

Modern research has isolated and propagated many strains of yeast. Several are grouped as *Saccharomyces*, which means "sugar fungus." The most common is *Saccharomyces cerevisiae* (*cerevisiae* meaning "of beer"), which is associated with top-fermenting ales. *Saccharomyces pastorianus* relates to bottom-fermenting lager yeast. Some strains have become iconic in brewing science. Chico yeast, for example, is strongly identified with American pale ales, especially those made by Sierra Nevada, as well as IPAs.

Wild yeasts such as *Brettanomyces* also play a role in beer. The lambic tradition of Belgium is distinguished by filling shallow, open vessels called "coolships" on the roof of the brewery, where fresh wort is exposed to airborne microbes as it cools. *Brettanomyces* has gained considerable use among craft brewers for its "funky" flavor profile; since it is a wild strain, however, it needs particular care to avoid contaminating other brews. Brett, as it is called, also factors into barrel-aging since the fungi can live in the wood.

WATER

It could be argued that water is the least sexy but most important ingredient in beer. Certainly, it carries the most weight, representing 85 to 95 percent of most brews.

Many of the world's prominent beers owe their character to local water. The soft water of Pilsen in the Czech Republic shapes the smoothness of Pilsner Urquell; the hard water of Burton-on-Trent, rich in calcium sulfate from area gypsum deposits, gives an edge to Bass Pale Ale; and the story goes on in Dublin, Munich, Vienna, and Virginia's Blue Ridge.

Much of water's character comes from the source, be it municipal, groundwater (think wells and aquifers), or surface water (think lakes and rivers). Technology avails various tools, such as filtration or reverse osmosis, to remove foreign and undesirable elements; chemical additives provide greater customizing options. Ions such as calcium, iron, sodium, magnesium, sulfate, and chloride each impact the character of beer, whether it be flavor (sulfate can give dryness and even a pleasant bitterness) or appearance (zinc boosts the foam).

Sustainability has become a growing concern among brewers, and water conservation is as important as sharing spent grain with local cattlemen. Wild Wolf Brewing Company in Nellysford received the Virginia Green Brewery of the Year award in 2015 and 2016

Spring-fed waters rather than beautiful sunsets led Coors
brewery officials to Elkton in 1987, back before the company was MillerCoors.

partially for its attention to water use. "Our water comes
from on-site wells, so water conservation is enormously
important to us," cofounder and president Mary Wolf
said in a news release. "We have streamlined all cleaning, brewing, and maintenance procedures to be as
water-efficient as possible. Flow meters are installed on
all appropriate equipment so that major water losses
can be quickly identified and stopped."

Richmond's wastewater authority on a mutually beneficial setup, where a treatment surcharge was removed (for other brewers as well) for use of the breweries' effluent, which contains ingredients still aerobically active and hungry to break down other waste. In 2017, Stone took things a bit further with an experimental "toilet to tap" beer—a pale ale called Full Circle made from sewage water recycled from a San Diego wastewater plant (Stone's home base is in Escondido, California, just outside San Diego). The batch was not offered for public sale, but it received complimentary reviews from local officials and enthusiastic backing from Steve Gonzalez, Stone's head of brewing innovation. Ballast Point, another California craft brewery that chose Virginia for an East Coast facility, stirred the pot in a similar fashion, producing Padre Dam Pilsner in a homebrew competition that stipulated using recycled wastewater.

The taste of place goes far beyond the four traditional ingredients. In making its acclaimed Gingerbread Stout, Hardywood Park uses baby ginger from Casselmonte Farm in Powhatan and wildflower honey from Bearer Farms in Oilville. Spencer Devon brewery in Fredericksburg also turns to local hives, using honey from Hungry Hill Farm in Nelson County for its Saison du Local. Like many breweries, Brothers in Harrisonburg brings in local pumpkins—nearly four hundred pounds for a 465-gallon batch—for its Five Pound Fall Ale. And the main ingredient for a historic persimmon beer made by Ardent Craft Ales? Strictly from Virginia.

Numerous factors weigh on the future of Virginia farms and businesses targeting growth by providing the ingredients used to brew beer. Much depends on the climate—political as well as entrepreneurial and environmental. Legislators in the Virginia General Assembly repeatedly introduced bills designed to give tax breaks to farmers providing barley, hops, or wheat to craft breweries in the state. The 2017 session saw a familiar fate; the bill languished in the House of Delegates Finance Committee.

No one predicts Virginia will compete with top-producing areas like the Pacific Northwest for hops or the Idaho/Montana/North Dakota region for barley. But interest remains strong, and developing ingredients for beverages that aren't cookie-cutter versions of brands offered elsewhere propels that quest for identity, that taste of place. With hops, for example, discovering or hybridizing a cultivar that grows well and is unique would create a valuable niche in the market, said hops guru Stan Driver: "That would be the magic bullet for our hop industry."

CHAPTER 3

Making It, Tasting It

Beer is a paradox. It's not necessary for survival, yet it has been a staple of life since humankind turned hunting spears into plowshares. Beer is a simple drink—just four ingredients, all of which occur naturally—yet "beer is the most complex beverage known to man," one authority says. Beer can be made at home, yet it drives a fiercely competitive, highly regulated global industry that in the United States alone counts for $108 billion annually.

So, how do we approach beer, in terms of understanding and valuing? One basic rule applies, and it involves another paradox: Beer takes only a moment to enjoy but can foster a lifetime of learning. Beer engages every sense, if we let it. Our eyes gauge the color; our nose, the aroma; our taste buds, the flavor; our touch, the mouthfeel. Even the sound of opening a bottle or can and hearing that effervescent fizz brings a smile to the soul.

While our level of enjoyment needs no sophistication, our degree of appreciation for each facet of beer's complexity grows with a grasp of the ingredients, the process, the stylistic parameters, the history, and the brewers' intent. Talking about or writing down what you taste is the best way to start; following your curiosity is the best path to knowledge.

The previous chapter dealt with beer's traditional ingredients—malt, water, hops, and yeast—in some detail, particularly as they apply to Virginia. The brewing process is more universal, and a quick overview might enhance the next sip you take, whether you're in a farmhouse tasting room or a Belgian brasserie. What follows is a simplified description; each step has variations that fill volumes.

First, go out and harvest a field of barley (it's not the only grain, but it's the predominant one for the malt that goes into beer). Strip the stalks so you're left with only the kernels. Steep those in water so that germination can occur. This promotes a natural growth process where enzymes inside the kernel (specifically, the endosperm) are activated to break down nutrients into building blocks for making beer. When the kernels are plump, soft, and have small sprouts called "chits," halt the germination, generally by air-drying. Then the malt can be roasted in a kiln at specific temperatures for specific times, depending on whether you want a light malt for a pilsner, or a dark, roasted malt for a stout.

Grind the malt to meet the specifications of the beer you're brewing and the nuances of your brewing system; the grain is called grist at this point. Now you're ready to begin the mash, the first real step in creating that beer you're thirsting for. Using a vat called the mash tun, combine the grains with water, then heat to form a porridge-like mix; this is called the mash. Times, temperatures, and processes differ according to whether you're making an ale or lager (and the various styles within each). Also, don't forget that the chemical composition of the water you're using is important in determining how the beer will taste. During this phase, those enzymes noted earlier are converting starches and proteins in the malt to sugars and amino acids that will be food for yeast during fermentation. But let's not get ahead of ourselves.

From Wort to Finished Product

Now, you'll want to separate the liquid in that porridge-like mushy mash from the grain husks. Various techniques are available, particularly using what's called a lauter tun, which acts like a big sieve. You can spray the remaining

TASTING BEER

The experience of savoring beer can be as simple or as involved as you like. You never have to apologize for the simple joy of a thirst-quenching swallow, but paying attention to various aspects can enhance your appreciation. Begin by being curious about the beer, either by asking a server or by perusing the menu or beer label to learn the style, ingredients, and alcohol level. Here are some basic sequential steps to evaluating beer.

AROMA. Your nose is more sensitive than your tongue. Immediately after the beer is poured, take a good whiff and see what you can detect in terms of malt (Is it toasty? Grainy? Roasted?), hops (Citrus? Herbal? Earthy?), and yeast (Spicy? Funky?). Fruity esters are common in ales. Now swirl the glass to release the volatiles and smell again.

APPEARANCE. Look at the head. Is it creamy or tawny? Are the bubbles tightly packed? Describe the beer's color (Straw? Amber? Brown? Black?). The Standard Reference Method (SRM) gives a range from one (straw) to forty (black) for the density of beer colors. See if you can guess the number of your beer. Also, look to see if the beer is clear or hazy (a quality of unfiltered or bottle-conditioned styles).

FLAVOR. What tastes do you experience on your palate? Sweet? Bitter? Caramel? Coffee? Chocolate? Herbs? Pay attention to different qualities affecting different areas of your tongue and mouth. A great beer will have a complex flavor that moves through your mouth (this is why beer judges don't spit out their samples, unlike wine judges).

MOUTHFEEL. This refers to the texture of the beer, with regard to three main attributes—carbonation, fullness, and aftertaste. Does your tongue tingle from the carbonation? Is there a sense of density or viscosity from the fullness? Is the aftertaste dry, bitter, smooth, or sticky?

OVERALL IMPRESSION. Put it all together. Think about balance—is it more on the malt side, with perhaps some sweetness or toasted qualities; or is it on the hops side, with perchance more bitterness and a dry finish? Judges use terms like "hop forward" or "malt forward." Is it full flavored, as with a stout, or light and refreshing, as with a kölsch?

Sources: The Beer Judge Certification Program, *The Oxford Companion to Beer*, the *CraftBeer.com Beer & Food Course, Professional Course*, and *Tasting Beer: An Insider's Guide to the World's Greatest Drink* by Randy Mosher (Storey Publishing, 2017)

grain with water to rinse residual sugars and attain the proper original gravity (a process called sparging). Now what you have is wort, a sweet concentration of liquid grainy goodness. Transfer this to your brew kettle, heat to a roiling boil, and add hops—a step intuitively called the boil. Here again, choices and decisions add to the complexity and creativity. The types and amounts of hops you use and the length of time they are in the boil determine much of the character of the beer, particularly the balance between sweet (from the grains) and bitter (from the hops). Hops also contribute their own flavor and aroma, elements you can adjust at various points in the process; dry-hopping, for example, is an option during fermentation or conditioning where hops are added largely to enhance the beer's aroma and flavor rather than bitterness.

After the boil, you're ready to filter out the hop residue, chill the wort as quickly as possible (to stop the chemical reactions in the liquid), oxygenate the wort, and add yeast (this is called pitching the yeast). Here again, yeast varieties abound—pale ale yeast, lager yeast, Belgian yeast, wild yeast—and each requires your careful consideration. These tiny microorganisms will begin gobbling up the sugars (maltose, dextrose, and others) in the wort and converting them mainly to alcohol and carbon dioxide (plus other compounds, some of which can be unpleasant if you're not a careful and sanitary brewer). You'll love the bubbling that occurs while this feast is under way. Ales mature more quickly than lagers, so this fermentation period is another variable. You will want to monitor the beer's specific gravity (its density at standard temperature and pressure) to determine alcohol content. When you've hit the bull's-eye, you'll transfer the beer (it's no longer wort) through a filter into tanks where it can be conditioned (a process of further maturing); prepared for packaging into bottles, cans, or kegs; put into barrels for long-term aging; or served directly to the customers in your tasting room, where they can savor the freshness, and where you can join them in sharing what you have created, another convivial link to the dawn of civilization.

For some folks, this process represents a way to make a commodity that can earn profits in the marketplace. For many others, brewing beer is a calling that forges unique bonds among passionate devotees. The combination of mastering the science needed to understand chemical reactions and channeling the artistic temperament for creativity hooks many a soul, none more than the homebrewers who provided the seeds for the craft beer boom.

Legally, the modern era of homebrewing can be traced to 1979, when legislation signed by President Jimmy Carter the previous year became effective. As noted earlier, it actually blossomed well beforehand, when travelers returned from overseas and began re-creating the flavorful ales and lagers they tasted on their journeys. In the Old Dominion, however, different circumstances led a student at the University of Virginia to embrace homebrewing in a way that would make history and forever change the brewing landscape in the United States.

Homebrewing Hobby Feeds Craft Surge

Charlie Papazian, an undergrad in UVA's nuclear engineering program, differed little from other students. He consumed beer mainly for alcoholic effect, not flavor. His buddies, however, told him about a man in Charlottesville who brewed his own beer, and they dropped by for a sample. As Papazian recalls, "He went down in the basement by himself and came up with a couple of brown quart bottles. He said, 'This is the good stuff. It's been aged a year.' He opened that, and we were quite impressed."

The process intrigued Papazian as much as the flavor, and he began experimenting on his own. Word spread until folks were coming up to him and asking how to make beer. "I would just say, 'Come on over—this is how to do it.'"

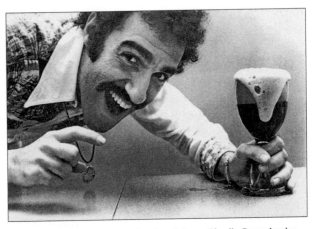

A seminal figure in the growth of craft beer, Charlie Papazian began homebrewing while a student at the University of Virginia.

After graduating in 1972, Papazian moved to Colorado, began teaching homebrewing, and eventually compiled his notes into a book called *The Complete Joy of Homebrewing*. First published in 1984 (an earlier version came out in 1978), it laid out the process in straightforward steps and reminded hobbyists to "Relax. Don't Worry. Have a homebrew." The book took off like a batch of bubbling wort, producing a legion of homebrewers nationwide. In 1978, he founded the American Homebrewers Association in Boulder, Colorado. As more homebrewers entered the commercial ranks, Papazian helped give shape to the groundswell through several efforts, most notably as president of the Brewers Association, the not-for-profit trade association that represents the nation's small and independent breweries.

Two other pioneering homebrewers, as noted in chapter 1, were Jim Kollar, a veterinarian, and Lou Peron, an orthodontist. In 1982, they began building Chesapeake Bay Brewing Company in an industrial park in the Lynnhaven area of Virginia Beach. It was the first commercial

WHAT IS A CRAFT BREWER?

There really is no formal definition of what constitutes craft beer. The Brewers Association, however, specifies three elements—small size, independence, and use of traditional ingredients—that constitute a craft brewer.

SIZE: Annual production cannot exceed six million barrels of beer (approximately 3 percent of U.S. annual sales). One barrel equals 31 U.S. gallons. Beer production is attributed to the rules of alternating proprietorship (see appendix C).

INDEPENDENCE: No more than 25 percent of the craft brewery can be owned or controlled (or have equivalent economic interest) by an alcoholic beverage industry member that is not itself a craft brewer.

INGREDIENTS: The majority of its total beverage alcohol volume must be in beers whose flavor derives from traditional or innovative brewing ingredients and their fermentation. Flavored malt beverages are not considered beers.

craft brewery in the South and, despite lasting only a few years, its beers achieved critical acclaim by medaling at the Great American Beer Festival.

At the same time that Kollar and Peron were going pro, clubs began sprouting up for homebrewers to share the passion as a hobby. In Richmond, a Vietnam veteran and chemist named Dan Mouer went into a local store that sold homebrewing supplies with the intent of posting a notice inviting interested parties to get together. To his surprise, a fellow named Mark Stansbury had already posted a similar message. "I was astonished, utterly astonished, at the fact that another person was trying to start a club or a group of homebrewers," Mouer recalled. The two corralled eleven others, and in early 1983 the James River Homebrewers was born.

That effort came on the heels of another club forming to the north. Eight hobbyists met at the home of Rick Gaskins in Gaithersburg, Maryland, in the summer of 1981 and planted the seeds for what evolved into a group with the endearing acronym of BURP—Brewers United for Real Potables. Membership extended into Washington, D.C., and Northern Virginia, and the group became instrumental in raising awareness of flavorful beer and creative brewing through festivals and contests, particularly its Real Ale Competition.

These days, hardly any region of the state lacks a homebrewers' club. In Charlottesville, where Papazian pitched his first yeast, the Charlottesville Area Masters of Real Ale, or CAMRA, meets monthly. Another acronym-spiffy group in the Richmond area is M.A.S.H., which stands for Mentoring Advanced Standards of Homebrewing. To the east, a club that started in 2005 as BARF (the Beer and Ale Research Foundation) changed its name to Seven City Brewers to draw from the entire Tidewater area. Roanoke boasts the Star City Brewers Guild; Winchester, the Shenandoah Valley Homebrewers Guild; Hampton, the Colonial Ale Smiths and Keggers (CASK).

These groups have been breeding grounds for great brewers, amateur and pro. Jamey Barlow of the CAMRA club won a gold medal in the specialty beer category at the 2016 National Homebrew Competition (one of his many awards, including Brewer of the Year at the 2014 Dominion Cup homebrew competition). Brandon Tolbert was a member of the James River Homebrewers before landing at The Answer in Richmond and winning the gold Best in Show Award at the 2015 Virginia Craft Brewers Cup.

Going pro doesn't mean forsaking roots. Collaborations with homebrewers yield some envelope-stretching results, such as at Center of the Universe Brewing Company in Ashland. Brothers and cofounders Phil and Chris Ray, both homebrewers, hold an annual "wort-sharing" event. Homebrewers gather on a particular day, pick up buckets of wort from a common batch, and then return home to concoct various brews in hopes of winning the grand prize—to have their beer commercially produced. The parameters were definitely increased by the 2017 winner, Mark Williams, with his Bloody Mary Beer. Hanover County is famed for its tomatoes, so he used them in his

Homebrewers gather at Center of the Universe brewery in Ashland to collect wort, which they customize for their own batches.

recipe, along with serrano peppers, horseradish, Worcestershire sauce, lime juice, sugar, celery salt, and pepper. A dash of Daddy G's Salsa, made by his friend Chris Galiffa, rounded out the mix and put him in the winner's circle. "Chris and Phil [Ray] both said it was great, a couple of other judges came by to congratulate me, and my homebrewing friends even admitted that they liked it, too."

Numerous other Virginia breweries nurture these bonds, for they represent the heart of the cultural shift that has brought flavorful beer to urban neighborhoods and rural retreats around the state. As the early months of 2017 were unfolding, members of the American Homebrewers Association were visiting sites in the state as potential venues for nationwide events, possibly even the marquee National Homebrewers Conference. That interest, combined with the continued blossoming of professional craft breweries, indicates that the beverage so vital to the settlers at Jamestown in colonial days is no less relevant to the health of the commonwealth in the twenty-first century.

CHAPTER 4

Pairing Flavors, Exploring Styles

On a sun-soaked fall day under crystal blue skies, Aaron Reilly stood inside a tent at the 2016 Top of the Hops festival in Charlottesville and addressed a standing-room-only crowd eager to hear about possibly the most seductive of food pairings—beer and chocolate. In general terms, one principle rules all possibilities. "If you like it, it's a good pairing. It doesn't matter what anybody else thinks," concludes Reilly, pilot brewer with Devils Backbone Brewing Company. "Having said that, there are several general rules to beer and food pairing."

Indeed, whether you're pairing Devils Backbone's Old Virginia Cream Ale with Gearhart's blueberry milk-chocolate bars made with lemon zest, or chasing a bite of pork barbecue with a swallow of Basic City N&W Porter, certain guidelines inform beer and food choices. As with most relationships, complexity and nuance are as valued as simplicity and soul. Here are three words to remember: complement, contrast, and cut. In the first, likes attract. In the second, opposites attract. In the third, one clears the stage and focuses the spotlight for the other.

Cheese holds a special spot on the menu of beer accompaniments. A full section of the national Brewers Association's *CraftBeer.com Beer & Food Course, Professional Course* focuses on the subject, offering six categories of pairings. A specialist in that beer-cheese niche is Margaret Bradshaw with Truckle Cheesemongers, based in Richmond,

PAIRING PRINCIPLES

Three principle interactions are at play in beer-food pairings.

COMPLEMENT: Look for harmonies in the aromas and flavors of the beers and food. For example, the roasted quality of malty beers such as porters and stouts finds resonance in the Maillard reaction that occurs when grilling or roasting meats. According to the *CraftBeer.com Beer & Food Course,* "The chemical reaction between amino acids and reducing sugars is the same whether it be in baking brioche, roasting a duck breast or kilning malt for beer."

CONTRAST: Think sweet versus sour, or bitter versus sweet. Contrasting flavors can have either a suppressing or an enhancing effect. A pale ale or IPA, with its hoppy bitterness, will contrast with the richness and fatty notes in a classic cream sauce. Bitter balances sweet in this case.

CUT: The carbonation and/or hoppy character of some beers can cleanse the palate by cutting away fat, sweetness, acidity, and any lingering fruity notes in food. A classic example noted by *CraftBeer.com Beer & Food Course* is "using the carbonation and citrus notes of a saison to cut away the buttery rich notes of . . . crab on the palate."

Source: The *CraftBeer.com Beer & Food Course, Professional Course*

who has taken her wares to numerous breweries—even to Black Heath Meadery and Blue Bee Cider in Richmond's Scott's Addition—always looking to find magic in the marriage of flavors. "I love pairings that go hand in hand and pick up on one another's qualities, such as aged gouda with caramel and meaty notes paired with a nice brown ale," she said. "I also like a pairing that does the opposite, by colliding, such as a sweet, spicy blue cheese paired with a good IPA. When I sit down to pair, I try to focus on one of these two approaches."

Given the diversity of beer styles among craft breweries, hitting a homer often depends on being able to handle the curveballs. Isley's Choosy Mother Peanut Butter Porter, for example, took an intuitive approach. "We tried it randomly with a goat gouda, and it ended up working. Pairings like that always remind me not to write something off until I've tried it," Bradshaw explained.

Therein lies the challenge as beer lovers have forged into territory previously dominated by wine aficionados. Brewers suggest food pairings with newly released beers. Starr Hill of Crozet, for example, recommended pairing its Double Bass Double Chocolate Stout with hoisin-glazed baby back ribs, as well as aged goat gouda (for cheese) and raspberry chocolate tart (for dessert).

Brewers also match taste buds with restaurateurs for meals that showcase pairings from soups to soufflés. Brothers Craft Brewing in Harrisonburg put together a six-course meal in 2016 featuring the culinary creativity of chefs from the city's Joshua Wilton House and Local Chop and Grill House. A tart saison accompanied Virginia blue crab salad with smoked salt dressing on challah slider rolls for starters. Subsequent courses featured a twice-cooked lamb and bacon dish paired with Brothers' Brown Out brown ale, smoked sausage tacos with guajillo peppers served with Scarlet Empire imperial red ale, and, to finish the evening, charred mushrooms stuffed with roasted

BEER LOVES CHEESE

Here are some cheese pairings to accompany suggested Virginia beers:

FRESH CHEESES: Pair with wheat beers and lambic-style ales: Starr Hill The Love, Port City Optimal Wit, and Seven Arrows Native Lambic.

SEMI-SOFT CHEESES: Pair with German styles (kölsch, bock, helles) and pale ales: Mad Fox Kellerbier Kölsch, Basic City Brazen Pan Bock, Lost Rhino New River Pale Ale, South Street My Personal Helles, and Brothers Lil' Hellion Lager.

FIRM/HARD CHEESES: Pair with pilsners, bocks, brown ales, and imperial stouts: Champion Shower Beer (a Czech-style pilsner), BadWolf Justin's Pilsner, Ardent Defenestrator Doppelbock, Midnight Not My Job Brown Ale, and Lickinghole Creek Enlightened Despot.

BLUE CHEESES: Pair with IPAs and imperial IPAs; beer choices are plentiful: Triple Crossing Clever Girl IPA, Deschutes Fresh Squeezed IPA, Stone IPA, Alewerks Bitter

chilies and a molé sauce using Resolute, the brewery's signature Russian imperial stout aged in bourbon barrels.

I also attended a similarly adventurous dinner hosted by Blue Mountain Brewing Company at the Jefferson Hotel in Richmond. Many of the details have faded, but I do recall being seated with folks who repeatedly professed not to be beer geeks. One woman had bought tickets for herself and her husband simply because she thought it would be fun. Beers appeared that none had tried before,

Valentine Double IPA, Smartmouth Notch 9 Double IPA, The Veil Master Shredder, Final Gravity Venus Rising Double IPA, Old Bust Head Graffiti House West Coast Style IPA, and any IPA from Ocelot.

NATURAL RIND CHEESES: Pair with golden or blonde ales, pale ales, and barleywine styles: O'Connor Green Can Gold Ale, Wild Wolf Blonde Hunny Ale, Blue Mountain Full Nelson Virginia Pale Ale, Legend Barleywine, and Seven Arrows Bear Mountain Barleywine.

WASHED RIND CHEESES: Pair with Belgian-style ales: Spencer Devon Sunken Road Belgian Blonde Ale, Studio Brew Dancing Monk Belgian Strong Ale, Strangeways Woodbooger Belgian-Style Brown Ale, and Soaring Ridge Belgian Dubbel.

Sources: Cheeses and styles from the *CraftBeer.com Beer & Food Course, Professional Course*; specific Virginia beer recommendations are by the author.

yet they sampled, savored, nodded, and puckered as their tastes dictated, all with smiles and open minds. They proved that being a beer geek need not be a prerequisite for enjoyment; an adventurous spirit suffices.

That said, an enhanced experience awaits those who develop a beer palate, particularly in refining one's assessment of the appearance, aroma, flavor, and mouthfeel associated with particular styles. Knowing that a West Coast IPA brewed with Cascade hops is likely to feature floral

A pairing of a saison with Virginia blue crab salad sandwiches at a beer dinner hosted by Brothers brewery in Harrisonburg.

and citrus notes in the nose helps guide food choices—pepperoni pizza, anyone? The malty sweetness of a stout is a well-known choice to complement the texture and briny goodness of oysters, yet the spice of a farmhouse saison can hit an equally satisfying spot.

The possibilities challenge the imagination, considering that each of the four ingredients that define traditional brewing (barley, hops, water, and yeast, discussed at length in chapter 2) carries myriad nuances within its family. Take hops: A guidebook published by a major hops contractor lists one hundred twenty-five cultivars from thirteen countries, from Australia-grown Ella to U.S.-grown Zeus. Each varies in bitterness, aroma, and flavor. Even in single-hopped beers, brewers can customize those qualities in assorted ways—by using freshly harvested rather than pelletized hops; by adding hops at different times in the boil; by dry-hopping (adding hops in the late- or post-fermentation stage); by serving the finished product unfiltered. Extend those options over every cultivar of hops. Now do the same with barley—two-row or six-row? Sown in winter or spring? Kilned to a toasted biscuit flavor or to a roasted coffee-chocolate darkness? Now yeast—ale or lager? West Coast Chico or Belgian saison? Or perhaps you'd like to try wild airborne yeast that makes a home in your wort while it is left cooling on a roof overnight? Finally, let's consider water—the "soft" water of Pilsen, home of pilsner beer, or the calcium/gypsum-rich "hard" water of Burton-on-Trent, famous for its pale ale. And let's not forget the water of the Blue Ridge Mountains, so ideal for brewing that it attracted a certain Colorado brewery to locate its East Coast facility in the charmingly rural environs of Elkton.

So, let's examine the possibilities. Four basic ingredients (with an emphasis on *basic,* because we're not counting the fruits, berries, sugars, spices, and adjunct grains that have found their way into brew kettles), each with hundreds of variations, multiplied by each other, factoring in nuances for locally produced ingredients, yield myriad options. Let's think of it in more manageable terms: If I eat exactly the same dinner each night, it would take about four months to pair that meal with one beer from each of the major categories listed in the Beer Judge Certification Program. And that doesn't allow me to experiment with which brown ale (Legend Brown? Newcastle? Three Notch'd No Veto? St. George Nut Brown? Lost Rhino Foxey Brown Smoked Brown Ale? Soaring Ridge Trail Head Nut Brown Ale?) tastes best with my meatloaf.

The Beer Judge Certification Program guidelines provide ample opportunity to learn about the specifics of such styles. They also frame the steps toward appreciating flavorful beer. Aroma, appearance, flavor, mouthfeel—each plays a role in the overall impression of a beer's character. You may not strive to memorize the difference between a Czech-style pilsner and a German-style pilsner (the latter

VIRGINIANS AT SAVOR

SAVOR, held annually in Washington, D.C., is the nation's premier beer-food pairing event presented by the Brewers Association. At the 2017 gathering, 86 craft breweries from around the country paired more than 170 beers with various dishes. Virginia was well represented with nine breweries participating. Here are a few examples of the Old Dominion's offerings with notes from the official menu:

ADROIT THEORY: All I see is Carrion (Belgian Quadrupel) paired with olive oil cake made with smoked plum and rosemary. "Smoked plum and sweet Belgian candi sugar brighten the palate. The rosemary provides a slight herbal note carried by the olive oil."

FAIR WINDS: Siren's Lure (Specialty Saison) paired with monkfish with nettle pistou and lemon. "The pistou works to tie in the saison yeast notes, while the monkfish adds a level of richness to dive deep into the complex notes of this beer."

HARDYWOOD PARK: Hardywood Ruse (Wood-aged Strong Stout) paired with brisket and confit potato. "Gentle smoke brings out the roastiness in this beer, while the confit potato holds the palate in check to dive deeper into the complex barrel-aged notes."

LICKINGHOLE CREEK: Magnificent Pagan Beast (Wood-aged Strong Beer) paired with an elk/pepitas/cacao mole. "Think of this pairing in the reverse. Let the elk play the role of the beverage and the beer play the dish. Take a bite of the mole first to coat the palate, then take a sip of the beer to let its complexities shine."

Source: SAVOR official menu

SAVOR, held annually in Washington, D.C., features pairings of various dishes with craft beers from around the country.

is lighter in color, flavor, and alcohol content), but knowing what's supposed to be there can lead to informed tasting and spirited discussions about styles.

And Virginia is fertile ground for exploring those styles. Unlike the West Coast, which has established a reputation for aggressively hopped IPAs, the mid-Atlantic has no signature style, at least not as I write. Here, diversity reigns, and in Virginia, unlike many other states, history also holds court. Ardent Craft Ales in Richmond's Scott's Addition gained international attention with a persimmon beer, brewed in conjunction with the Virginia Historical Society. That group's "History on Tap" program also included a molasses beer based on a colonial recipe researched by Frank Clark and brewed in Williamsburg at Virginia Beer Company. Another historic style, Lichtenhainer (a smoky East German ale), earned Hardywood Park Craft Brewery's Große Teufel a silver medal at the 2016 Great American Beer Festival.

Some Popular Beer Styles in Virginia

The diversity of beer styles can be bewildering as well as beautiful, particularly for those just beginning to sample the variations available in Virginia's taprooms. Informed choices can enhance enjoyment and add to lively discussions with fellow beer explorers. Here's a brief overview of some of the scores of styles you're likely to encounter in the Old Dominion, accompanied by representative examples from many of the breweries profiled in chapters 5 through 12.

LIGHT-COLOR, LOW- TO MID-ALCOHOL BEERS

American light lager: Here you find the country's biggest sellers—Bud Light, Coors Light, Miller Lite, and others. They are straw to pale yellow in color, have little or no malt aroma, have possibly some light hop aroma but little hop flavor or bitterness (8 to 12 IBUs), are highly carbonated, and have a light, crisp finish. *Example:* Yuengling Light Lager, Yuengling Brewery.

Kölsch: Associated with Köln (Cologne), Germany, kölsches are top-fermented in the ale tradition but lagered for extra conditioning. They are gold in color and have a subtle aroma that can be grainy from the malt or spicy from the yeast, a delicate grainy-sweet malt flavor, medium hop bitterness (18 to 30 IBUs), medium body, and a crisp finish. They can range in ABV from 4.4 to 5.2 percent. A highly drinkable and flavorful beer. *Example:* Kellerbier Kölsch, Mad Fox Brewing Company, Falls Church.

Pilsner: One of the few styles with a historically evident starting date, pilsners can be traced to the Czech Republic town of Pilsen, where Joseph Groll brewed the first batch in 1842. Now pilsners dominate the global market. A brilliant gold color with refreshing carbonation, a blend of moderate grainy sweetness and floral/spicy Saaz hops (30 to 45 IBUs) in the aroma and flavor, a soft roundness from the water, plus a modest alcohol content (4.2 to 5.8 percent ABV) make this style a favorite (with German versions lighter in ABV and a less aromatic hop profile). *Example:* Safety Dance, Smartmouth Brewing Company, Norfolk.

Saison: A farmhouse ale that originated in Wallonia, the French-speaking area of Belgium. Saisons vary widely in many aspects—in color from pale gold to dark brown; in aroma from fruity and spicy to peppery and malty; in flavor from moderately fruity and spicy to earthy and herbal. The body is generally light to medium; hop bitterness (20 to 35 IBUs) should be balancing rather than dominating. High carbonation makes saisons a companion for many foods. Generally, this is a highly refreshing, accessible style with broad appeal. *Example:* Salad Days American Saison, Pale Fire Brewing Company, Harrisonburg.

Weissbier: You often see the description "hefeweizen" ("hefe" means yeast; "weizen" refers to wheat). Straw to gold in color with a haze from being unfiltered, these beers are known for the banana esters and clove-like phenols that characterize the aroma and flavor. You might even catch a hint of bubblegum. With high carbonation, light body, low to moderate alcohol content (4.3 to 5.6 percent), and extremely little hop presence (8 to 15 IBUs), these ales are another German offering for thirst-quenching occasions. *Example:* The Love, Starr Hill Brewery, Crozet.

LIGHT-COLOR SOUR, TART BEERS

Berliner weisse: A wheat beer associated with Berlin and dubbed the "Champagne of the North" by Napoleon's troops in 1809. These effervescent ales are pale straw in color with a hazy appearance and have a sharply sour aroma and flavor from lactic acid, very little hop presence (3 to 8 IBUs), and range in ABV from 2.8 to 3.8 percent. A light, refreshingly sour beer perfect for summer afternoons, often blended with raspberry or woodruff syrups. *Example:* Berliner Weisse, Ardent Craft Ales, Richmond.

Gose: Another quirky German wheat ale that has found favor with craft beer brewers and drinkers, largely for the tart, refreshing zing. Goses (pronounced *GO-zehs*) are hazy gold (unfiltered), with a light fruity (sometimes lemony) aroma that can carry a briny tang from sea salt, a mild sourness in the flavor, high carbonation, and often a nuanced coriander character. Expect little if any hop presence (5 to 12 IBUs) and modest alcohol content (4.2 to 4.8 percent). *Example:* Gose Both Ways, Parkway Brewing Company, Salem.

LIGHT- TO AMBER-COLOR HOPPY ALES

ESB (Extra Special Bitter): The term "bitters" describes a range of British styles generally low in alcohol, high in drinkability, toasty in malt character, and moderately hoppy with floral and earthy notes. American brewers have adopted ESBs and made them slightly darker (deep copper in some), more midstream in alcohol content (4.6 to 6.2 percent), and more wide-ranging in hop profile. The emphasis is on balance and drinkability. *Example:* River Runner ESB, James River Brewery, Scottsville.

IPA: The acronym stands for India Pale Ale, based on beers that were shipped to India from England in the 1800s. IPAs are the nation's most popular style. They are gold to reddish-amber in color and high in hop bitterness (40 to 70 IBUs), aroma, and flavor. ABV ranges from 5.5 to 7.5 percent. Hopheads delight in high-octane imperial and double IPAs (DIPA), which can have bitterness values as high as 120 IBUs but with added malts for balance. *Example:* Face Plant IPA, Lost Rhino Brewing Company, Ashburn.

Pale ale: This style has English and American interpretations; the latter favor greater hop presence in the aroma and flavor and generally are more available in the Virginia marketplace. They are pale gold to light amber in color and moderate in alcohol content (4.5 to 6.2 percent). Citrus, pine, and grapefruit notes are common from New World hops, which should not overshadow the malt character (bready, toasty, or biscuity). In English versions, floral, spicy-peppery, and slightly grassy notes are common in the hops. *Example:* Lord Fairfax English Pale Ale, Lake Anne Brew House, Reston.

AMBER, BROWN BEERS

Amber ale: Developed as a slightly darker and maltier version of American pale ale with some interpretations bridging into the red ale category. Color is self-explanatory. Expect some citrus hop notes blending with a moderate caramel malty character in the aroma and flavor. Medium carbonation and body make this a welcome bridge between lighter and darker styles, with hop bitterness (25 to 40 IBUs) and alcohol content (4.5 to 6.2 percent) straddling extremes as well. *Example:* Red Nun Red Ale, O'Connor Brewing Company, Norfolk.

Bock: This German lager reputedly originated in the northern municipality of Einbeck but found its stride in Munich in the seventeenth century. Variations include Maibock (brewed in May, or *Mai*), helles Bock (*helles* means "light"), weizenbock (a wheat beer), and doppelbock ("double" bock). The standard is the "dunkels" ("dark") bock. It is light copper to brown in color and has a bready, toasted malt aroma and flavor with little or no hops presence (20 to 27 IBUs) and slightly elevated alcohol content (6.3 to 7.2 percent). *Example:* Hermenator Doppelbock, Seven Arrows Brewing Company, Waynesboro.

Brown ale: Here again, English and American versions differ, largely with more hop bitterness (20 to 30 IBUs) and alcohol (4.3 to 6.2 percent) in U.S. brews. Look for a light tan head on a clear brown body, and expect malt (with some sweetness and caramel, nutty, or toasted qualities) to dominate the aroma and flavor. *Example:* Brown Ale, Legend Brewing Company, Richmond.

Fest beer: These seasonal beers are associated with the fall harvest and with the Oktoberfest celebration in Munich. They are deep yellow to deep gold, with a moderate malty aroma and flavor with lightly toasted notes, a light hop character (18 to 25 IBUs), and medium body, ranging in ABV from 5.8 to 6.3 percent. Pumpkin beers also have become popular as a fall seasonal. *Example:* Oktoberfest, Old Bust Head Brewing Company, Vint Hill.

Vienna lager: Developed in Vienna in the 1840s and later popularized in Mexico by Austrian immigrant brewers, these beers are reddish amber to copper in color and have a toasted malt aroma and flavor with balancing low hop bitterness (18 to 30 IBUs), medium body, medium alcohol content (4.7 to 5.5 percent), and a smooth finish. *Example:* Crossroads Vienna Lager, Caboose Brewing Company, Vienna.

DARK BEERS

Porter: This ale, George Washington's favorite, evolved from strong brown beer popular in London in the 1700s and became a favorite during the Industrial Revolution. Brown in color, porters have bready, toasted malt traits in the aroma and flavor with perhaps a touch of chocolate and caramel. Hop bitterness is medium (18 to 35 IBUs) in the English version and more aggressive (25 to 50 IBUs) in American interpretations; traditional British hops give a floral or earthy character. Overall, this is a medium-body, medium-strength beer (4 to 6.5 percent) with lots of malt character. *Example:* Ghost Rider Porter, Big Ugly Brewing Company, Chesapeake.

Stout: By many accounts, an offspring of porter due to the description of strong versions as "stout porter." Variations abound—milk stout, oyster stout, oatmeal stout, Irish stout, tropical stout, imperial stout, and more. Irish Stout, brewed by world-renowned Guinness, borders on black (or dark ruby, the company says), has a tight, light-brown head (often using dense nitrogen gas), and accentuates complex coffee, chocolate, and roasted notes in the aroma and flavor. Some versions are aggressively hopped (25 to 45 IBUs is the traditional range) and can combine with the malts for a dry finish. Alcohol content is a deceptively low 4 to 4.5 percent ABV in this Irish version, but can range as high as 12 percent in imperial stouts. *Example:* Blackreach Stout, BadWolf Brewing Company, Manassas.

Wee heavy: This style is sometimes called Scotch ale and is not to be confused with lighter Scottish ales. Rich malt dominates every facet, from the caramel in the aroma and flavor to the copper-brown color and tawny head. Sometimes a hint of smoke comes through from the roasted malt; expect a sweetness in the flavor and finish, and a full-bodied mouthfeel with alcohol warmth. This is a rich, strong beer (6.6 to 10 percent ABV) with minimal hop presence (17 to 35 IBUs). *Example:* The Ferminator, Backroom Brewery, Middletown.

Belgian-style dubbel: One of several Belgian styles rooted in the monastic tradition, this is a step up from the Belgian singel in alcohol strength (6 to 7.6 percent), color (reddish-copper), and complexity. A rich malt character dominates the aroma with notes of raisins, plums, or cherries; those traits come through in the flavor as well. The body and carbonation are medium, and hop presence is low (15 to 25 IBUs). *Example:* Lustful Maiden, Apocalypse Ale Works, Forest.

Belgian-style tripel: Another step up. Be careful—the golden color can belie the potency of the alcohol content (7.5 to 9.5 percent). This beer rewards those who seek complexity and harmony. Spiciness dominates the aroma and flavor, along with fruity esters and occasionally a banana or clove-like note. A hint of honey and a suggestion of pepper might pop up as well, and the hops and yeast combine for medium bitterness and a dry finish. All in all, this is one of the loveliest beers in the brewing realm. *Example:* Duke Belgian Tripel, Belly Love Brewing Company, Purcellville.

History Combines with Innovation

The deep roots of some of these styles have found new expression with modern methods. At The Veil, the Belgian lambic tradition of open-air fermentation, where fresh wort is left exposed overnight to airborne microorganisms (aka wild yeast), finds fresh interpretation by head brewer Matt Tarpey. His résumé includes a stint at the Cantillon Brewery in Anderlecht, Belgium, renowned for its lambics (including the kriek, made with cherries) and for housing a museum devoted to the gueuze style (made by blending various ages of lambic, which is then laid down for an additional period of fermentation).

The Veil also created a buzz when fans stood in line on Tuesdays for the weekly release of the latest canned batch of juicy, fruity IPAs. As does the rest of the country, Virginia loves India Pale Ales. Nationwide, IPAs claimed more than 25 percent of the dollar share among craft beer styles in 2016, well ahead of the second-place seasonal category (13 percent). No similar statistics exist for Virginia's market, but rare is the brewery that does not offer at least one IPA. More likely, you will encounter multiple choices—imperial IPAs, session IPAs, black IPAs, rye IPAs, Belgian IPAs, coffee IPAs, fruit-infused IPAs, pepper-packed IPAs, and red, white, or brown IPAs—all within the state's border.

Another style that Virginians have embraced—saison—flies just under the radar. This farmhouse ale, with roots in Belgium's Wallonia, lends itself to broad interpretation, given its history of being brewed with an assortment of grains, herbs, and spices. In Richmond alone, I counted sixteen different saisons brewed by seven breweries. In Tidewater, Smartmouth welcomed summer with Farmer's Tan Hoppy Saison, loaded with fragrant Citra hops, and Commonwealth conjured the dark side with Dysphotic Black Saison—malty, fruity, and dark as ebony. To the north, Ocelot of Sterling used wildflower honey for its *biere de miel* Honey Pie Farmhouse Ale. In the Star City of Roanoke, Deschutes of Oregon celebrated the announcement of its Virginia facility by brewing Roanoke River Saison, dry-hopped with El Dorado hops and featuring a traditional saison yeast yielding notes of banana, bubblegum, clove, and a hint of melon. And in Charlottesville, Champion took the style from its rural heritage to the Downtown Mall in 2017 by opening Brasserie Saison, a restaurant with crisp linens and bright lights where

Belgian-style beers and French wines are matched with Franco-Belgian cuisine (think steamed mussels, crispy scallops, raw or fried Brussels sprouts, and more). Hunter Smith, Champion's founder and owner, partnered with restaurateur Wilson Richey to develop the concept, a combination of internationally inspired cuisine and locally sourced agricultural products.

With the abundance of styles and interpretations, it's risky to single out specific Virginia beers as exceptional. Two, however, rise to the challenge. Devils Backbone's Vienna Lager has won awards from every festival and competition imaginable, from the Great American Beer Festival to the World Beer Cup. The recipe is the brainchild of Jason Oliver, DB's founding brewer. Always a fan of German-style lagers, he began by studying index cards he'd assembled over the years. "I put a lot of thought into it," he said, "but once we started using it, the recipe didn't change much." The beer succeeds on two important levels. First, it's a comfortable gateway beer for mainstream drinkers, with a middling 5.3 percent ABV and minimum bitterness (18 IBUs). Second, it's complex enough to satisfy discriminating beer geeks with its blend of caramel, toasted malts, and subtle hops. As of early 2016, before Devils Backbone was acquired by Anheuser-Busch InBev, the recipe used Vienna, pilsner, dark Munich, and caramel malts; Northern Brewer and Saaz hops provided sufficient bitterness to balance the sweetness and a delicate floral, spicy aroma.

The other style (and exceptional Virginia example) worth noting is kölsch, specifically that introduced by Bill Madden while he was head brewer with Capitol City Brewing Company in the D.C. area (Madden is now cofounder of Mad Fox, and his kölsch is still a flagship). It's incredible to think of this style, now a staple of many breweries, as being so new that people stumbled over the pronunciation. When I interviewed Madden in 2000, he said people

Bill Madden, cofounder of Mad Fox brewery, has been a longtime champion of kölsch beers.

were pronouncing it as everything from *Grolsch* to *klosch*. That aside, it quickly established its popularity as a gateway beer. "People come in and the first thing they'll say is, 'What's your lightest?' And the bartender, without even asking, will just pass them a kölsch." As noted, the style and the name derive from the German city of Köln (Cologne); a story holds that Madden once was told a proper kölsch couldn't be brewed outside of the shadow of a certain cathedral there. No worries—he ordered a souvenir of the cathedral and placed it on top of the brewery's lauter tun.

Madden credits Capitol City's original brewer, Martin Virga, with the initial recipe, but notes that "this is a beer style that I have worked on for years getting right." A silver medal at the 2001 Great American Beer Festival confirmed that he did indeed get it right. Initially, the recipe called for all-German ingredients (except for the water), including signature Tettnanger hops. After moving to

Mad Fox, which he opened in 2010 with business partner Rick Garvin, Madden launched another version, a Kellerbier Kölsch. It also has medaled (gold at the 2011 GABF), and because it's unfiltered, it gives a fuller mouthfeel and a fruitier flavor. Both versions sport the low alcohol level (4.4 percent ABV) that has characterized the trend toward sessionable beers.

"Kölsch has been a very successful product for us. It's a very small beer, a delicate beer to make. It really is a challenge," Madden said in an interview with *Virginia Craft Beer* magazine. "It's a beer in which a brewer really stands naked. There's nowhere to hide with a kölsch."

Mentioning medals begs the question: How good are Virginia beers and breweries? Gold, silver, and bronze awards reflect only one aspect of quality, though the consensus of experienced judges carries considerable weight. At the Great American Beer Festival, Virginia breweries counted seven medals in 2010, eight in 2011, and rose to a peak of fourteen in 2013, which they matched in 2016. By comparison, in 2016 craft brewing centers such as California won sixty-eight; Colorado, thirty-eight; and Oregon, twenty-one. Devils Backbone twice won back-to-back GABF awards for Small Brewpub and Small Brewing Company; when it outgrew that category, it won again for Mid-Size Brewing Company and Brew Team in 2014. (It moved out of the craft brewer category after its acquisition by AB InBev in 2016.) In 2015, Port City of Alexandria received the award for top Small Brewing Company in the nation.

In other measures, Hardywood Park in Richmond raised eyebrows in 2012 when its Gingerbread Stout received a perfect 100 rating from *BeerAdvocate,* a rare achievement. Neighboring Strangeways was twice named one of the South's best breweries by *Southern Living* magazine. *Frommer's* travel guide listed the craft beer scene among the reasons it highlighted Richmond as a top destination in 2014. Add to the kettle the fact that four major

West Coast breweries—Green Flash, Stone, Deschutes, and Ballast Point—have settled on sites in Virginia (with Green Flash closing its Virginia Beach operation in 2018), and you get an indication that the state, while not on the level of California, Colorado, or Oregon, certainly belongs in any conversation of thriving craft beer communities. "There is a lot of quality beer being brewed in the state," said Dave Gott, vice president of operations at Legend Brewing Company.

CHAPTER 5

History and Innovation in Northern Virginia

The region of the state closest to Washington, D.C., combines some of the most historic brewing sites with some of the most innovative. At Port City, founder Bill Butcher and his head brewer have developed and patented a special hopping process. Portner Brewhouse in Alexandria draws on the legacy of Robert Portner's brewing enterprise, the largest in the South in the late 1800s. Fair Winds in Lorton has garnered critical acclaim with its medal-winning Howling Gale IPA, Siren's Lure saison, and other beers. Lake Anne Brew House in Reston focuses on creating a community destination rather than pursuing widespread distribution. Bill Madden displays his love of kölsch and malty styles at Mad Fox in Falls Church. Sarah and Jeremy Meyers showcase their quirky approach to brewing at Bad-Wolf, the first craft brewery in Manassas. Mustang Sally's spacious facility has allowed it to host numerous events, including the Fairfax County BrewFest. Tying them all together is the Beltway Beer Trail, which links twenty-five breweries in Fairfax, Manassas, Alexandria, Falls Church, Arlington, and beyond.

Port City Brewing Company

When Bill Butcher was setting up the brewing system for Port City before its opening in 2011, Jonathan Reeves, his head brewer, insisted on a piece of equipment that might not have seemed as essential as the tanks, hoses, kegs, and coolers. It was a D.O. meter—a device to measure the beer's amount of dissolved oxygen, an element that impairs shelf life and quality.

"This piece of equipment is about the size of a toaster and costs about as much as a Hyundai—about $14,000," Butcher noted with a chuckle. "But Jonathan emphasized how important that instrument was in assuring beer quality. So we bit the bullet and bought the D.O. meter, and that formed the basis of our lab."

It also formed the basis of Port City's philosophy of emphasizing quality in every aspect of brewing its beers, a focus that has led to numerous awards and consistent growth. After being named Small Brewing Company of the Year at the 2015 Great American Beer Festival and launching a multiyear $3 million expansion program, Port City climbed into the ranks of regional breweries with production at 16,000 barrels in 2017 and expected to hit 20,000 barrels annually in 2018. "I like to tell our people that we're swimming in the deep end of the pool now," Butcher said.

Sales and awards have been led by Optimal Wit, a Belgian-style white ale brewed with Virginia wheat that accounts for more than 35 percent of production. In addition to the traditional coriander and orange peel, the brew uses grains of paradise to give a peppery finish. "Other wit beer producers generally don't give it that ingredient," observed Butcher.

Brewing traditional styles with a unique twist or unusual ingredient defines another tenet of Port City's approach. You won't find some of the creative extremes that fill the tanks at some craft breweries. "We like to say we focus on beer-flavored beer," Butcher said. "We do focus on classic styles. Basically, what we're trying to do is brew beer that is complex with layers of flavor that also is approachable and easy to drink." Flagships Monumental

IPA, balanced and accessible at 57 IBUs and 6.3 percent ABV, and Port City Porter, chocked with coffee and chocolate notes from its malt depth, fit that bill.

While creating a deeper footprint through its production side is an obvious goal, Port City values the role its tasting room on Wheeler Avenue serves as a community center. Trivia nights, bluegrass and jazz bands, yoga workouts, a running club, and political events create a hub in the densely populated area around Duke Street. Even extraterrestrials and Star Trekkers found a niche on Halloween, along with lumberjacks, pirates, ghosts, and ghost-busters.

As one of the state's veterans, Butcher has seen the warp-speed rise of craft breweries in Virginia. As we spoke in June 2017, a media release was announcing that the number of licensed breweries had risen to 206—a five-fold increase in five years. Butcher believes the numbers don't mean that standards for excellent beer are being diluted.

"The level of quality in Virginia is extremely high, and the bar has been set very high by the people who opened from the very beginning," he said. "We've all been focused on quality. And that is what I believe is going to drive the business in the future."

And just as that D.O. meter played a role in Port City's evolution, a new dry-hopping device developed by Reeves figures in the future. It's called a Hopzooka, and Port City received a patent on the design in 2016. It stands about head high, has three wheels, and is shaped like a small fermenter. You put in pelletized hops, purge the container of oxygen by infusing carbon dioxide, build up the pressure with CO_2, then shoot the hops into the fermenter. "It helps with the aromatics, and because you're adding virtually zero oxygen during this process, it's increasing the shelf life and stabilizing the beer," Butcher said. "So, overall it's an improvement in the quality of the beer."

Bill Butcher (*left*), founder of Port City, and head brewer Jonathan Reeves developed and patented a Hopzooka.

Try this: Port City's Optimal Wit was not the first of its beers to win an award (Monumental IPA did in 2012), but it has won repeatedly at the Great American Beer Festival and the Virginia Craft Beer Cup. "Tastes like sunshine and happiness," the website reads. For me, it's the crisp wheat character, the classic coriander flavor, and the citrus edge from orange peel that mark the beer's appeal. Pay close attention and you'll get a peppery note from grains of paradise. Drinkability also is a factor; ABV is 4.9 percent and IBUs are 15.

Portner Brewhouse

More than a century had passed since Virginia saw a tap list with these names—Tivoli Cream Ale, Vienna Cabinet Lager, Hofbrau Pilsner, and Portner Porter. They were proudly displayed on placards inside a certain Alexandria

Four pre-Prohibition beers add historic authenticity to the Portner Brewhouse in Alexandria.

brewpub that opened its doors in March 2017, and the connection with history was no marketing ploy.

Sisters Catherine and Margaret Portner offered versions of those pre-Prohibition beers to celebrate the legacy of their great-great-grandfather, Robert Portner, who steered the original Portner company to prominence as the South's leading brewery before closing in 1916 (see chapter 1). Photos, documents, and other memorabilia graced the walls and added an air of venerability to the otherwise freshly minted sheen of the brewpub.

What I didn't know when I plopped down at the bar a week after Portner Brewhouse's opening was that the young man sitting next to me was head brewer Brian McElvaney. And as I worked through a flight of those four beers with historic pedigrees, he told me about the research that the sisters put into the recipes and how his own background—he spent two stints in Germany and was trained at a brewery in Einbeck—helped shape the brews. The beers' names and much of the original marketing material were well known, and sleuthing by the Portner sisters had unveiled additional clues about brewery operations. But no written recipes surfaced.

"We are of the opinion that brewing was a skill passed down from one individual to the next," Catherine told *Mid-Atlantic Brewing News*. "Since breweries produced fewer unique beers than we see today, it would not have been difficult for a brewer to memorize one or two recipes and then try a new one every once in a while. Thus, a strong need to write down the recipes did not exist."

McElvaney uses a 3.5-barrel system to re-create the pre-Prohibition styles. They score high in drinkability, with appropriately low bitterness and with ABV ranging from 5 percent for the Vienna Cabinet Lager to 6.3 percent for the Portner Porter. The Tivoli Cream Ale (recall that Tivoli is "I Lov It" spelled backward) offers fruity esters, while the Hofbrau Pilsner is appropriately crisp and has a dry bite at the finish.

"The Hofbrau Pilsner and the porter are the two favorites so far," Catherine told me. "The porter is a big surprise because the recipe includes a lot of brown malts. It has a very strong coffee flavor, so it's one that deviates from what people expect from a porter."

Portner Brewhouse also offers seasonals—a Belgian dubbel, a pale ale, a German IPA, and a chocolate stout during my visit—and a Craft Beer Test Kitchen where homebrewers and other individuals can ply their skills. The restaurant menu emphasizes German options such as Bavarian pretzels, potato pancakes, bratwurst, and sauerkraut as well as contemporary American cuisine.

The culinary side of the operation reflects Margaret's interest in cuisine, while the beverage part is an outgrowth of the homebrewing Catherine started a decade before launching the brew house. They'd been raised in Virginia Beach on stories about the Portner brewing business, "but when you're ten years old, it doesn't impress you much," Catherine said. Friends in college with a love of history showed such interest that the Portners began to appreciate their heritage more and to consider combining their interests commercially. "We grew up in an entrepreneurial family, so it was only a matter of time until we started our own business."

In its first eight months of business, the brewery produced nearly five hundred barrels of beer. Catherine foresees limited distribution of kegs to local retailers, but the small size of the current system precludes anything on a grander scale.

Try this: Rarely do you get a chance to try four pre-Prohibition beers that have a stamp of legitimacy like Portner's. So order a flight and get a range of old-school flavors. Hofbrau Pilsner and Vienna Cabinet Lager were flagship brews for Robert Portner; I particularly liked the latter for its copper color and the toffee notes from the Vienna and Munich malts. Portner Porter is malt-forward in a bigger way, with just a touch of sweetness to go with the coffee roast.

Mad Fox Brewing Company

A restrained dryness, preferably from German noble hops; a touch of wheat malt character; a crisp finish; and maybe a hint—just a hint—of sulfur: That's what Bill Madden would like you to get from the kölsches he brews at Mad Fox.

Madden is passionate about kölsches, a style he has been associated with since starting at Capitol City Brewing Company in 1995 (see chapter 4). While other brewers scramble to make their mark in a landscape dominated by IPAs, Madden's first love is malt.

"I've been called a malt-head by many," he said as we relaxed at the bar in the Falls Church location (a Mad Fox taproom is located in D.C. on Wisconsin Avenue in Glover Park). "I've had to change my ways, especially since we opened Mad Fox. I've also been known for wee heavy and some of the British cask ales. I've learned to train myself to do more hoppy beers. But the thing I do differently from West Coast brewers is I always like to have that malt backbone." That's borne out by the Orange Whip IPA, brewed with Citra hops to 75 IBUs and brimming with fruit aroma, but particularly notable for its caramel and crystal malt balance. It's rated "outstanding" by *BeerAdvocate* magazine.

Madden enjoys rare stature in Virginia. He's been brewing beers and managing pubs in Virginia nearly continuously since graduating from the renowned brewing program under Dr. Michael Lewis at the University of California–Davis. "Capitol City hired me before I even graduated," Madden recalled. He inherited recipes from a German brewer, Martin Virga, who managed to add a touch of Deutschland to nearly every style. And kölsch, originally from Köln in Germany's Rhineland, was a flavorful answer for the most common question of the day: "What's your lightest beer?"

"Nobody was doing kölsch then, but there weren't many breweries then, either," Madden said. "We used to kid ourselves and call it the Köln on the Potomac." There was more cheering than kidding when Capitol Kölsch won a silver medal at the 2001 Great American Beer Festival.

Madden left Capitol City and served a stint at Founders Restaurant and Brewing Company in Old Town Alexandria before taking a short break from the beer world. Four years at Vintage 50 in Leesburg followed; then he cofounded Mad Fox with his wife, Elizabeth, homebrewer Rick Garvin, and others. That was in 2010, before Virginia law allowed breweries to sell beer retail on-site without selling food.

"A friend of mine, another brewpub owner, and I talk a lot, and we both have the experience of people walking in and saying, 'My gosh, you have food, too!' The brewpub model is less and less the experience, and less and less brewpubs are opening," Madden said.

Mad Fox's production in 2017 was about 1,700 barrels; the Falls Church tap selection featured fourteen beers, including several IPAs, an altbier, a saison, an 80-shilling Scottish ale, and, of course, kölsch. Barrel-aging and kettle-souring with *Lactobacillus* were finding favor in the brewing regimen as well.

With plenty of capacity at 3,800 barrels, Mad Fox was moving beyond sales at its two brewpubs into distribution. As Madden observed, "Ten years ago, I never thought I would be in distribution. We sold all the beer we could produce out of the brewpub."

What is less of a surprise is that Madden still rocks the kölsch style. The Kellerbier Kölsch, an unfiltered interpretation, won gold at the 2011 GABF and silver at the 2016 Virginia Craft Beer Cup. And there is still plenty of passion in Madden's approach. "The combination of art and science—that's what is so attractive about this job," he said. "We take all these agricultural products and bring them all together to produce beer—beers of all different flavors and profiles. Golly, what you can do with beer is phenomenal."

Try this: Kölsches sometimes fly under the beer geek radar because they are considered "gateway" beers, for craft newbies rather than aficionados. Kellerbier Kölsch proves the opposite. Being unfiltered gives it more body and a slight haze in appearance; the wheat crispness combines with lemon notes and a mildly dry finish to provide ultimate drinkability at 4.4 percent ABV.

Lake Anne Brew House

It's a sunny, temperate afternoon in mid-August 2017, one of those days that straddle Virginia's muggy summer heat and brisk autumn brilliance. Lively chatter bubbles around a finger of Lake Anne that pokes at a cluster of shops and apartments in this Reston neighborhood. A bevy of colorful kayaks and paddleboats moored at the water's edge bob like flower petals lilting in the breeze.

Moments earlier, an armada of paddlers had taken to the water for the inaugural Lake Anne Cardboard Boat Regatta. Melissa Romano, her clothes still damp, smiled as she recalled her nautical misadventure. "We capsized, but it was still great fun," she said.

Being part of this charity event (which benefited the Reston Historic Trust and Museum) was just one expression of community involvement for Melissa and her husband, Jason. They've lived on the lake for years, raising three kids and working in the area, she as an architect, he as a government contractor. Now they are extending that sense of community with Lake Anne Brew House. The space is intimate—47 seats, mostly on a tiered patio overlooking the lake—and their goals are modest. Jason, a longtime homebrewer and certified beer judge, says he's content using a two-barrel system to supply the taproom only. Visions of distributing beers to a broader market are not part of the business plan.

That said, Jason's beers have gained wide attention and respect. In the brewery's inaugural year, Lake Anne won two medals in the 2016 Virginia Craft Beer Cup competition. Three more medals followed in 2017, putting Lake Anne among the elite of Virginia breweries. Lord Fairfax English Pale Ale was a repeat medalist, winning in the Extra Special Bitter/English Pale Ale category. At 5.5 percent ABV and 33 IBUs, it is among several accessible beers that anchor Lake Anne's lineup.

"We set out in this business to just make really high-quality beer, not to be too crazy and experimental, not to do too many trendy things," Melissa explained. That said, North Shore New England Style IPA was a nod to one of the hottest styles going with its juicy, orange-peel tropical fruitiness and hoppy bitterness (45 IBUs).

Melissa and Jason Romano have won numerous medals for Lake Anne's beers, but their main focus is on serving the Reston community.

The couple split duties at the brew house. While Jason oversees the beer operation, Melissa runs the front of the business, where her background in architecture informed the choice of decor. During renovation, she removed the tile to expose the original concrete floors, which were then polished. Furnishings glow with bright orange accents, and walnut in the bar area gives a woodsy touch. "We tried to take [the space] back to its vintage, original state and kick it up a notch," Melissa said. The goal was to reflect Lake Anne's Brutalist architecture, a style that caught on in the 1950s and flourished for more than two decades.

As the afternoon breeze tickled the surface of Lake

Anne, and a flight of fresh handcrafted beer awaited tasting, I could only agree with one of Melissa's comments: "Brews with views . . . what more could you ask for?"

Try this: While the Lord Fairfax English Pale Ale warrants serious attention, I suggest you first ask for a sample of 2017.5 Golden Ale (a Belgian golden strong ale in the mold of Duvel, the definitive example of the style). The beer was introduced originally as New Year's Golden Ale at the dawn of 2017 and returned that summer after winning gold at the 2017 Virginia Craft Beer Cup (hence the .5 in the name, which will probably change by the time you read this). It was the biggest and most complex of the beers when I visited. Jason notes pear and pineapple notes from the fruity esters; I fully enjoyed the spiciness from the yeast, always a hook among Belgian styles. It weighs in at 9 percent ABV and 28 IBUs, and is served in ten-ounce pours (unless in flights).

Fair Winds Brewing Company

Ask any brewer—winning a medal in a significant competition is a thrill. It signals the ability not only to make excellent beer but also to meet the criteria of a specific style. The next step up the ladder of acclaim is winning multiple medals; the highest rung is taking home awards repeatedly for diverse beers in the portfolio.

Fair Winds opened in Lorton in March 2015. A month later, its Howling Gale IPA was named Best IPA in Northern Virginia by a regional magazine. Shortly after that, Siren's Lure saison won gold at the Great American Beer Festival, the toughest competition in the country. In 2016, Fair Winds brought home three awards in the Virginia Craft Beer Cup, with Siren's Lure again a medalist.

How does such a string affect such a young brewery? "Our brew crew and the entire crew has sort of adopted this mantra of 'it doesn't matter how old we are,'" said founder Casey Jones. "As long as we're putting out quality product, that product competes without an age to it. It competes solely on its merit."

Though he's homebrewed for decades, Jones decided from the outset that he wanted a professional with a proven record to head the brewing operation. Charlie Buettner, who was commuting from Burke to Falls Church to work at Mad Fox, fit the bill. In terms of recipe development, quality assurance, and actual brewing, Jones said, "I tell him, 'Charlie, this is your brewery.'"

The business, though, was founded by Jones and has been a dream since he was at the Coast Guard Academy. Sierra Nevada Pale Ale was a game changer in his beer appreciation, and homebrew batches flowed—not always with stellar results. One recipe requiring jalapeño peppers was so over the top that Jones couldn't even finish a pint. That was an aberration, though, and didn't discourage him. Just after leaving the Coast Guard, he moved to Northern Virginia and began shaping a serious business plan.

His first choice for the brewery's name, Topsail, ran aground, thanks to a challenge from a certain brewery in Bend, Oregon. The fallback to Fair Winds was a natural offshoot of the sailors' expression, "May you always have fair winds and following seas." Doors opened in 2015 on a twelve-thousand-square-foot space housing a ten-tap tasting room and a thirty-barrel system primed to supply both the taproom and the packaging side of the business. Two years after opening, Fair Winds was cranking out an estimated 4,500 to 5,000 barrels on an annual basis and distributing beers throughout Virginia and D.C.

The top seller, Howling Gale IPA, follows the national trend toward hoppy beers. Loaded with Simcoe, Mosaic, and Citra hops used both in "massive" kettle additions and double-dry hopping, it weighs in at 80 IBUs and has the signature West Coast citrus and tropical fruit profile.

Quayside Kölsch and Siren's Lure are the second- and third-best sellers.

Jones's goal in 2018 is to expand the canning line from three to six beers, including seasonals such as Pohick Bay Pilsener, Hells Navigator (a Maibock/helles bock), and Nautifest (an Oktoberfest).

Try this: Any beer that wins gold at the GABF (not to mention bronze at the 2016 and 2017 Virginia Craft Beer Cup competitions) deserves special mention. Siren's Lure puts a hoppy imprint on the traditional saison style. Jones points out that dry-hopping with Hallertau Blanc hops gives the ale a tart, dry white-wine finish; Galaxy and Zythos are used as bittering hops in the boil (32 IBUs). The grain bill includes pilsner and Vienna malts, and of course the Belgian yeast adds its characteristic spice and fruity esters. Alcohol content is 7.2 percent by volume.

BadWolf Brewing Company

Sarah and Jeremy Meyers like to sprinkle a little offbeat fun in their business. Take, for example, the You Will Not Like This IPA. Jeremy cranked it out because IPAs are not his favorite style to brew, but his customers were eager for a high-octane West Coast option. He made it big and bold, a lupulin challenge for hopheads. The joke, however, turned out to be on him.

"It's been a hit," Sarah said in a 2016 interview, as have other beers from BadWolf. After opening doors in June 2013 with a one-barrel system in an intimate space on Center Street, the Meyerses added a ten-barrel production brewery on Kao Circle and partnered in a full-service brewpub on Battle Street in Manassas's historic district. However, in April 2018, the Meyerses announced making "the incredibly tough decision to downsize" and closed the Kao Circle facility. "We want to focus on our family, quality of life and go back to our roots with BadWolf." They still have retained their quirky approach at Center Street, though, with beers such as Funky Lil' Meemaw (a sour grisette) and Mabel's Mystery Milk Stout (made with a bag of "mystery grain").

"Our philosophy is we do not want to be super niche. Our goal is to be centered around the community, to poke a little fun, and to have a good time," Sarah said when I talked with her in 2016. That involvement is reflected in programs on area beer history and their use of local ingredients for brews and food.

Their approach evolved during a class Sarah took on entrepreneurship. Sarah, who has lived in Manassas since the age of two, was working for several businesses while attending George Mason University. Jeremy, who also came to the area as a tyke, fell in love with flavorful beer on a trip to Germany and took up homebrewing at age

Sarah Meyers and her husband, Jeremy, built BadWolf from a one-barrel system in a tiny space to three locations in Manassas.

seventeen. The project Sarah's group tackled for class was to plan a brewery; their effort earned an A. They put it aside until "Jeremy had a rough day at work one day and said, 'I want to start that brewery,'" Sarah recalled. They talked with industry folks and learned about the game-changing law (Senate Bill 604) in the works. "I said, 'Let's do it.'"

Jeremy doesn't brew that contrarian IPA anymore, but hopsters will find satisfaction in offerings such as Kaiju IPA (65 IBUs and 7.1 percent ABV), Jalapeno IPA (low in bitterness but with plenty of hop flavor and zing from the pepper), and Virginia Hooligan IPA (aged in gin barrels). Fans of barrel-aged big brews can also look to Cygnus X1, a Belgian-style quad aged in A. Smith Bowman bourbon barrels; it's another sipper at 11.2 percent ABV. Before the downsizing, Mother Pucker Witbier (made with raspberries and soured using *Lactobacillus*), Jesse's Girl American Amber Ale, and Aces High American Pale Ale headed up a canning line for distribution, which the Meyerses kept centered on the Manassas area. "I think people get caught up in this idea that if you're not growing you're dying," Jeremy said, "but I want to ensure I can have full control of my product."

Try this: Virginia Hooligan exemplifies BadWolf's brashness in brewing. Technically, it's a double or imperial IPA at 10.5 percent ABV. Notes of juniper from the gin-barrel aging join citrus from the use of fresh Virginia-grown Cascade hops (82 IBUs) for a nuanced complexity. The version I had was released in December 2016; a bourbon-barrel variation also was available in 2017.

Mustang Sally Brewing Company

Common wisdom in the entrepreneurial world says that before you get into a business, you should know how to get out of it. Sean Hunt, a former corporate attorney familiar with the twists and turns of mergers and acquisitions, knows that, but when it comes to Mustang Sally, he makes it clear he's all in.

"At the end of the day we see ourselves as a classic American brewery with a commitment to doing things right," Hunt said. "Experts always say, never start a business without an exit plan, and I sit here, making that fatal flaw. I don't want an exit plan."

Doors opened in April 2016 on a fourteen-thousand-square-foot facility in Chantilly. The space includes a four-thousand-square-foot taproom, big enough for arcade games, indoor cornhole, barrels, benches, tables, a wood-slat bar, and, if the need arose, an indoor skating rink. It's big. The walls sport educational posters about beer styles and the brewing process as well as photos documenting how the thirty-barrel brew house took shape. The tap list during my August 2017 visit highlighted six beers—an amber lager, a Dortmunder, an Irish red ale, and three IPAs, including a feisty East Coast IPA at 75 IBUs and a sessionable pilot IPA using unnamed "experimental hops."

The size of the tasting room fosters Hunt's goal of establishing a community center. "We'd like to use our large tasting room to showcase local talent, partner with local causes and charities that are important to our community, and, of course, bring the community together over good conversation and great beer," he said.

Bret Kimbrough, former head brewer for Vintage 50 in Leesburg, is in charge of making sure the beer is great. Traditional styles—a kölsch, an IPA, and a porter—characterize the flagship beers. Mustang Sally Dortmunder Lager won a bronze at the 2017 Virginia Craft Beer Cup in the Pale Bitter European Beer category.

That style provides a link to Hunt's initial passion for flavorful beer. He experienced the lagers of Bavaria while in Germany for several years before heading to the University of Virginia to study engineering. The desire to open his own brewery tickled his fancy as he entered the business world at Booz Allen Hamilton. "Another engineer and I talked about opening up a brewery . . . but then it went away. The name [of the brewery] comes from the same era, when I was also working on a boat called Mustang Sally. That boat, Mustang Sally, is a memory of being carefree and not having a lot of worries."

A homebrewer for more than twenty-five years, Hunt would occasionally bring up the idea of a brewery with his wife, who had started her own engineering company. "We always came to the conclusion that one startup company was enough for a family." Finally, Hunt recalled, "She said 'Go ahead.'"

Increased competition as the number of breweries reaches record levels doesn't sway his confidence. "It's a crowded field if you just look at the number of breweries opening up, but the amount of beer they're producing is just not that great," Hunt said. Numbers from the Brewers Association back that up. In 2016, the U.S. counted 5,301 breweries; 3,132 of those were microbreweries, producing less than fifteen thousand barrels a year. Bart Watson, chief economist for the association, noted that "the average brewer is getting small, and growth is more diffuse within the craft category, with producers at the tail helping to drive growth for the overall segment."

The initial capacity at Mustang Sally on the thirty-barrel system is four thousand to five thousand barrels a year with a ceiling of twenty-five thousand to thirty thousand barrels when fully built out. Kimbrough also has a twenty-gallon pilot setup for one-offs and test batches. The size of the facility enabled Mustang Sally to host the first two Fairfax County BrewFests; the 2017 event included seven Fairfax breweries, three more than when Mustang Sally opened.

Try this: The Dortmunder style, according to my Beer Judge Certification Program guidelines, was developed in the 1870s, then enjoyed great popularity after World

War II but declined in the 1970s (as did many European styles). Gold in color, smooth with a mild noble hop aroma and bready malt character, Mustang Sally's version is clean and crisp, with 5.5 percent ABV and 15 IBUs. Balance is the key; drinkability is a major plus.

CHAPTER 6

Loudoun Experiences a Growth Spurt

On Monday, January 23, 2017, brewers from around Loudoun County gathered at Ocelot Brewing Company and formed the Loudoun County Brewers Association. The charter document was signed by nineteen brewery representatives. The organization signaled a growth spurt and a sense of cohesiveness that would have been hard to imagine five years earlier, when wine defined the area. "Loudoun County is D.C.'s wine country, but there's absolutely no reason on earth we shouldn't be D.C.'s beer country," said Chris Burns, head of Old Ox Brewing Company and the association's newly minted chairman.

The scene goes beyond brew kettles. Lucketts Mill & Hopworks became the first business in Virginia to establish a hops processing facility. Its companion operation, Black Hops Farm, and other farms have experimented with hops cultivation, and in July 2017 growers formed their own organization, the Loudoun County Hops Association. The LoCo Ale Trail encourages tourism by connecting dots from Dirt Farm and B Chord breweries in Bluemont to Lost Rhino and Old Ox in Ashburn. Purcellville, with Adroit Theory, Belly Love, and others, is a destination in its own right, and the intimate settings of Loudoun Brewery and Crooked Run in Leesburg provide a contrast with Lost Rhino's high-volume operation in Ashburn. The LoCo Brewfest has become an annual event, and county brewers have contributed to several collaborations, including a milk stout brewed at Beltway Brewing Company in 2016.

Dirt Farm Brewing

Stand on the patio at Dirt Farm brewery, and on a clear day you can see a jigsaw patchwork of fields, pastures, vineyards, trees, and streams rising to a distant ridge of blue on Loudoun County's eastern horizon. Janell Zurschmeide looks at the same view and sees something else—the future.

On a brilliant Saturday in June 2017, she pointed to a pocket of land adjoining the plot of hop bines in the valley below and told me about a possible production facility to boost the output of Dirt Farm beers. All around us, patrons sat at tables under charcoal-and-white umbrellas seeking shade and sipping those beers. A few yards away, Nick Zurschmeide and Wes Schoeb, Janell's nephews, tended to brewing another batch on the ten-barrel system housed in a converted shed. It was easy to see the need for the thirty-barrel brew house Janell envisioned—the demand for those seeking the combination of flavorful brews and soul-expanding vista has made Dirt Farm a bucket-list destination among Virginia breweries.

Before there was beer, there was wine. And before wine, there was simply a love for growing things. "Bruce is passionate about being a dirt farmer," Janell said of her husband, the second generation in his family to work the land in Loudoun. Great Country Farms, begun in 1993, led to Bluemont Winery in 2007, and when the opportunity arose to add one hundred acres at the foot of the Blue Ridge Mountains, visions of a brewery crystallized. A few visits to Dogfish Head brewery in Delaware in previous summers had started wheels turning toward the brewing side of things. The concept of farm breweries was still taking shape in Virginia, so working with state and local officials became an important chore. (Janell would later

Bruce and Janell Zurschmeide (*foreground*) have made Dirt Farm Brewing a bucket-list destination in Loudoun County.

join Lisa Brotherton Pumphrey of Lickinghole Creek in cochairing the Farm Brewery Committee of the Virginia Craft Brewers Guild.)

As with the farm in general, the brewing became a family operation. Bruce started homebrewing; a small Sabco system and kegerator sufficed for the opening in 2012, but not for long. Serious brewing chops were needed to work the ten-barrel setup, so cousins Nick and Wes made use of the online courses offered by Chicago's Siebel Institute of Technology. One of the early brews was Ogden Pale Ale, named in honor of the man who in 1941 built the stone house on the mountain that now houses Dirt Farm's taproom. The ale's re-release on Father's Day 2017 featured their barley—no surprise as beers such as Tart 31 Cherry Ale, Peter Peter Pumpkin Ale, Som Peach Ale, and Fluster Cluck Ale make use of fruit and produce from the farm. The three-acre hop yard also supplies Cascade, Chinook, Nugget, and Centennial cones for their brews. The ultimate goal is to brew beer made exclusively from homegrown ingredients, including yeast cultures gathered on-site.

Try this: During this visit to Dirt Farm, my flight of four beers—Scott Brown Ale, Awe Dang IPA, Pants Off DIPA, and Milk Stout Ale—were clean, flavorful, and worth the trip. But one beer I had been eager to sample had just kicked. Red Merl, an Irish red ale, won a gold medal at the 2016 Virginia Craft Beer Cup. At 6.2 percent ABV and a grain bill yielding caramel and chocolate notes, it promised drinkability as well as complexity. Given that my visit coincided with Dirt Farm's annual oyster festival—and the famous pairings of Irish ales with those bivalves—no wonder it was the first to kick.

Corcoran and B Chord Breweries

Before breweries started popping up like mushrooms in Loudoun County, the fertile hills of horse country sprouted vineyards and established a reputation as the top destination for wine lovers in the D.C. region, with forty-some vineyards by 2017. One of the bunch was Corcoran Vineyards & Cider, which planted its first vines in 2002 on one hundred acres north of Purcellville by the town of Waterford.

Owners Jim and Lori Corcoran saw the swell of interest in craft brewing as the decade advanced, and in 2011 they put a half-barrel system in a barn near the property and established the first combined winery/brewery in Virginia. "The brewery business and the winery business are similar in the sense we take products on our farms and ferment those products and turn them into adult libation," Jim said.

The brewing venture proved so popular that in 2014 the Corcorans opened a taproom in Purcellville on Hirst Road, within a golf cart ride of Adroit Theory's brewery. The contrast of the two made for interesting bookends—while you are likely to hear vintage Black Sabbath and sample unorthodox, adventurous beers at Adroit Theory, the Corcoran taproom was more apt to offer classic British rock (Kinks, Stones, Small Faces) and traditional brews.

In 2017, however, Corcoran began a transition, merging with B Chord Brewing Company as the latter prepared to open on sixty-four acres in western Loudoun County. The farm brewery had run into resistance from Bluemont residents when it applied for a license there in 2015, but the arrangement with Corcoran and its reputation of excellence gave B Chord new life in a location on the outskirts of Round Hill. B Chord opened in early 2018, with brewing continuing temporarily at Corcoran under the direction of Favio Garcia, a figure familiar to me from his days as head brewer at Richbrau brewpub in Richmond's Shockoe Slip.

On a sunny afternoon when the calendar said spring but snow still lay in patches in the adjoining woods, B Chord resonated with the impetus behind its name—music. "We did a lot of research," said Marty Dougherty, CEO and director of operations. "We wanted something that sounded like music, and B Chord does that."

As we spoke, a circle of a dozen musicians played classic Celtic tunes on instruments ranging from mandolins to a bouzouki—with guitars, fiddle, penny whistle, and banjos in the mix. The brewery also hosts "neighborhood nights" devoted to bluegrass and other musical styles. The smell of fresh popcorn wafted from a machine as children skipped between wood picnic tables where parents munched on tacos and burritos. Outside, more picnic tables awaited warmer weather; poles rose in the beginnings of a hop yard, and construction sheds hinted at future amenities.

Garcia has proved his brewing mettle many times over with stints at Old Dominion, Lost Rhino, and Beltway breweries. The flight I tasted included an IPA made with El Dorado and Chinook hops, a hearty coffee stout, a refreshing Helles lager, and a malty Scotch ale—all tasty and easy to recommend. Dougherty said Garcia's time at

B Chord, however, is limited. "He's starting his own brewery, so at some point he will bail and get out on his own." Nonetheless, as Corcoran's presence in Purcellville fades into memory, B Chord promises to keep flavorful beers and foot-tapping music a fixture in the county.

Try these: Finding a light but complex German lager and a roasty Scotch ale on the same tap list was a treat. The Helles lager uses a blend of German hops and two English varieties—Northdown and Goldings; ABV is 5.2 percent, adding to the easy-drinking appeal. Not many details were available on the Scotch ale, other than its 7.6 percent ABV. A rich whisky color, sweet but not cloying malt, and subtly warming alcohol made this a nice bookend to the Helles.

Adroit Theory Brewing Company

It's 10:30 on a Monday morning in April 2017, and Mark Osborne is pouring beers for a group of media folks on a tour of Loudoun County breweries. The front of his black T-shirt reads "Adroit Theory," the brewery he opened in 2014 in Purcellville. As he turns to pull a tap, you can read the back: "Brewed to destroy." And considering that the first brew offered to the group—a New England–style double IPA called EBK (after "Eastern Bushido Knight")—weighs in at 8.5 percent ABV, any thoughts of easing into the session are quickly destroyed. "Eight and a half percent for us is very sessionable," he says, to general laughter. "We make primarily big, boozy beers."

Hazy, hoppy IPAs such as EBK made the draft list at Adroit Theory only after adventurous, challenging imperial stouts, Belgian-style quads, and American barleywines—all made with outside-the-box blends of ingredients—built the brewery's reputation. Take, for example, Death of Cthulu, a Russian imperial stout made with marshmallows and seaweed and aged in Jamaican rum barrels. The sweetness and the brine play off each other, with the dark rum adding complexity; the 12 percent ABV takes no prisoners.

Adroit Theory has produced five hundred distinct beers in its three years, Osborne says. Some are made on the ten-barrel brewing system that sits behind partitions in the tasting room, and additional brewing is contracted out to Old Bust Head Brewing Company in Fauquier County (see chapter 7). Distribution in early 2017 included all of Virginia and parts of Maryland, and being able to buy a huge beer like B/A/Y/S (Black as Your Soul) Imperial Stout in Costco says a lot about the market for creative brews. "Consume Life, Drink Art" is part of Adroit Theory's mission statement.

Adventurous concoctions and vivid graphics are a signature of Mark Osborne's Adroit Theory brewery.

In an increasingly competitive market, creating identity is crucial, and Adroit Theory succeeds with a Vaderish appeal to the Darth side, the Black Sabbath side, the "tear off your suit-and-tie straitjacket" side. Variations of brews are marked as "ghosts"—EBK (Ghost 523) is the prototype of that IPA; EBK (Ghost 545) is the triple IPA version, hopped with Citra, Mosaic, and Galaxy hops. "We're trying to paint a picture that it's not just beer," Osborne says.

An artist who sold his painting business in 2017 after getting Adroit Theory on its feet, Osborne looks more like an average Joe businessman than a heavy metal–loving big-beer fiend. The contradiction played out during my first visit to the brewery in 2015. As Ozzy Osbourne droned "Iron Man" on the sound system, I struck up a conversation with the mild-mannered woman next to me who, it turns out, was Mark's mother, there to taste her son's latest concoction.

All of the beers aren't big and brawny. Adroit Theory's Antithesis Line features Dr. M's Cream Ale at 3.8 percent ABV. "It's something you can drink, not just sip," Osborne says.

On this April media morning, Osborne closes out the session with Persona Non Grata, a saison made with hibiscus and fermented with *Brettanomyces*, a wild yeast, and *Pediococcus* bacteria for an interplay of earthiness and tartness. We sample a batch made in 2014 and aged in wine barrels. "We actually forgot about them," Osborne says. "This beer sat for almost two and a half years."

Try this: It's hard to guess what might be on tap at Adroit Theory at any given time, but you can't go wrong with any of the imperial stouts. That said, if you can find Tenebris (Ghost 552), you're in for a treat. This English-style barleywine boasts flavors of figs, raisins, dates, and brown sugar, plus unmistakable bourbon notes thanks to barrels from Loudoun's Catoctin Creek Distilling Company.

Belly Love Brewing Company

Anybody who can turn a grumble into a chuckle deserves a pat on the back. My dad had a good technique—when I got into a tussle with one of my brothers, he would make us kiss each other on the cheek. Anger gave way to humiliation, which gave way to laughter.

Tolga and Katie Baki have a good method, too, and it led to the name of their brewery. "After a fight, I'd pull his shirt up and my shirt up, and I'd rub my belly on his," Katie said. "It really was an offering of peace, no matter how mad we were with each other or how stupid it was. It would always make us laugh. So I called it belly love once."

They add that it's hard not to be happy when you have a bellyful of craft beer, and they keep their 3.5-barrel system busy churning out five year-round beers, a handful of seasonals, and special batches to that end. Demand is spread across the styles, but Tolga said that the best-selling brew in the taproom probably is Narcissist, an easy-drinking (5.4 percent ABV) Munich helles lager. More adventurous palates can sample Eye of Jupiter, an oatmeal stout with notes of coffee and chocolate, and 50 Shades of Gold, a Belgian golden strong ale. For a taste of tart, there's Duchess, a seasonal Belgian tripel brewed with cranberries and hibiscus; for hopheads, there's the seasonal Flying Unicorn Crotch Kick, made with Mosaic and Galaxy hops and clocking in around 104 IBUs.

The more challenging beers seem to appeal to out-of-town weekenders from D.C. and elsewhere, who are in the area visiting Loudoun County's wineries as well as breweries, Tolga says. During the week, the taproom attracts more of the local crowd, who might sample something new or edgy but more often go with a familiar favorite. Either way, he says, Purcellville benefits from having five distinctly different breweries, from hyper-creative Adroit Theory to the more traditional Corcoran (now B Chord) brewery. "We're all somewhat unique in our approach to brewing and in the feel of our taprooms," Tolga said.

Belly Love's tasting room eschews the modern industrial-park feel of some breweries for a more polished-but-casual ambience. Located in the underbelly of a strip shopping center off East Main Street in Purcellville, the brewery isn't the easiest place to find, and the buzz of conviviality makes it hard to leave. Brick walls with wood-slat accents and wooden tables (many of them made by Tolga's father) create a neighborhood hangout feel. The design reflects combined input from Tolga and Katie. "I wanted to do something that represented him, the balance between the female and the male, a place women would want to come to, too," she says. "All of those things come together to evoke who he is as a person, but also a little bit of me is in it as well."

Their love of craft beer grew from different directions. Tolga was born in Turkey and raised in Vienna in Northern Virginia; he developed a taste for flavorful beers during travels abroad. Katie grew up in North Carolina, and during her college years a friend who was Dutch introduced her to a variety of European beers. About two decades ago, Tolga began homebrewing, sporadically at first but more in earnest in 2008. Visions of going pro danced in his head. "All homebrewers, to some degree, have that in the back of their mind, 'Oh, one day I'll start my own brewery,'" he said. Belly Love went live in 2014, with Katie running the taproom and Tolga heading the brewing and business side of things. They have no plans to distribute; annual production is roughly three hundred barrels. The goal is to sustain the business and be a part of the community by putting beer in bellies. Every indication is that that's rubbing people the right way. "We love making people happy, and that makes us happy, too," Katie said.

Try this: Check out 50 Shades of Gold if, like me, you are a fan of Belgian strong ales. This pours gold with a creamy head, and the Belgian yeast offers spicy notes in the aroma. The flavor is fruity with some pear and citrus; the mouthfeel is smooth and rich, bordering on a tripel. Alcohol is high (9.2 percent ABV), and bitterness is low (29 IBUs).

Crooked Run Brewing

When the economy took a nosedive in 2008, the recession that followed made life difficult for a lot of folks. Jake Endres was no exception. His political science degree from James Madison University wasn't getting much traction in the job market. He'd begun to take his homebrewing seriously, so the idea of starting a brewery spurred him to develop a business plan and raise money through a crowd-funding source.

He put out a notice for an assistant brewer and landed Lee Rogan as a business partner. "He'd applied to a bunch of places and said he was open to volunteering. None of them would give him the time of day," Endres said.

A cozy spot in the Market Station section of Leesburg proved ideal for starting brewing on a 1.5-barrel system, and Crooked Run, named for a creek that runs through Loudoun County, opened in 2013. Endres was twenty-five; Rogan, twenty-six. "I believe we were the youngest brewery owners in Virginia at the time," according to Endres.

The intimacy of the taproom and the quality of the beers gained a following. Loudoun regulars rubbed elbows in the six-hundred-square-foot space, creating a "Cheers" ambience. The eight taps flowed with IPAs, some featuring locally grown chilies, and Belgian-style ales. One of those, the Supernatural imperial saison, won a gold medal in the 2016 World Beer Cup judging. The same year, the *Washington Post* dubbed Crooked Run the best nanobrewery in the D.C. area.

Despite upgrading the brewing capacity with a three-barrel system, Endres and Rogan found that the demand for Crooked Run beers was testing the limits of their setup. Expansion seemed warranted. They found a suitable spot for a ten-barrel system and an inviting taproom on Davis Drive in Sterling, and the second location was launched in February 2017. The larger setup allowed them to produce about four thousand barrels in 2017. "We expect to hit 4,500 barrels in 2018, and then we're going to cap it," Endres noted. A partnership with Senor Ramon Taqueria taco restaurant enables them to serve food on the premises (during one of my visits a Taco Olympics was under way).

The Leesburg spot has become a fermentation laboratory, with barrel-aging and a coolship installed to capture wild yeast. *Brettanomyces, Lactobacillus,* and *Pediococcus* all are tools for producing the sour and funky beers that have become Crooked Run hits. "Sours weren't that popular when we started, but now there are a lot of fans," Endres observed. A 4-percent-ABV Berliner weisse made with blackberries, vanilla beans, and milk sugar called Blackberry Vibes proved a tart and refreshing option in late summer.

When Endres and I spoke in September 2017, he said Supernatural was going through some rethinking. The original recipe was designed by head brewer Brad Erickson using organic hibiscus petals. It has been billed as a saison, but the high alcohol content—10 percent ABV—and richer mouthfeel might lead to rebranding it as a tripel. The farmhouse ale tradition will still be represented by the likes of Skyline, a 5-percent-ABV saison made with navel oranges and Lemondrop hops.

The hoppier taps are anchored by Heart and Soul IPA, brewed with Mosaic and 007 hops; aroma and flavor are accented more than bitterness (30 IBUs). Crooked Run's penchant for peppers and fruit comes through in brews such as Cherry Cayenne Storm IPA, made with cherries and fresh cayenne pepper.

Upsizing to the ten-barrel system has allowed Crooked Run to distribute some beers—Raspberry Empress (a sour IPA) and Heart and Soul IPA were among selections going into cans. But Endres counts his blessings that the business stuck with a modest setup. "I'm very happy we don't have a larger system. It's been extremely difficult to sell beer. A lot of people think that local beer will sell itself, but that really is not the case," he concluded. Distribution in 2017 was focused in Northern Virginia and parts of D.C. with a goal of expanding to Winchester, Fredericksburg, and, eventually, Richmond.

Try this: Supernatural stood out on my visit to the Sterling taproom. The hibiscus petals create a ruby-magenta color, and the Belgian yeast and barrel-aging give it a crisp, dry finish. It's deceptively light on the palate, given its high alcohol content (the 2016 version weighed in at 10 percent ABV). As one reviewer wrote, it's a "monster that's dangerously drinkable."

Loudoun Brewing Company

Tucked away in a small strip of businesses off Leesburg's East Market Street, Loudoun Brewing Company opened its doors in September 2015 as a quintessential nanobrewery. With a thirty-gallon system (just shy of one barrel), the brewery had the capacity to do little more than supply patrons who came to its nook of town. "We had a pretty simple vision, and that more or less has come true," said Patrick Steffens, cofounder with his wife, Alanna, as LBC celebrated its first anniversary.

By the time the second anniversary rolled around, nearly 170 batches had flowed from LBC tanks. More important, LBC came under new ownership. The Steffenses decided to sell in March 2017 to Shannon Burnett and Phil Fust. Phil had begun volunteering there as a brewer, out of curiosity and simply to pitch in. "I did very little home-brewing ahead of that time," he said.

Now he's brewing five to seven times a week, and he and Shannon have visions of taking the business to a new level. As we sat on the brewery's deck in September 2017, they described what has become a common model among Virginia breweries—establishing a production facility that feeds multiple taproom locations, each of which would have a small pilot system.

Still, "we want to continue focusing on the strength of being small," Phil noted. The flexibility of brewing different beers appeals to him despite the hours put in with multiple batches: "Playing with flavors is what craft beer is all about." Patrons seem to agree. Styles rotate often, and even the flagships—Loud & Brewing IPA and Oh My Darlin' DIPA—kick quickly. Phil decided to test the competitive waters and entered two beers for judging at the 2017 Great American Beer Festival.

While Phil is quick to acknowledge a lack of formal training in his brewing background, Shannon brings depth to another side of the business. She is director of finance for a defense contractor and rides herd on the financial side of LBC. "All I do is tell him how much money he's spending and make sure the bills get paid," she said. She's also a Loudoun County native, so she knows the community and its tastes. They chuckled about a visit from a group of residents of a neighboring elderly care facility who took a shuttle to LBC. The youngest was eighty-two; the oldest was ninety-seven. And, according to the taproom person on duty, "They drank the beer and had a nice time."

One of the signature brews is Completely Nuts, an English-style nut brown ale. The recipe includes pistachios, almonds, cashews, and walnuts, and Phil uses the family kitchen to do the roasting. British hops (East Kent Golding and Fuggle) and barley (Maris Otter two-row) help define the ale's UK profile. At 5.2 percent ABV, it goes down easy. "I like to focus on brewing little beers, in terms of ABV, with big flavor," Phil said. The philosophy seems to resonate—LBC was voted the county's favorite brewery by readers of *Loudoun Now* in 2017.

Try this: Check out Completely Nuts if it's on tap. The combination of nut flavors is nuanced, leaving the emphasis on drinkability. If that's not available, try Loud & Brewing IPA. Phil gets a kick out of naming his beers, and this one is not hard to figure out. It also reflects one of his brewing mottos: "Beer should not go hopless."

Old Ox Brewery

Growing up in Burke in the 1950s and 1960s, I would have been hard-pressed to imagine the evolution of Northern Virginia. Back roads that my family took to places like Sully Plantation on scenic Sunday drives have become multilane parkways, and Sully's site is now home to Dulles International Airport. (Did you know that Burke initially was the site for that airport? And that a historic black community was forced out to make way for airstrips?)

Back in the day, we would have driven on Old Ox Road to reach that part of NoVa. And if you'd told me that one day there would be a brewery honoring that stretch of highway—well, you might as well have told me that one day I'd be writing a book about beer.

Time chuckles at such changes. And Old Ox Brewery could hardly be a better place to relax and contemplate the vagaries and vicissitudes wrought by Father Time. The brewery itself has seen its share of change—only four breweries existed in Loudoun County when the Burns family opened the doors in June 2014. "Now there are twenty-five licensed breweries, twenty-one of which are in operation," Chris Burns said during my second visit in the spring of 2017.

Old Ox reminds me of Steam Bell brewery in Chesterfield County for its family-oriented operation. Chris was inspired to begin homebrewing by his father, Graham. Now they and others—Chris's siblings, Mike and Katy;

his wife, Kristen; and Graham's wife, Mary Ann—have built a business that takes pride in its community involvement, its spread of beers, and its local orientation. With production targeting five thousand barrels in 2017, Old Ox keeps its distribution in a tight circle. "We're very focused on being a local brewery first and foremost," Chris emphasized.

Being small, however, doesn't mean being bullied. Even before the first beer was tapped, Old Ox found itself locking horns in a trademark dispute with the makers of Red Bull, the energy drink. The latter wanted Old Ox to change its name and logo, citing intellectual rights to all things bovine. In recalling the episode, Chris smiles wryly and says, "Three years later, we're still here, and the logo didn't change. It's safe to say that both Old Ox and Red Bull are pleased to have put this matter behind us."

The Old Ox spirit plays out in several other ways. Large American flags hang from brewery tanks. The tasting room walls sport local artwork provided by members of the Loudoun Art Council. The service is friendly and informed. And the beers provide a range of options, from the approachable Golden Ox Golden Ale (5.9 percent ABV and 18 IBUs) to the double-barrel Hoppier Place imperial IPA collection (various batches feature Citra, Mosaic, Amarillo, and Simcoe hops). Experiments with lupulin powder show that Old Ox is hip to new techniques.

When Chris says you can find more than two hundred unique beers at any time among the breweries on the county's LoCo Ale Trail, you sense his appreciation for being a vibrant part of a bigger picture. As a sign says, "Even if you don't think you're connected to beer, you are." And these days you can access the brewery via bicycle from the Washington and Old Dominion Trail as well as Old Ox Road.

Try this: Being a hophead, I could easily recommend the Hoppy Place and Hoppier Place collection of IPAs. Instead, I'll steer you to Black Ox Rye Porter. I found that the rye succeeds in adding crispness to the malt character, which favors chocolate over coffee in a complex, roasted mix. Cascade hops provide sufficient balance (more than the 20 IBUs might indicate). I favor the nitro version for its smoothness, and the 6 percent ABV lends itself to easy drinkability.

Lost Rhino Brewing Company

Providing a taste of place goes further than most beer drinkers realize at Lost Rhino. For starters, Native Son Table Beer took local to a new level as the first beer in the Old Dominion made from all-Virginia ingredients. Bone Dusters Amber Ale used yeast found on protocetid whale fossils near the Dismal Swamp for its fermentation factor. Locally sourced oats and yeast gave Saison D'Anomaie, an American-style saison, a complexity that warranted a grand championship in its category in the 2015 U.S. Beer Tasting Championship.

What most folks don't see, though, is the equipment that handles the in-house brewing. Like much of the grains, yeast, water, and hops, it comes from a local source—the remains of a one-time Loudoun County neighbor, Old Dominion Brewing Company.

Lost Rhino cofounders Matt Hagerman and Favio Garcia benefited from stints at the Old Dominion brewery, run by Jerry Bailey, one of the state's early craft giants. Garcia landed there after jobs at Arlington's Bardo Rodeo and Richmond's Richbrau, now both memories. Hagerman got his start at Old Dominion, cleaning floors at first, then brewing root beer, and finally moving onto the beer crew. When Old Dominion morphed to a new identity and a new location in Delaware, Hagerman and Garcia raided the facility for equipment to launch Lost Rhino in 2011. Some of the apparatus is so old-school that when Ken Grossman, founder of Sierra Nevada Brewing Company, came through for a tour, he recognized a keg washer similar to one that his California brewery used back in its infancy.

And there are no apologies. "There's a lot of brewing left in these tanks," observed Chris Drummond, vice president of operations, during a 2017 tour. That's not to say Lost Rhino is antiquated. New fermenters, state-of-the-art lab equipment, rows and racks of barrels, and an in-house canning line have kept pace with the growing demand and the evolving needs of creative brewing. During the same tour, Hagerman showed off the latest purchase—a six-figure German-made centrifuge used to clarify beer before packaging.

The combination of new and old reflects Lost Rhino's overall blend of being both traditional and hip. Face Plant IPA and Rhino Chasers Pilsner are the flagships, and both reflect traditional approaches. The pilsner sports Hallertau and Saaz hops—nobles of European tradition grown in the U.S.—and pilsner and Munich malts. The IPA has a satisfying hop bite (65 IBUs) featuring whole-cone Centennial and Cascade varieties, with pilsner, Vienna, and crystal malts providing balance.

On the hip side, the brewery's name comes from a surfing term. A rhino chaser seeks epic waves, wherever they break. The brewery also makes donations to help rhinos through the African Wildlife Foundation and contributes to the care of Andatu, the first Sumatran rhino born in captivity.

The brewery's nontraditional side also shows in the Genius Loci Series. Along with Native Son, it includes funkadelic delicacies such as Alphabrett, a barrel-aged brown ale fermented with *Brettanomyces* (a wild yeast); Execus Sanctum, a fruit sour beer also aged in barrels; Bramble Frumenti, another American fruit sour; and Double Z, a barrel-aged double IPA.

Much of the unique quality of these and other beers comes from the expertise of Dutchman Jasper Akerboom,

Chris Jacques, Matt Hagerman, and Jasper Akerboom (*from left to right*) keep the beer flowing at Lost Rhino in Ashburn.

a microbiologist. He harvested a yeast strain in Ashburn for Native Son, swabbed fossils for Bone Dusters, and turned a backyard expedition into a yeast extraction for the brewery's Wild Farmwell Wheat beer. Using science to push the envelope is important at Lost Rhino. "We're trying to set the standard for some of these smaller [breweries]," he told a local publication.

Using as many local agricultural products as possible is equally high on the priority list. Some grain is grown in the Northern Neck, while malts come from Copper Fox Distillery in Sperryville and hops from farms in Madison County and Leesburg.

In 2015, Lost Rhino Retreat, a full-service restaurant with guest taps, a downstairs patio, and upstairs bar and deck, opened in the nearby Brambleton Plaza. A one-barrel brewing system there has cranked out monthly releases, including a milk stout and an imperial brown ale called Sumatran Solstice. A regular feature is the Hangover Brunch every Sunday midday. (BTW—Lost Rhino makes its own

A SPECIAL ALE

One of my favorite stories about Lost Rhino beers concerns New River American Pale Ale. It initially was the brewing brainchild of Kenny Lefkowitz, who finished graduate school at Virginia Tech in 1995. He had an exceptional recipe for this beer and took it to Old Dominion brewery, where it was first produced in 1999. At its debut in judging at the 2000 Great American Beer Festival, New River Pale Ale won bronze in its category, a feat beyond the pale of any reasonable expectation. I was there, and Kenny was filled with hope, humor, charm, boyish charisma, and vibrant vision.

In 2001, Kenny died of a massive coronary attack at the age of thirty-two. The news stunned Virginia's brewing community. His family and fiancée persisted in the brewing enterprise, and Old Dominion produced New River Pale Ale until 2007. Lost Rhino took up the reins, and though brewing took a short hiatus, it now is offered in a recipe with Amarillo and CTZ hops—used in the boil and dry-hopping—and pilsner, Munich, and crystal malts. The golden brew has a classic citrus aroma "with a touch of sweet tropical fruit"; ABV is a moderate 5.4 percent and hop bitterness is 34 IBUs.

root beer as well, although Hagerman now is able to delegate the role he once had at Old Dominion.)

Try this: Native Son requires a place on the palate simply because of its all-Virginia pedigree, with details of its ingredients discussed earlier (see chapter 2). I also like the designation as a table beer, echoing Thomas Jefferson's description of the beers brewed at Monticello. I was surprised by the honey aroma and sweetness when I had my first sample at the Virginia Craft Brewers Fest; there's enough dry finish, however, to balance the flavor. It's highly drinkable at 6.1 percent ABV and 35 IBUs.

Ocelot Brewing Company

Early in its existence, Ocelot gained a reputation for big beers—highly hopped and high in alcohol content. Founder Adrien Widman had cut his teeth on the bold brews of San Diego, and the edgy West Coast style became an initial signature of the brewery.

At the 2016 Great American Beer Festival, however, when the Ocelot crew took the stage for a gold medal, it was Sunnyside Dweller—a light, crisp, German-style pilsner created by brewer Mike McCarthy—that brought them into the spotlight. "It was awesome when we heard our name called, but we were not that shocked because we love that beer," Widman recalled. "It's the staff's favorite, and it's our favorite."

It's also an indication that Ocelot isn't a one-style-fits-all brew house, especially considering that its Baltic porter (an ale style actually brewed as a lager) medaled at the 2017 GABF. Yes, there are IPAs aplenty—more than a hundred versions in two and a half years—but even those have evolved since doors opened in mid-2015. Softer, less bitter profiles are more likely to pop up on the beer menu, which itself is renowned for always having something new and different. Widman explained, "We sit down every Monday and ask ourselves, 'What are we going to

The Ocelot Brewing Company team, led by founder Adrien Widman (*far left*), joins Charlie Papazian (*second from left*) onstage after winning a medal at the Great American Beer Festival in Denver.

brew? What will we feel like drinking in a month, when it's ready?'" The result is a range of lagers, stouts, red ales, farmhouse ales, and IPAs.

Part of Ocelot's evolution involves keeping up with technological advances, and Widman said the advent of lupulin powder "is a monster for us." He had just returned from hop heaven (aka Yakima Valley in Washington state), where he contracted for more hop powder. The primary attraction spurring its use is increased yield in each batch because the vegetal component of hops, which soaks up lots of water, is removed. Widman says they get an extra two barrels of beer from every thirty-barrel brew.

That adds up quickly for a brewery with a modest production level. Output in 2017 was expected to total 1,800 barrels, with a 20 percent increase in 2018. Only about a quarter of that goes beyond taproom doors, and Ocelot works mainly with two distributors, Hop and Wine Beverage in the D.C.–Northern Virginia area and Reverie in the

Richmond region and to the east. But Ocelot beers have popped up in taprooms and at festivals in unexpected places—Vermont, Maine, Massachusetts, Florida, and South Carolina.

The taproom at Sterling is the real magnet, though. Big and bright, it buzzes with cheerful chatter and music—always music. That passion plays out in the names that Widman has given his tanks—Dave Grohl, Robert Plant, Jimi Hendrix, Eddie Vedder, George Harrison, and more. The lettering on the "Barrel Wall" drips in Pink Floyd fashion. Ocelot's logo is shaped like a guitar pick, and the name itself comes from a Phish song. Even a small fridge behind the bar has a Marshall amp facade.

The beer menu has expanded from just three brews initially—Tangerine Trees IPA, Lemon Yellow Sun Imperial Hoppy Wheat Ale, and My Only Friend Russian Imperial Stout—to a dozen or more on a regular basis. In September 2017, you would have found four of twelve beers under 6 percent ABV, with Sunnyside Dweller on the low end (5.1 percent ABV) and bourbon barrel–aged Capsized, an imperial milk stout, on the opposite side at 11 percent ABV. Another barrel-aged beer, Hearts & Thoughts saison, was fermented with *Brettanomyces* yeast and conditioned in white wine barrels. The list included two IPAs made with lupulin powder—Time After Time, with Citra and Cascade, and Break My Balls, which featured Mosaic hops.

There's a sense of fun in some of Ocelot's brewing. Two beers, From the Top and From the Bottom, were identical except for the ale yeast used in the former and lager in the latter. Customers could ask for a blind tasting to see if they could tell which was which. Brews offered at the one-year anniversary included The Gallows and Hangman, both imperial red ales, and two versions of My Only Friend, a Russian imperial stout with and without barrel-aging.

One final note—Widman said all of Ocelot's beers are gluten-reduced.

Try this: As much as I love pilsners, I should have taken home a growler of Sunnyside Dweller during my last visit. But I have to rave about the brew I did choose—Time After Time IPA, made with lupulin powder. Slightly hazy and juicy with tropical fruit, tangerine, and grapefruit notes, it showcased the Citra and Cascade hops in both aroma and flavor. At 6.4 percent ABV, it is slightly above sessionable level. IBUs were not available.

CHAPTER 7

The Outer Reaches of Northern Virginia

From Fredericksburg to Culpeper, and from Sperryville to Spotsylvania County, the breweries ringing the outer reaches of Northern Virginia offer a diverse set of brews and destinations for beer lovers in the state. Maltese, founded by two firefighters, creates a unique setting dedicated to emergency service personnel. Pen Druid, begun by three brothers in a rock band, explores the world of wild yeast and spontaneous fermentation, while at nearby Hopkins Ordinary a more genteel ambience frames the offerings of Sherri Fickel and Kevin Kraditor. Red Dragon's cask-conditioned and Welsh ales evoke the British spirit of brewing. Fär Göhn features two beers inspired by the owner's grandfather's homebrewing recipes, while nearby Beer Hound showcases founder Kenny Thacker's brewing skills. Strangeways' Fredericksburg location, discussed in the Richmond brewery's profile in chapter 8, adds a bit of quirkiness to the local scene. At Adventure, you can taste the offspring of some of the first craft beers brewed in the Fredericksburg region. Old Bust Head in Vint Hill also pays tribute to famous figures and colorful landmarks in Fauquier County. The full history of commercial brewing, however, reaches back to John Mercer's efforts in the 1760s at Marlborough in Stafford County (see chapter 1).

Adventure Brewing Company

In 2002, about two dozen breweries existed in Virginia, and so every brewer's flag that was planted in the Old

Dominion staked out new territory in the landscape of craft brewing. Blue & Gray Brewing Company was the first in the Fredericksburg region when it opened in Spotsylvania County that year. Owner Jeff Fitzpatrick built a following with Fred Red, Stonewall Stout, Blue & Gray Classic Lager, and other brews; the companion Lee's Retreat Brewpub fed hungry beer aficionados and satisfied the existing state law requiring food with on-site beer.

By the time Adventure Brewing Company planted its own flag as the first modern brewery in Stafford County in 2014, Virginia law had changed and small breweries were simultaneously creating and being driven by a growing thirst among beer consumers for flavorful, innovative brews. The three-barrel system used by founders Tim Bornholtz, Stan Johnson, and John Viarella—homebrewers all—quickly reached capacity. Simultaneously, Fitzpatrick was ready to end his run at Blue & Gray, so in January 2016 Adventure acquired Blue & Gray and its twenty-barrel system as a production facility while keeping the original site for pilot batches and as an additional taproom. The agreement included continuing to produce some of Blue & Gray's beers, which took on new meaning when Fitzpatrick died in October 2016.

As Adventure has grown—annual production stood at about one thousand barrels in 2017—Fred Red has led expansion into new markets. It accounts for 30 to 40 percent of sales, followed by Adventure IPA. "We have new beers coming out every week," said head brewer Bryan Link. One weekend in September 2017 saw a Vienna lager and a Belgian tripel join Adventure's Oktoberfest on the tap list, with Mary Washington Gingerbread Ale, Runaway Pumpkin Ale, and others in the tanks maturing. "We have tweaked some of the Blue & Gray recipes since we use a different source for our grains," Link noted. "One of our biggest changes is from Canada Malting to Briess, which is an American maltster, for the base grains."

Bornholtz said that before they made the gingerbread ale, they actually made gingerbread based on a Mary Washington recipe. "Colonial breads like that were not so sweet because they used very little sugar—it was expensive. It was a non-sweet bread, so we made a non-sweet beer."

The taproom in the main Bowman Center facility combines an industrial feel (the space previously housed a cellophane manufacturer) with the warmth of wood. Church pews line one wall, and the towering wood facade behind the bar contrasts with the adjoining cinderblock walls. Wood is an important feature as well at the north taproom, where a thirty-foot slab from a historic sycamore tree anchors the bar and provides a possible link to the commercial brewing venture at Marlborough in the 1700s. "We cling to the possibility that the tree spans the time between Stafford County's previous brewery and Adventure," Johnson observed.

Links to the past and to the community are important to the three founders. They invited friends to join them in their homebrewing pursuits, and the Stafford Brewers Club grew from that interest. When they began searching for a commercial brewery site, being local was a priority. "We're in Stafford County because it's where we live. We love it here," said Johnson.

Some of the beer names and the company's logo reflect their active lifestyle and their involvement in the Boy Scouts. "I've been in every Boy Scout job you could possibly do," Bornholtz noted. Backpack Wheat (a hefeweizen) and Adventure IPA are among year-round offerings from the production facility, while Campfire Smoked Lager (a rauchbier using malts from Copper Fox), Night Hike Black IPA, and Pathfinder IPA (similar to their Expedition IPA but experimenting with different hop profiles for every batch) have flowed from the north's smaller system.

Try this: Fred Red's flagship status and its link to the Blue & Gray days give it special appeal. True to the Irish red ale style, it pours a lovely copper color with a tawny head and is malt-forward with notes of toffee and caramel. It hits the drinkability bull's-eye at 5.2 percent ABV and is not shy on the hops (30 IBUs) while keeping perceived bitterness low. Being a paddler, I particularly like the label showing a kayak's prow pointed toward the railroad bridge over the Rappahannock River.

Red Dragon Brewery

Some places have you at "hello." The first time I entered Red Dragon Brewery—after an afternoon of exploring the downtown streets of historic Fredericksburg—the buoyant lilt of Celtic music, the mid-June sunlight beaming through the windows, the high ceilings, the intriguing beer list, and the vibrant greeting of the waitstaff put a hook in me.

What set the hook, though, was a taste of Welsh ale from a beer engine. Whereas having a cask-conditioned ale on tap is standard procedure at nearly every pub in the United Kingdom, the custom is far less pervasive at breweries in the United States, and even less so in Virginia. Daffodil Welsh Ale, brewed as an English bitter, poured a hazy gold (the color of the Welsh national flower, the daffodil) and blossomed with herbal notes in the aroma from the English hops. The mouthfeel had that soft, full texture that comes with cask conditioning, and the low alcohol level (4.1 percent ABV) also captured the sessionable character of many British ales. Another Welsh ale, Rose the Sharon, and David's Stout, a roasty treat with the typical coffee/chocolate notes, displayed the Anglophile chops of head brewer Cody Natale.

Co-owners Dan Baker and Thomas Evans are long-time Fredericksburg residents, but they wanted the Red Dragon to reflect their Celtic heritage. "I have Welsh, Irish, and Scottish ancestry, and Dan does also," Evans said.

English beer styles, including cask-conditioned ales, are a specialty at Red Dragon in Fredericksburg.

The location, on Princess Anne Street, allows a walkable, neighborhood feel unlike many breweries forced to locate in industrial settings to comply with zoning ordinances. "When we found the building on Princess Anne Street, we knew it had to be here," Evans recalled. "We looked at industrial parks, but they just don't have the character of the building we are leasing. We were able to get a bigger space [four thousand square feet] than we had originally planned." As he noted, "The building has been a lot of things over the years—a Goodwill laundry, a Chevy dealership, a Safeway, a pool hall, and a motorcycle shop. It was just a shell when we got it."

Evans started as a homebrewer, focusing on English styles. The beer selection when I was there, however, ventured outside traditional UK offerings with a kölsch, an American-style hefeweizen, a New England–style double IPA, and the promise of a gose sour ale called "Here Be Dragons" soon to emerge from the tanks. Road Rash Red, a red IPA loaded with citrus from four types of hops, is one of the flagships, though distribution does not fit into their present plans.

As if I wasn't already in love with the place, one of my favorite pop songs, "New Slang" by The Shins, came on after the fiddles and pipes.

Try this: Anything cask-conditioned; not only does Natale nail the delicacies of producing what are called "real ales" in the UK, but manager Hilary Kanter showed an equal deftness in drawing a lovely pint. That's half the beauty of this beast, and it's a treat for those able to appreciate it.

Maltese Brewing Company

If a fire ever breaks out in the Spotsylvania County business park that houses Maltese brewery, I can guess where the first responders would go first. With two career firefighters as founders, the brewery often serves fire, rescue, and police personnel, and they no doubt would put a top priority on protecting a setting designed to make them feel right at home.

The taproom here is decked with gear and equipment to evoke a firehouse atmosphere. The door leading into the brewery is propped open by an antique brass fire extinguisher with a fire hydrant perched nearby. The first big wall you see is painted fire-engine red. Coats and helmets hang from the wall behind the bar; above the taps, a mounted ax is flanked by dozens of patches representing regional squads. A hose hangs like a flaccid anaconda from light fixtures. A red, white, and blue poster labeled "Flag of Heroes" highlights the names of emergency service personnel who died on September 11, 2001.

The ambience is the handiwork of cofounders Bobby Cook and Joe Smith, Prince William County firefighters. So are the beers, which have evolved from recipes they developed as homebrewers. Maybe that explains the heat in one of the brews I tried, a saison called Song of the Siren that is "dry-hopped" with Tabasco and brewed with oysters. The hot sauce came through loud and clear. "It's one of the variants that we have based on our traditional saison," said Michael Cooper, the taproom manager. "That's the beer we play with the most."

The best seller is the Pineapple IPA, or PIPA, made with pineapple "nectar." Though it's labeled an English-style

What better than a fire extinguisher to prop open the door to Maltese brewery, cofounded by two firefighters?

IPA, it's hopped with American varietals. "I think we call it an English style because of the malt-to-hops ratio. It's not a West Coast IPA," according to Cooper. Among emergency service patrons, the Fireman's Blonde Ale is clearly the top thirst-quencher for its light flavor and accessibility (5.3 percent ABV and 13 IBUs). On the adventurous side, A Luz, a Belgian blonde ale, is aged in oak port-wine barrels, and a bourbon barrel–aged porter called Founding Fathers came from a recipe of George Washington's that used molasses.

The brewery's name comes from the symbolic Maltese cross. Each of the eight points refers to a value or quality, such as sympathy and dexterity, while the four curves emphasize ideals—bravery, courage, compassion, and loyalty to duty. "Trust us with your life? Then trust us with your beer," say the plastic mats used to mark flights.

Maltese has gone through several upgrades since opening in June 2015. Head brewer Stephen Matters uses a three-barrel system, double the capacity of the original setup. The tasting room has expanded, and Maltese has begun distributing in the area.

Try this: I'm not a huge fruit-in-beer lover, but the Pineapple IPA surprised me. Much of that comes from the low perceived bitterness of the hop blend—Horizon, Citra, and Simcoe. It's rated at 68 IBUs, but hopheads will find it below usual expectations. The pineapple is understated, resulting in a smooth-drinking, medium-bodied, mid-alcohol beer (6.5 percent ABV).

Beer Hound Brewery

I'm sitting in the tasting room at Beer Hound on Labor Day weekend 2017, sipping a just-released Oktoberfest. Outside, a three-piece local band is powering through hits by the Clash, Spin Doctors, and Van Morrison as a crowd gathers for Culpeper's second annual Hoptoberfest. Blue and white Bavarian pennants flutter in the breeze as the sun plays peekaboo through billowing clouds.

A pair of screens in the tasting room—a historic train station warehouse that now is a rustic mix of oak barrels, recycled barn wood, and chalkboards chocked with colorful notes (including "It was a wise man who invented beer")—give a rundown of the ten beers on tap. The Oktoberfest I'm drinking, Skrappy Dew, is crisp and clean, malty and bready. Also in my flight are a couple of medal winners—Teddy Cream Ale and Kujo Imperial IPA—and Teufelhunde Belgian tripel. In one corner of the room rests a sixteen-gallon brewing system that owner-brewer Kenny Thacker used for the original batches.

It's one month shy of three years since Thacker moved into this spot in Culpeper's historic district. Before that, Beer Hound was an outgrowth of Fermentation Trap, a spot north of Charlottesville that combined homebrewing supplies with a half-barrel brewery. Thacker had spent twenty-five years working in the construction industry, but the collapse of the housing market left him unemployed—until the opportunity to open a nanobrewery arose. "I think the initial investment was $25,000," he recalled. "It's not a lot to start a brewery, but my background in construction allowed me to go in and actually do the infrastructure myself." He went four years without a salary. "There were several times I wanted to fire myself, because I wasn't sure if I was going to be able to make it work."

It worked. Opening day in Culpeper on October 3, 2014, proved as much. "Everybody here in town was drinking Miller and Coors. We were wondering, how were we going to do with a craft beer," Alan Moyer, a former taproom employee, told me on a previous visit. "We opened and then sold out of beer in five days. . . . In order to keep up with demand, we had to close for two weeks."

Five medals won at the Virginia Craft Beer Cup are another indication that Thacker has made it work. Brewing is now done on a seven-barrel system, with annual

Kenny Thacker moved Beer Hound to Culpeper after starting the brewery in a homebrew store north of Charlottesville.

production around one thousand barrels in 2017. In March, Beer Hound began its first foray into distributing bottles, Teddy Cream Ale and Olde Yella Pale Wheat Ale (a two-time medal winner).

I tell Thacker how much I enjoy the beers, particularly Teufelhunde. Belgian tripels are one of my favorite styles, and this version has that spicy yeast complexity and soft malty fruity character that appeal to me. At 9.1 percent ABV, it is nearly as big as the alpha dog, Kujo. Thacker smiles and tells me that when he was revising the recipes to go from the sixteen-gallon setup to the larger system, he miscalculated the grain bill, resulting in higher alcohol levels. "Both those beers were mistakes at first. But they worked out," he said.

Try this: Who can argue with a gold medal at the 2017 Virginia Craft Beer Cup? Kujo has that big-dog bite (never mind that the hound in the Stephen King novel was less than balanced). Big means 11.6 percent ABV and 110 IBUs. The Beer Hound profile describes Kujo in this way: "It features a blend of citrus, spicy, and piney hop characters with a balanced maltiness."

Fär Göhn Brewing Company

Fär Göhn is a mere 125 paces away from Beer Hound; the two combine for a multifaceted beer magnet in Culpeper's historic district. While Beer Hound has ventured into bottling and small-scale distribution, Steve Gohn has been content for his "tavern brewery" to be destination-oriented. "We don't have a distributor, and we might never have a distributor," he said at the opening. "We're not looking to dominate the world. The only place you can get my beer is between these four walls."

Fär Göhn had been open less than a year when I entered for the first time in January 2016. I felt like I was walking into a friend's den rather than some fancy parlor. Wood paneling created a warm glow, and a middle-age fellow with long hair greeted me with a welcoming smile, as if to say, "C'mon in, you're among friends."

The building is more than a hundred years old and once housed a lumber mill, observed owner Gohn, who was behind the bar pulling taps on this Saturday afternoon. He wore a short-sleeve black T-shirt with the company logo. Motown music played on a component stereo system sitting on a shelf above a rotary dial telephone; boxy speakers were nestled in the corners. The latest brewery offerings were spelled out in neatly handwritten notes on a blackboard.

The umlauts in the brewery's name and some of the styles on tap—kölsch, altbier, hefeweizen, radler—pay homage to the area's German influence. Other offerings—the IPAs, Scottish ale, two stouts, and Coons Process Historical Pale Ale—show the influence of the current American craft boom.

"Every effort is made to produce beer true to the history of the style," Gohn says on his website. "European-styled beers use imported malts and hops wherever possible, and American styles use ingredients 100 percent produced in the USA." He also takes pride in serving beer that hasn't been filtered or pasteurized.

I sampled Madden's IPA, fragrant with the citrus-pine aroma of hops, and noticed a garland of hops draped over one of the gleaming mugs lining the board. Another IPA, Sleeping Elefant, had more of an earthy flavor, and Gohn explained that it wasn't his customary recipe because he had difficulty getting the usual hops. Still, both brews were tasty, and I followed the advice of the guy sitting next to me and got a sample of the Helleschwarz, a black IPA. The roasted coffee and chocolate notes of the malt balanced the dry finish of the hops nicely.

A young man greeted Gohn familiarly, with a name and a number. Gohn deftly used a long, hooked stick to secure one of the hundreds of stainless steel tankards that belong to members of Fär Göhn's mug club. The entry fee is $100,

Steve Gohn offers two beers based on his grandfather's home-brew recipe called Coons Process Pale Ale.

which gets you twenty-ounce pours rather than sixteen ounces, plus other benefits.

Gohn joined Virginia's brewing community through a familiar route—as a homebrewer. He brought more than fourteen years of experience in the food service industry to the job—plus his wife, Shelby, provides support and a helping hand in the tasting room.

Though Fär Göhn is no sports bar, the owner's love of pro football is readily apparent. On the day of my first visit, the playoff-bound Washington Redskins were a day away from ending the regular season with a game against the Dallas Cowboys. The chalkboard read "Skins/Cowboys @ 1 P.M. Cowboy fans welcome." Apparently Gohn needed to clarify a quote in the local newspaper about being open on Sundays during football season. "Only Redskins fans are allowed in," he had joked. Even football rivalries take back seat to sharing good craft beer.

Try this: On my second visit to Fär Göhn, I sampled both versions of Coons Process Pale Ale, the original and the historical. The original featured the authentic homebrew recipe used by Gohn's grandfather. At 10.4 percent ABV, it was boozy and a bit cloying. The historical revision is lighter in color, flavor, and alcohol (5.3 percent ABV) and fills an often-overlooked low-IBU spot in pale ales (16 IBUs).

Old Bust Head Brewing Company

You won't find a spot called Bust Head featured on the Fauquier Historical Society's website. Morven, Oak Hill, Belle Grove, and other landmarks figure more prominently, and understandably so because they boast connections with such notables as Chief Justice John Marshall.

Bust Head was important enough, though, that it caught the attention of Ike and Julie Broaddus when they were pondering a name for their brewery (and they live on Old Bust Head Road). "Our name comes from the nickname given to one of the first local watering holes in Fauquier County," Julie said. "It reminds us of why we're here—to bring people together, build community, and share our quality craft."

The past plays into much of Old Bust Head's present. Beer names bear local references—Wildcat India Pale Ale, for example, refers to Wildcat Mountain, which now harbors a nature preserve outside Warrenton. The label shows Charlie Ashby, last king of the Free State in Fauquier. Graffiti House IPA, which accounts for 20 percent of sales, is named for a historic spot in Brandy Station that is covered with inscriptions, signatures, and messages from Civil War soldiers on both sides.

Unlike some nanobreweries that also emphasize their community ties, Old Bust Head wants to carry the tales and the tastes of the area to a broad audience. Annual production on the thirty-barrel system reached six thousand barrels in 2017; distribution extended throughout Virginia and into D.C. The eventual goal, through adding fermenters and other equipment, is to reach forty thousand barrels annually.

That business plan and the investment in growth are shaped by the three founders' vision of trends. "While many local markets still have room to grow, it is unlikely that any additional regional breweries will be able to develop," Ike observed. "It is more likely that a good number of regional folks will retreat to their local markets after determining that the cost of distribution and supporting a sales team is not profitable until a much higher level of sales can be sustained."

Making sure the beers support that approach is mainly the job of head brewer and co-owner Charles Kling. A native of the Ozark Mountains in Missouri, Kling learned to make moonshine at the hands of the old-timers there. He studied chemical engineering and became intrigued by the process of brewing beer. By the time he moved to Fauquier County, he'd already worked at craft breweries in the western U.S. He, Ike, and Julie developed a business plan that initially focused on a brewpub, with a restaurant, but morphed into a production operation after state law changed in 2012.

Their search for a facility hit a few dead ends, but the beer gods smiled when a complex of buildings at Vint Hill, a former military site, came on the market. It provided twenty thousand square feet of space for brewing tanks and a bottling line as well as a spot for a taproom. "The 1952 post-and-beam warehouse that houses our taproom was part of the original high-security military facility where the government worked on and stored electronic warfare equipment," Julie noted.

Making it work as a beer hall took some doing. "This was not a pretty building," she recalled. Touches such as using walnut from the Broaddus farm for the thirty-foot bar added warmth, but she felt "the thing that was important to me was that when you came here, you could tell this was a military building at one time." Now the tasting room offers brews from forty-eight taps, a stage for live music, access to the outdoor beer garden, and a venue for community activities such as yoga and 5K runs.

Another expression of Old Bust Head's connection to the locality comes through harvest ales made with Virginia ingredients. The 2014 version featured freshly picked hops—Cascade, Zeus, Chinook, and Nugget—from two area sources, and the grain bill included apple- and cherry-wood smoked malt from Copper Fox Distillery in Sperryville. And, of course, Fauquier County well water was part of the mix. "[People] like to feel a connection to their local brewery," Kling explained. "That's one thing really nice about the craft industry. All of these small breweries are popping up in all these small locales, and people feel a connection to a local business."

Try this: If you're looking for that West Coast citrus hop profile, Graffiti House IPA is your ticket. But don't overlook Bust Head English Style Pale Ale. Goldings and Fuggle hops give it some earthy British character; Cascade hops boost the aroma while keeping bitterness low (21 IBUs). Look for some bready notes from the two-row malt. Drinkability is a plus at 5.6 percent ABV.

Pen Druid Brewing

Julie Spiezio and Carolyn Cobb have been craft beer fans since the first wave of microbreweries in the 1990s. Mention Old Dominion Brewing Company or any of several other veterans, and their eyes light up. On this Saturday in August 2017, they've come from D.C. to sit at the bar of Pen Druid in Sperryville, savoring samples of the three beers on tap—a fourth has already kicked. "This is a destination for us. The beers are unique, and we really enjoy it," says Spiezio.

The tasting room bustles with energy. Kids play with plastic blocks as parents chat. Couples line the wooden tables, voices raised above the rock music playing from speakers flanking the bar. Stacks of grain sacks and oak barrels—the word "spontaneous" conspicuous on several—form a low wall, partially hiding brewing tanks beyond. Posters with psychedelic lettering—"Cannablis" and "Big Brother"—adorn the walls. A man holding four metal horseshoes stands at the chestnut-and-poplar bar, patiently waiting for a glass of hazy beer to find him. The rough-hewn ambience reflects the past of the space (a former apple packing warehouse) and the cofounders (three brothers who toured in the rock band Pontiak).

Jennings Carney is one of those brothers (Lain and Van share his DNA). They grew up outside the nearby town of Woodville, and the brewery's name and logo reference the family farm. You get the sense talking with Jennings that "taste of place" is more than a slogan for him and his brothers. Local grains and hops go in the beer, and the yeast is a homegrown specialty.

"The yeast is from outside the brewery," Carney says, pausing between filling glasses. "It was grown up from a small flower out of about fifty samples. The one sample we took, we threw it into a culture, and that's the culture that we use to brew all of our beers."

The process included considerable analysis and test batches to develop that culture. Other elements of the brewing process further the goal—to create beers you can't find anywhere else, not just for the sake of being different but to convey local and regional identity. Copper-lined coolships enable spontaneous fermentation in some batches. Sour beers also benefit from a customized blend. Wood fires the brew kettles. Even Pen Druid's water is pure Rappahannock; "We don't do anything to it" in terms of adding chemicals, Carney observes.

The offerings on this Saturday are scrawled in different colors of chalk on a board by the bar—Penelope Wild Southern Brown, Mars Wild IPA, and Odysseus Wild Oatmeal Blonde, all keg conditioned. Suzersain and Golden Swan, wild blonde ales made with a variety of local grains (the former is aged on fresh chardonnay lees from Rappahannock Cellars), are available in bottles.

When I tell Carney I get some raisin notes from the Penelope, he one-ups me. "I totally get raisin off of it. Raisin, leather, tobacco, chocolate—it's great," he says. "What fermented the Penelope is the exact same culture that fermented the Mars and fermented the Odysseus. So you can see that just by doing different things to the yeast, like adding different malts and hopping it differently, it changes how the culture expresses itself. People will call something wild because they're taking *Brettanomyces* [yeast] from a lab and adding it. We're not doing that. We got the yeast from the wild, brought it into the brewery, and we're just using that."

You can walk on the wild side at Pen Druid or have more traditional styles at Hopkins Ordinary in Sperryville.

Suggested theme song for the Carney brothers: "Wild Thing" (although I really like the clip of Led Zeppelin performing "Dazed and Confused" on their website).

Try this: The appeal of Pen Druid is that you will have a unique experience with each visit. No flagships here. No West Coast IPA clones (not that there's anything wrong with that). Come. Try. Taste. Talk to one of the brothers. Play horseshoes.

Also in Sperryville: Before landing at Pen Druid, I spent a delightful half hour getting to know the folks and the beers at **Hopkins Ordinary Bed & Breakfast** on Main Street. Kevin Kraditor and Sherri Fickel came down from D.C. to follow their passion for hiking (Old Rag, White Oak Canyon, and other popular destinations are nearby). They bought the historic building, formerly an inn, about sixteen years ago and spent more than three years renovating before opening. In 2014, the Ale Works was added featuring Kraditor's beers. A former homebrewer, he originally intended just to share his brews with guests at the ordinary, but ABC laws prohibited that. So a one-barrel system was installed in a cozy cellar space that doubles as the taproom, which is open to the public. Outside, a magnificent American elm tree offers shade, and hand-hewn wood furnishings provide seating in the beer garden.

The tap list during my visit included eight beers, all containing at least some malt from Copper Fox Distillery. The Farmer's Tan Saison caught my attention with its refreshing blend of lemon thyme and mint (from the ordinary's garden) and cucumber (also locally sourced). Only one of the beers is always on tap—the Innkeepers' IPA. Centennial, Citra, and Cascade hops provide a citrus aroma and mild bitterness (53 IBUs), and a blend of two-row and six-row barley malts provides full body. Alcohol content is 6.6 percent ABV. It's a perfect thirst-quencher after a rigorous hike.

A short drive from Hopkins Ordinary—and only paces across the parking lot from Pen Druid—is **Copper Fox Distillery.** If you're curious about the process of converting barley from grain to malt, Quinlan Ashwell or one of the other assistants will explain the nuances during one of the tours, which are offered every half hour. There is much to learn about the distilling art, but my beery antennae went up when Ashwell said Copper Fox provides malt to more than one hundred and fifty breweries, including the Stone facility in Escondido, California. As noted elsewhere, Copper Fox opened a Williamsburg facility in 2016 on a six-acre plot fronting Capitol Landing Road.

CHAPTER 8

Breweries Change the Face of Richmond

Could Richmond be the most "beeristoric" city in the country? A persuasive argument could be made for a number of reasons: If you consider that in 1607 beer was part of a full-fledged party on Fulton Hill, where Powhatans greeted Captain John Smith and others who came upriver from Jamestown. If you count a continuous brewing scene through colonial times, the Revolutionary War, the Civil War, and the First and Second World Wars. If you factor in that the first canned beer in the world made its debut in Richmond in 1935. And if you take into account programs such as the annual Beeristoric bus tour, the BrewHaHa festival hosted by the Virginia Historical Society, and the Hops in the Park Harvest Festival at Henricus settlement, which dates to 1611.

The power of the past holds only partial sway in assessing the story of beer in the state's capital. Breweries have transformed urban areas. Scott's Addition was a dead zone of empty warehouses and abandoned businesses in 2012, before a string of five breweries, two cideries, a meadery, and a distillery gave the area new spirit(s). Nearby, Hardywood Park has created a cultural destination. Legend's established presence across the James River helped attract new business to Manchester. Stone and Triple Crossing have chiseled a new visage on the city's eastern face. Strangeways (which also has a location in Fredericksburg) brings its quirky approach to the world as expressed in art as well as beer. Ardent Craft Ales blossomed as one of the

Hop bines growing up twine provide a decorative feature as well as a brewing ingredient at Fine Creek in Powhatan County.

early brewing sites in Scott's Addition. The Answer Brewpub on West Broad gives shape to beer icon An Bui's "Beer is the Answer" motto. The city's neighboring counties add to the mix with Steam Bell in Chesterfield, Fine Creek in Powhatan, and Midnight and Lickinghole Creek, which helped shape the footprint of farm breweries, in Goochland. Now Richmond is cited frequently as a top tourist destination, with its vibrant brewing culture as a major attraction.

Legend Brewing Company

Superlatives can cut two ways. Legend Brewing Company, for example, ranks as Virginia's oldest existing craft brewery, a position that commands respect for an established line of solid beers. But brand loyalty is a wandering child; market trends show that many beer lovers seek the latest, the hippest, the most exciting, and the most extreme.

Since tapping the first keg of Legend Brown Ale at

Commercial Taphouse and Grill in 1994, the brewery's founder and owner Tom Martin and such longtime employees as its vice president of operations Dave Gott, its head brewer John Wampler, and its vice president of distributor relations Rick Uhler have steered the brewery over bumps and past pitfalls. The early business strategy encompassed starting with four beers on a ten-barrel system, forming a separate company for self-distribution, and setting up a small kitchen in a nook of the building to satisfy a state law requiring breweries to serve food in order to sell beer on-site.

Martin soon added a deck, giving patrons an unparalleled view of the city skyline from Manchester, an industrial ragamuffin on the south side of the James River. The sandwich nook morphed into a restaurant. Beer lovers embraced Legend Brown Ale as Richmond's iconic brew. And Legend's measured growth gave it legs to survive turbulence in the early wave of microbreweries. In fact, after Richbrau Brewing Company closed in Shockoe Slip

The view of Richmond's downtown skyline from Manchester has been a part of Legend Brewing Company's appeal for decades.

in 2010, Legend stood as the lone craft brewery in the city limits. (Extra Billy's Smokehouse and Brewery in Midlothian had a small presence.)

As it always does, the pendulum then swung in a new direction. Hardywood Park opened on Ownby Lane in 2011, preceding a fresh spurt of breweries spawned by the 2012 state law removing the food requirement. Tastes changed. IPAs became the darling of aficionados, and adventurous brews such as Hardywood's Gingerbread Stout and Lickinghole Creek's Enlightened Despot drew crowds and raves. For Legend, relevance became as much a priority as respectability.

Brian Knight, a Legend brewer at the time, came up with the idea of developing new beer recipes paired with local stories and myths, and developing collaborations along those lines with other Virginia breweries. The Urban Legend Series was born, and the first batches included offbeat brews such as a red IPA created with Lost Rhino brewery focusing on the story of a Northern Virginia man who dressed in a bunny suit and terrorized area residents.

"The Urban Legend Series is one of those things that's allowed us to change up," explained Gott. "Having an established line is a great thing. But it's like anything else. It makes it a challenge when you've got a product that's kind of iconic, to keep that in the news, in people's minds, and keep it exciting. So we're constantly looking at ways, honestly, to keep ourselves relevant in the marketplace."

One of Legend's original marketplaces was in Portsmouth, and in 2017 the brewery expanded into that area with a 120-seat full-service brewpub in a historic building fronting on the Elizabeth River. The three-barrel system there and a five-barrel pilot system at the hub in Richmond allowed Wampler to play with new recipes without having to use the full thirty-barrel production equipment.

In 2017, about 60 percent of Legend's ten-thousand-barrel annual production comprised Legend Brown Ale.

The recipes for it and the three other founding brews—Legend Pilsner, Porter, and Lager—were developed by Martin with the help of his father, who worked for Anheuser-Busch as vice president of European Brewing Operations and as the original brewmaster at the A-B Williamsburg plant. A career in making beer sounded good to young Martin, so he attended the University of California–Davis and earned a master's degree in brewing science. He did the corporate brewing gig briefly, but the efforts of pioneers such as Anchor's Fritz Maytag and Sierra Nevada's Ken Grossman prodded him to branch out on his own. "While I was at UC-Davis, we'd go around and tour different breweries that had just started. Sierra Nevada had just started at that time," Martin said.

In 1993, the view from a then-trashy spot in Manchester spoke to Martin, and the deck of great renown followed. A sunny day, a glinting downtown skyline, a churning historic river, and a pint of Legend beer defined many a good time over the years. For better or worse, boom times in Manchester in the mid-2010s led to construction that compromised the view. The satellite in Portsmouth and plans for additional expansions showed that there has been little compromise in Legend's vigor.

Try this: Well, duh—Legend Brown Ale. Even if you've had it scores of times, as I have, try it again and rediscover the beer that built Richmond's craft scene. It's a bit of a hybrid—slightly nutty with notes of caramel consistent with English styles but with enough hops to give it a dry American edge (19 IBUs). Be careful, though. The 5.8 percent ABV belies this beer's ability to produce a surprisingly substantial buzz.

Hardywood Park Craft Brewery

It's the Fourth of July 2017. I stand in a shadowed nook of Hardywood's lot, by a grain elevator, sipping a Great Return IPA and waiting for my favorite cover band, Zep

Replica, to take the stage. People bump and elbow and jostle their way among food trucks and beer wagons; some line the bocce and cornhole courts, rolling or tossing, chatting and chuckling, drinking and lolling in the heat. Soon the sky will come alive with bursts of color and crackling booms as fireworks from The Diamond, Dogwood Dell, and elsewhere celebrate the day.

It's a community time at an iconic Richmond community place. Hardywood is at the heart of the city's craft beer scene, and though it doesn't have the veteran status of Legend across the river, it beats with a pulse more in time with RVA's new hipness. Here is the site of the signing of Senate Bill 604. Here is brewed the "flawless" Gingerbread Stout. Here is the home of the Community Hopping Project and RVA IPA. Here you can hear indie bands, classic rockers, and the Richmond Symphony. You can stand among cryptically marked barrels filled with nuanced brews while sipping the latest release. You can stroll by a mural depicting the original Hardywood Park, an Australian sheep station where two boyhood friends tasted their first flavorful beer. And you're just as likely to bump into those friends, Eric McKay and Patrick Murtaugh, still following their passion for flavorful beer.

It's been a long and winding freeway since Hardywood's doors opened on Ownby Lane in 2011. In calendar time, it's a blink; in beer time, eons. Legend was the only other craft brewery in the city then, and the state counted a total of about forty. By mid-2017, Richmond's metro area counted thirty-some breweries and brewpubs; the state, more than two hundred. Hardywood managed to surf the wave with big-board authority and elegance, expanding its footprint on Ownby Lane, growing distribution to the point of straining its twenty-barrel system, planting a taproom in Charlottesville, winning medals galore, and breaking ground on a $28 million facility in Goochland County that promises to be a game changer for the brewery. "Basically, we're going to have the capability of making three times as much beer at once," observed Kate Lee, director of operations.

As with many breweries, Hardywood's growth has appeared neck-snapping. For example, the production target in 2017 was sixteen thousand barrels, more than double the volume of just three years earlier. But the pace belies the care that McKay, Murtaugh, and their investors took in developing a methodical plan—and the homework that the two did over the course of years. After having their palates popped in Australia, the lads took up homebrewing and expanded their knowledge with jobs in bartending, in distribution, and at breweries. Murtaugh studied at the Siebel Institute of Technology in Chicago (where his great-grandfather and great-uncle trained to become master brewers) and Doemens Academy in Munich, Germany; McKay excelled in marketing, got an MBA from Fordham, and became a Certified Cicerone®.

They scoured the country for the ideal place to plunk down their brewing boots. The Southeast region, they learned, was growing by three times the national average in craft beer volume but still had low market share. "We knew that from a portfolio standpoint, we wanted to brew beers that were a little more unique, more outside the box. So we were looking for a region that would appreciate creativity," McKay explained.

Richmond, however, was more of an acquired taste than an immediate favorite. McKay transferred with his job to Specialty Beverage, a distributor in RVA, and was impressed by the flourishing local restaurant scene, the strong artistic and cultural vibe, and the sense of community. "Ultimately, it took just being in Richmond to feel like this was the perfect place to start what we wanted to start," McKay recalled.

Speaking of perfect . . . a game-changing 2012 rating of Hardywood Gingerbread Stout in *BeerAdvocate* magazine—one hundred out of one hundred, a perfect beer—made headlines and drew lines to the brewery. "I would say it was arguably the most impactful credibility booster to our beer," McKay concluded.

Medals aplenty have cemented that credibility. Beers as diverse as the Raspberry Stout, the Pils (a classic German-style pilsner), Ruse, and Große Teufel (based on a historic Lichtenhainer eastern German ale style) have won awards. Just as important, Hardywood enjoys a reputation for high quality along its product line and in its consistency. "It's really quite easy to make a beer taste good once," said Lee, who worked in quality control for Anheuser-Busch before landing at Hardywood. "Quality is all about consistency and the ability to make the beer taste good over and over and over again."

It's the sense of community, though, that defines Hardywood's character. Local history gets a nod in the Cream Ale, which pays homage to the 1935 world debut of canned beer in Richmond. (Hardywood's can even has a tongue-in-cheek guide to popping the top, mirroring instructions on the original Krueger Cream Ale cans.) Great Return IPA celebrates the revival of the James River and the return of sturgeon. RVA IPA is the annual culmination of Hardywood's Community Hopping Project, where free rhizomes are distributed to hobbyists who later provide the cones for the special brew. Within the professional ranks, McKay has had repeat terms holding the gavel for the Virginia Craft Brewers Guild.

The next time Zep Replica takes the Fourth of July stage, perhaps it will be at Hardywood's West Creek plant. The opening in April 2018 marked the most ambitious chapter in the business's expansion. The twenty-two-acre site on Tuckahoe Creek houses a sixty-thousand-square-foot brewery with accompanying taproom, beer garden, and amenities such as self-guided tours of the brew house. Plans include an amphitheater and trails along the creek.

Most important, a sixty-barrel system gives Hardywood a significant leap in brewing capacity from the original twenty-barrel setup.

Try this: The opinions of beer critics should be taken with a grain of sea salt (for gose lovers). But there's no debating the excellence of Hardywood Gingerbread Stout. It's received accolades and awards on state, national, and international levels. Made with baby ginger and wild-flower honey, both locally sourced, this imperial milk stout (lactose and oats are used for a creamy smoothness) surprises with subtlety. It's not a cloying-sweet confection but a layered adventure with notes of chocolate, cinnamon, vanilla, and honey. It's a heavyweight at 9.2 percent ABV, but elegant hopping (55 IBUs) not only provides balance but also adds some snap. Review after review says it evokes the beer equivalent of Christmas morning.

The Answer Brewpub

Well before An Bui announced plans for The Answer Brewpub, he had established a reputation in Richmond and beyond as one of beer's most engaging and influential personalities through Mekong Restaurant. Twice voted the nation's top beer bar in online balloting by *CraftBeer .com*, Mekong is renowned for eclectic choices of Belgian and craft beers as well as for its Vietnamese cuisine. Visits by personalities ranging from Jerome Rebetez of Brasserie des Franches-Montagnes in Switzerland to GWAR's Oderus Urungus made Mekong a local favorite among beer geeks and a must-go for tourists. Bui's "Beer is the answer" comeback to nearly every question achieved celebrity status on its own. Still, curiosity bubbled when Bui announced his next venture would feature on-site brewing; beer would literally be the solution as well as the answer.

A vacant building a few paces from Mekong on Richmond's West Broad Street was renovated for the brewpub, which opened on a steamy, rain-spattered July evening in

2014. Brewing had yet to begin, and the following months saw a five-barrel direct-fire Premier system take shape with seven five-barrel fermenters and seven bright tanks. Brandon Tolbert, who had made a mark at Extra Billy's Smokehouse and Brewery in Midlothian with an aggressive IPA called Citra Ass Down, was hired as brewer. He and Bui shared a common vision—serve the freshest of fresh beers with the spotlight on hoppy styles.

The first brews ran from the taps in May 2015. Response was uniformly favorable. The long-awaited moment when all questions were answered came at that year's Virginia Craft Brewers Fest in Nelson County. Host Devils Backbone had dominated the awards in previous years, including a sweep of the three Best in Show medals in 2014. On August 22, however, a mighty roar went up when Tolbert took the stage to hoist the trophy for Virginia's best beer—Larceny, a single-hopped IPA made with Citra hops.

The months that followed fixed The Answer's star status in Richmond's vibrant brewing community. And although stouts, porters, goses, browns, and more styles have flowed from Tolbert's Star Wars–themed tanks, IPAs still occupy center stage. "People really seem to like what we're doing here," said Tolbert, who has since departed The Answer. "I've set out to do exactly what I said I was going to do from the start here, which is that we were going to focus on IPAs to begin with and get that down. I think I've achieved that. Not only personally do I feel I've achieved that, but we've gotten recognition."

In addition to the house beers, The Answer offers a variety of guest beers and ciders in its fifty-nine taps, plus there's the Andall, which allows for adjuncts to be infused into existing beers. Take, for example, the Cuban-style Guava Mangito Gose, flavored with pink guava, mangoes, fresh lime juice, habanero, and sea salt.

Rather than one answer, The Answer is helping provide

Richmond with multiple choices. "So many breweries, so many awesome beers," Bui told the *Washington Post* in 2017. "The beer crowds in town are more educated and have more options to pick. It's incredible."

Try this: Brandon Tolbert had a deft touch with most hops, but when it came to Citra, he wielded a magic wand. Larceny is a case in point; Citra Secret is another. Single-hopped with Citra, Larceny not only won Best in Show at the 2015 Virginia Craft Brewers Fest, but also is rated outstanding by *BeerAdvocate* magazine. It is slightly hazy (not to be confused with New England styles), blossoms with citrus aroma thanks to triple dry-hopping, and makes no apologies for its hop-forward bitterness. The double IPA Citra Secret was a treat offered at The Answer's second anniversary celebration in May 2017, and it upped the ante in alcohol content (8 percent ABV), fruity flavor (think mandarin orange, tangerine, papaya, and guava), and hop profile with the use of Australian Vic Secret hops.

Ardent Craft Ales

Search Google for "three guys and a . . . ," and the results you get are, in this order: "three guys and a truck," "three guys and a baby," ". . . and a grill," ". . . and a baby ghost," ". . . and a pizza pie." Search for "three guys and a homebrew setup in a garage on Church Hill in Richmond, Virginia," and you still don't get anything close to Ardent Craft Ales.

But that's where the first bubbles of the brewery that would be Ardent rose to the surface. Tom Sullivan, Paul Karns, and Kevin O'Leary established a brewing cooperative in said garage after gaining a following for the saisons and other beers they crafted on a half-barrel Sabco system. The decision to go commercial led to a citywide search ending in historic Scott's Addition, where Isley had recently established a craft brewing presence and new lofts and apartments were drawing fresh souls into the

Tom Sullivan, cofounder of Ardent Craft Ales, describes the brewing process to a group of patrons.

area. "It was a central location—accessible from the interstate, right next to a number of great neighborhoods, and close to attractions like museums and The Diamond," recalled Sullivan, cofounder and general manager. "But Scott's Addition also had its own identity, and we were excited to potentially be a part of it."

That potential has been realized. Though Karns and O'Leary are no longer part of the day-to-day operation, they helped guide Ardent to prominence, and Sullivan's steady leadership has secured the brewery's reputation as one of THE places to go in Richmond. There's an unpretentious, welcoming vibe to the walnut-bar taproom and umbrellaed beer garden that exudes conviviality.

Part of the appeal has to do with the adventurous and collaborative brewing spirit. Even before Ardent opened on Leigh Street in June 2014, word of the subtly sweet Honey Ginger Ale, the crisp and fruity Virginia Common, and the farmhouse-style Saison had whetted appetites and expectations. "The beers we were brewing weren't beers that you could readily go out and buy at the time," according to Sullivan. "It made perfect sense to us to try to perfect those styles."

Several brews in particular have been outside the box. Ardent chipped in with historic beers for programs sponsored by the Virginia Historical Society; one, a persimmon ale, received international attention. The brewery also had a hand, along with Hardywood Park, in Give Me Stout or Give Me Death, an imperial stout that saw then-governor Terry McAuliffe pitching in, literally, on brew day at Stone.

Lupulin lovers gravitate toward Ardent's IPA series, numbered for reference according to the particular hop profile; No. 14, for example, put the spotlight on Citra hops. In a separate building (a former garage they fondly call "the donkey barn"), you'll find barrels with résumés of bourbon, chardonnay, Madeira, and port imparting unique flavors, often with the help of *Brettanomyces* yeast strains. Saisons in particular showcase Ardent's range, with wild yeast, wine barrel–aging, dry-hopping, and herb or fruit puree additions giving the farmhouse tradition fresh fields of flavor. Specialties such as Roggenbier (think rye) join more mainstream ales such as the seasonal Robust Porter (think roasty) in the rotation.

Following Wild Ale releases using the unruly *Brettanomyces,* the brewery launched a line of sours in July 2017 with two variations—one featuring mango, the other raspberries. Two years in the making, the ales debuted in handsome 330-milliliter bottles and packed a tongue-tingling blend of acidity, tartness, funk, and fruit. On a totally different note, Ardent experimented with gluten-free recipes developed by taproom manager Lincoln Smith, whose son has celiac disease. Quinoa, a grain rich in protein but devoid of gluten, replaced barley in the recipes of an imperial stout and a Belgian white ale. Smith also engineered a rye kölsch ale that was one of the batches first brewed in that garage on Church Hill. Upon its release in 2016, Sullivan noted, "Our whole team worked together to make this beer perfect, just like the one brewed years ago in our little co-op."

Try this: A hard choice, but Ardent's straight-up Saison gets my nod. The farmhouse ale tradition of using a variety of ingredients has stretched the parameters of the style with a bounty of interpretations. Ardent has its share of horses in the stable, and the straightforward offering at the top of the menu gives a wonderful taste of this classic. Light gold in color, spicy in aroma from the Belgian yeast, slightly fruity in the flavor with a pleasant, subdued bitterness (31 IBUs), and refreshingly carbonated—this is a go-to standard. The 6.7 percent ABV is a little more than sessionable, but sometimes you have to let the donkey kick.

Triple Crossing Brewing Company

History surrounds Triple Crossing. Take a quick walk north on Hatcher Street from the production facility, and you can look up at Fulton Hill. In 1607, Captain John Smith, Christopher Newport, and other newly arrived colonists shared beer, wine, and brandy with Powhatan Indians living there. Look across the bottom to Chimborazo Hill, where a lager brewery provided beer, seen as a medicinal beverage, to wounded and sick Civil War soldiers. Look west to Rocketts Landing, where you can go see the caves that James River Steam Brewery, built in 1866, used to store beer. Even Triple Crossing's original Foushee Street location, housed in a historic building, rubs elbows with a spot at the corner of Adams and Canal streets where a Maryland-based brewery offered beers in the late 1890s.

This sense of history is not lost on Triple Crossing's cofounders—Scott Jones, Adam Worcester, and Jeremy Wirtes. The release of Liberty or Death Porter in 2014 featured a costumed actor giving a stirring rendition of Patrick Henry's famous 1775 speech, delivered at St. John's Church on East Broad Street.

By no means are these three stuck in the past, though. Nearly every Friday features a release of something new, something interesting, something tasty. It might be "super dank" Surprise Valley Imperial IPA made with Mosaic lupulin powder. It might be a gluten-free version of Element 79 Golden Ale, one of their original beers. Or someday soon it might be a funky ale fermented with wild yeast using the lambic-style coolship, or *koelschip,* installed in 2017.

While the tap list might sport everything from a light-bodied farmhouse grisette to a brawny imperial stout brewed with toasted coconut flakes, hoppy beers are Triple Crossing's trademark. One weekend in September 2017, for example, six of the dozen beers being poured were IPAs or double IPAs. Falcon Smash and Clever Girl IPAs have become standards among RVA hopheads. Producing old-school British ales was a goal of Wirtes's from the beginning in 2014. "English beers today—some of the bigger brands—are seen as more subtle than their American counterparts. But English beers back then were anything but. They were just as strong then as they are today on the West Coast," explained Wirtes, the head brewer. "That's what we're all passionate about, the big, dry hoppy beers."

That passion brought the three together in the first

place. Jones and Worcester have been friends since child-hood days in the Smoketree area of Chesterfield County. They went to the same schools and later became increas-ingly interested in craft beers. Wirtes, originally from Newport News, moved to Chesterfield in 2005, and the three immediately plugged into a shared vision when they sat down together at Sedona Taphouse in Midlothian in October 2012.

Their search for a suitable space took them to a 1930s building on Foushee Street. The 2,800 square feet of space was adequate for a seven-barrel system, and the old-school brick-and-wood taproom proved a draw for downtown workers and students, many of whom could walk from the nearby Virginia Commonwealth University campus.

It didn't take long, however, to exhaust capacity. Stone's choice of east Richmond for its brewery cast a new light on that part of town, and Worcester, Jones, and Wirtes saw opportunity in a 30,000-square-foot building between Fulton Hill and the James River. This time, they chose local artists to create a more vibrant ambience with strung lights, acid-stained tables, a pizza oven, and vi-brant art—on one wall an alluring woman with blue skin keeps a steady eye on patrons. "We wanted the space to re-mind people of downtown Richmond," Jones said. "Every-thing from the lights to murals reflects what we wanted the space to look like."

A twenty-barrel system and the use of a canning line also allowed them to expand the product line and boost distribution. Barrel-aging and kettle-souring broadened the creative aspect of brewing, as did the wild fermenta-tion project (a day at Pollak Vineyards near Charlottesville yielded eight grape varietals for fermentation trials). The Fulton site also has become a center for happenings such as the RVA Street Artist Pop-up Event and the East Coast Covenant Beer Fest.

The story of the brewery's name is well-known—it

refers to a spot in Richmond where three railroad lines cross vertically. It's a morsel of locomotive trivia now blended into a tasty part of beer history.

Try this: Falcon Smash IPA put Triple Crossing on beer lovers' map for its artful complexity and uncompromised hop-forward profile. The recipe showcases Falconer's Flight hops, with Centennial and other rotating varieties. Heavy dry-hopping boosts the citrus-pine-grapefruit aroma and flavors. It pours hazy and golden orange, almost a hybrid between West Coast and New England styles. Alcohol level is 7 percent ABV; no IBU rating is listed, but perceived bitterness is satisfyingly high.

Stone Brewing

The single most common question I have received over the years is "What's your favorite beer?" It's a question I dislike, because beer favoritism depends on mood, food, my thirst level, time of year, cycle of the moon, and, to some extent, whatever beer happens to be in front of me. In my early days of writing about beer, I parried the question by saying I had two desert island beers. One of those was/is Arrogant Bastard Ale.

So imagine my excitement when Stone Brewing, the ninth-largest among craft breweries in the nation, announced in 2014 that it had selected Richmond for its East Coast location. I'd had Arrogant Bastard fresh from the tap at Stone's headquarters in Escondido, California. The prospect of having it available fresh from the tap approximately 2,657 miles closer to my home was delightful to contemplate.

Still, I had concerns, as did many others. The deal to land Stone's $74 million facility was a generous one, sweetened with roughly $7 million in city and state grants plus more money in incentives (and the brewery itself was constructed using city bonds). Was this fair to homegrown breweries, some of which have had to machete their way through tangles of local bureaucracy? Would Stone's immensity overshadow the locals? Was Stone, renowned for its aggressive beers and in-your-face marketing, be a good fit for a region still known for its Southern gentility?

Beer started flowing from Stone's tanks in 2016, but the goodwill flowed much earlier. Frequent visits by co-founders Greg Koch and Steve Wagner, accompanied often by former head brewer Mitch Steele and other Stone dignitaries, built rapport. Sharing recipes and forging collaborations with local breweries—including a three-way imperial stout brew with Hardywood and Ardent that featured then-governor Terry McAuliffe pouring hops into a brew kettle—signaled a mutual embrace. Wagner had lauded Richmond's "impressive craft beer culture" at the outset, and Stone signaled it wanted to be in the pews rather than in the pulpit.

That first year of full brewing yielded roughly 100,000 barrels; the eight-year goal is 600,000 barrels (Stone's

Greg Koch (*right*), cofounder of Stone, talks about the process of brewing Give Me Stout or Give Me Death with Governor Terry McAuliffe (*center*), McAuliffe's wife, Dorothy, and other state and brewery officials.

total annual production was 325,645 barrels in 2015, a 13.4 percent increase from the previous year). The full measure of Stone's impact on the region won't be felt until the thirty-thousand-square-foot restaurant and beer garden open on Wharf Street facing the James River.

For all of Stone's stature, it started just like Hardywood, Triple Crossing, Ardent, Garden Grove, Reason, Wolf Hills, and so many others across the land—by friends following a passion. Koch and Wagner were musical buddies when they decided to go pro with their homebrewing in 1996. (BTW—ask Steve about guitars and you're guaranteed a lively conversation.) From the outset, they chiseled a distinctive face on their brand, with gargoyles, hop-forward beers, and labels that warned "You are not worthy." That attitude probably attracted me to Arrogant Bastard Ale in the first place.

Stone doesn't hang its reputation on one beer. In 2017, readers of *Zymurgy* magazine, the official publication of the American Homebrewers Association, voted Stone as having the top-ranked beer portfolio in the nation. All told, the brewery cranks out twoscore or more different beers, everything from Stone Enjoy By IPA, which carries a date beyond which it is not to be consumed, to cellar-able brews such as Stone Old Guardian Barley Wine. Stone IPA is a definitive version of the West Coast style, with bountiful grapefruit/citrus aroma, zingy hop bitterness (71 IBUs), and slightly elevated alcohol (6.9 percent ABV). That collaboration with Governor McAuliffe yielded an imperial stout called Stone Give Me Stout or Give Me Death, loaded with Virginia blackberries and raspberries and packing a wallop with 9.5 percent ABV and 94 IBUs. You can get Arrogant Bastard Ale aged in oak bourbon barrels, a brew that one aficionado described as "like the steak of beer in a glass." And as much as I like my Arrogant Bastard Ale, I've become a huge fan of Who You Callin' Wussie, a bold but elegant pilsner that's part of the Arrogant Brewing line (a separate company formed in 2015 with Arrogant Bastard Ale as its flagship). I enjoy Wussie so much that I might have to make room for two pilsners on my desert island. (I knew you'd be curious—Pilsner Urquell won a spot long ago.)

Try this: Arrogant Bastard Ale lives in myth as much as in your mouth. It allegedly was a recipe malfunction in 1995 when Koch and Wagner were doing a batch of pale ale. "We did not create it. I did not name it," Koch says on the website. "It was already there. We were just the first mortals to have stumbled upon it." Its official style is "classified." I find it hard to describe. It's like unleashing a friendly beast in your mouth, a creature so provocative your senses can't turn away. For the record, its ABV is 7.2 percent. Its IBUs? Also classified.

Strangeways Brewing

It doesn't take long after entering Strangeways' taproom on Dabney Road to realize that you have entered an alternate beer universe. The first clue might be the portrait of a chimp squatting on a barrel pondering a glass of beer, a pose repeated on tap handles. Or maybe it's the Twilight Zone art with banged-up hubcaps and twisted metal. Or the mounted boar's head, wearing a red-banded hat and eyeglasses with a medal hanging from its tusks (or other apparel appropriate for the season).

Pay close attention to one of the photos spread out under the glass-covered bar and to a vinyl disc on the wall for insights into owner Neil Burton's perspective. The photo is of Robert Smith of The Cure; the record, a copy of The Smiths' "Strangeways, Here We Come." Both reflect his passion for music; the latter provided the name for the business spawned by his passion for beer. And it's the beer—the salty-sour Wake Me Up Before You Gose, the aromatic Hop Howler IPA, the flagship Woodbooger Belgian-Style Brown Ale, the apocalyptic Ape Armageddon

Barrel-Aged Imperial Stout, and nearly three hundred other varieties—that's brought you through the door.

From the brewery's beginning in 2013, Strangeways has celebrated individualism, uniqueness, and creativity. Mike Hiller, director of brewing operations, and Brian Knight, head brewer, get considerable leeway in putting together beers several steps off the beaten path. "We want to approach [brewing] from a creative standpoint rather than to find a particular niche in the marketplace," Burton noted. As a result, the business has succeeded in creating and sustaining an identity in an increasingly crowded industry. The taproom has repeatedly been voted Virginia's Best Brewery Taproom by RateBeer.com users.

The same quirkiness marks Strangeways' second facility on Lansdowne Road in Fredericksburg, Burton's hometown. The 10,100-square-foot site, which opened in late June 2017 with Matty Eck as head brewer, features similar art oddities and eye-catching curios in a former warehouse that once was part of the family clothing business. That location was designed to provide not only a second retail taproom but also a "launch pad" for distribution into the Northern Virginia market, according to Burton. Though the ten-barrel system in Fredericksburg is half the size of Richmond's setup, the newer facility offers nearly one hundred taps at the indoor and patio bars.

The connection between family clothing and craft beer might seem strange in itself. Burton was a student at Wake Forest University when he signed up for a study abroad program that took him to Munich. It just happened to be during Oktoberfest, and a waitress at a small restaurant he visited recommended trying Schneider Aventinus, a wheat doppelbock. "She brought it to me in this beautiful custom glass," Burton recalled. "I took my first sip and I was like 'What am I drinking?' It was remarkable. That's what changed my life right there; that's what got me into beer."

Fredericksburg beer lovers wasted little time in checking out Strangeways' new brewery when it opened in late June 2017 on Lansdowne Road.

It's no coincidence that bocks have their own niche among Strangeways beers. One of Hiller's most adventurous brews was an eisbock, a style that requires the liquid to be chilled until the appearance of ice, which is removed to boost alcohol content and concentrate flavor. Sours using *Lactobacillus* bacteria and *Brettanomyces* yeast also have become staples in the brewery's portfolio. And Belgian brewing tradition inspires three flagships—Woodbooger Belgian-Style Brown Ale (6 percent ABV, 20 IBUs), Albino Monkey Belgian White Ale (5 percent ABV, 25 IBUs), and Phantasmic Belgian IPA (7 percent ABV, 70 IBUs). The production area of the brewery is lined with barrels of beer, soaking up flavors of oak, vanilla, bourbon, and more as it ages.

Burton has been involved on several fronts in promoting the craft beer scene. His involvement with state legislators helped secure passage of a bill allowing manufacturers to lease space to small breweries for production (renting space was part of Strangeways' original business plan but has not been exercised). Strangeways has also helped increase the visibility of Virginia beer by pouring at the Great American Beer Festival in Denver. And serving on the marketing and tourism committee of the Virginia Craft Brewers Guild has given Burton a platform for attracting beer aficionados to the Old Dominion in general and Richmond in particular. "Richmond used to be just a place to drive through," he noted. "Now it's a place where people stop, realize how cool our town is, and stay. That's magic."

Try this: The German gose is a quirky style that befits Strangeways' image, and Wake Me Up Before You Gose Sour has been a hit since it was introduced. *Lactobacillus* and *Brettanomyces* combine for tartness and funk in the fermentation, and French sea salt, combined with coriander and ginger, puts a refreshing twist in the taste. It is a light beer at 4.6 percent ABV but has more spunk than the radlers on Strangeways' menu.

Steam Bell Beer Works

In 2014, Brad Cooper was fired from his job at a mining company. Two years later, he opened a brewery in Chesterfield County. In between, he sold his truck, moved in with his parents, rounded up some investors, leased space in a business park, and jumped a series of hurdles that would test anyone's mettle.

The payoff, though, has been to introduce creative brewing to a part of the Richmond region that might have been challenged to know the difference between an IPA and a PBR. Steam Bell's beers have not only helped clarify that distinction but broadened the possibilities with beers such as The Grisette, a low-alcohol Belgian-style saison, and Harwood's Entire Porter, a malty American-style porter with ginger and clove notes from masala chai.

Steam Bell's success can be measured by a couple of

benchmarks. In May 2017, then-governor Terry McAuliffe and other government officials filled the tasting room for the ceremonial signing of a bill increasing the number of banquet licenses allowed annually (from four to eight) at breweries and wineries. The same month, Cooper announced plans to expand to a second location named Canon and Draw in Richmond's Fan District. The five-thousand-square-foot site on Main Street feeds off the nearby campus of Virginia Commonwealth University and offers a new aspect of Steam Bell's vision.

"It's really a completely different concept," observed Brittany Cooper, Brad's sister and the company's marketing guru, before Canon and Draw's opening in 2018. "It will be higher end, with leather couches and darker wood—cool, eclectic, old Southern atmosphere." It also features a seven-barrel setup, slightly smaller than the ten-barrel brew house in Chesterfield.

Brittany is just one of the Cooper clan to pitch in at Steam Bell. She moved to Richmond to help with the brewery's marketing while continuing to work remotely for IBM in New York. Tom Cooper, Brad's dad, scavenged hundreds of pallets from Lowe's and similar places to put together tables and other furnishings in the Chesterfield tasting room. "We got them wherever we could find them," Tom recalled. Connie Cooper, Tom's wife and Brad's mother, helps with a variety of chores; perhaps most important, she gave Brad support and encouragement as he recovered from the job loss and began shaping plans for the brewery. "Tom and I both were just on board with it," Connie said. "We felt like he had that entrepreneurial spirit."

The six-thousand-square-foot space in the Oak Lake Business Park takes advantage of a densely populated suburban chunk of metro Richmond. The beers benefit from Brad's experience as an assistant brewer at Hardywood Park and his years of homebrewing. The tap list reflects diversity and collaboration, such as with the bourbon barrel–aged wee heavy Scotch ale made in cahoots with the local M.A.S.H. homebrew club. And though Brad says he originally "didn't even want to do an IPA," he couldn't ignore the most popular style among craft aficionados. So Time is Money IPA joined the selections, offering a floral, farmhouse approach with a healthy 50 IBUs and 6.3 percent ABV.

Steam Bell's name shouldn't be confused with any reference to steam beer, the style trademarked and made famous by Anchor Brewing of San Francisco. The reference is to a piece of equipment used by coopers (get it?) to shape the staves of wood by using steam. Correspondingly, Canon and Draw plays off the same theme—*canon* is French for "barrel" and a drawknife, or drawshave, is used in making hoops for barrels.

Along with his family, Brad credits Richmond's beer community for helping him get past bumps and building his dream: "Everybody has been amazing. I don't know how else to say it."

Try this: Steam Bell eschews strict stylistic guidelines with many of its beers, and that's the case with Tiramisu Stout. It is a milk stout, offering lactose sweetness, and a big beer, at 9 percent ABV, which puts it in the imperial category. What makes it unique is the use of vanilla beans, rum-soaked oak chips, and Brazilian coffee. It won a bronze medal at the 2016 Virginia Craft Beer Cup competition.

Midnight Brewery

Trae Cairns couldn't have known it when he opened Midnight Brewery in May 2012, but the boat he had just launched was about to catch the biggest tailwind ever to hit Virginia's brewing scene. Cairns was just following his passion—rather, his obsession. Seven years earlier, his wife had given him a homebrewing kit. One batch led to another, and soon he was burning the midnight oil washing bottles, starting yeast cultures, and tweaking recipes. The "midnight brewer" became his nickname, and his information technology job began to pale beside his desire to make ales. Support from his family and a course at the Siebel Institute of Technology in Chicago provided the impetus to become the professional Midnight brewer.

Funding came from his own pockets. "I went to the banks, and it was like 'We're not loaning any money.' This was probably 2010," Cairns recalled. "Probably the worst thing to do is to tell me no or tell me it's not going to work, because I'm going to prove you wrong. That's kind of what I did."

Starting with a kölsch named, appropriately, New Beginning and a follow-up Banana Pancakes collaboration with Eric McKay and Patrick Murtaugh of Hardywood Park, Cairns built a stable of solid, straightforward styles. Rockville Red, an Irish-style red made with four malts and East Kent Golding hops, and Not My Job Brown Ale, which uses an assertive hop blend of East Kent Golding, Liberty, and Willamette hops, drew a following to the small taproom in Rockville, a nook of Goochland County just off Interstate 64.

A few weeks after the dawn of Midnight, a state law (the legendary SB604) completely changed the realm of craft brewing in Virginia by allowing breweries to sell beer on-site without having to sell food. Cairns's brewing quickly expanded from a 1.5-barrel system to a three-barrel setup, and in March 2014 Cairns took another step with construction of a 5,400-square-foot facility that featured a new tasting room and a ten-barrel brewing setup with twenty-barrel fermenters, all purchased from O'Connor Brewing Company in Norfolk.

Special beers raised the brewery's profile. Christmas at Midnight, a seasonal spiced beer; Purdy Mechanic IPA, a showcase for Nugget and Chinook hops at 66 IBUs; and

Virginia Midway, an American wheat beer brewed specifically for the State Fair of Virginia—all brought new fans and broadened the base for Midnight aficionados. I found the 2017 Vernal Elixer saison memorable, thanks to dry-hopping with Mandarina Bavaria hops; monthly brewery-only releases also add variety to Midnight's lineup.

In addition, Midnight has succeeded in building a clientele of regulars, patrons who know Cairns (including his mother, who volunteers in the taproom), enjoy the beer, and appreciate what he's dedicated to the business after putting that boat in the water in 2012. "I've not regretted my decision one bit," Cairns said in 2017. "It's been a great journey."

Try this: If you want to try the backbone of Midnight's lineup, the flagship Rockville Red is the beer for you. The Maris Otter in the grain bill gives the malty side a slight bready, biscuit element in addition to the caramel notes, and the British-born EKG hops add an earthy touch. At 5.5 percent ABV, it is highly drinkable and a ready companion to Irish stew and other hearty fare.

Lickinghole Creek Craft Brewery

Part of the challenge of farm breweries is creating a destination so appealing that folks are willing to drive along winding country roads to reach pockets of rural tranquility where the beer and the ambience reward the effort. Such was the goal when Lisa Brotherton Pumphrey and her then-husband, Sean-Thomas Pumphrey, pioneered the farm brewery concept in Virginia by starting Lickinghole Creek in 2013 on 260 acres in Goochland County. A long white building arose on a commanding knoll, giving the impression of a gleaming stable in an area known as horse country. That equine association goes deeper than meets the eye, for Lisa's grandfather David P. Reynolds owned Tabasco Cat (sired by Storm Cat, a grandson of the legendary Secretariat), the winner of the Preakness and Belmont Stakes in 1994.

It is beer rather than horses that has made Lickinghole Creek a destination. The brewery inside that stable-like structure has won its own share of medals—and produced a Secretariat-themed beer, an imperial red IPA named Secretariat's Meadow. It's a big beer, double-dry-hopped with Mosaic hops and 8.5 percent ABV, perfectly in step with Lickinghole Creek's other aggressive beers. Enlightened Despot, for example, is a Russian imperial stout made with ten specialty grains, hopped to a robust 78 IBUs, and aged in Pappy Van Winkle bourbon barrels. At 11.5 percent ABV, it's a sipper to be savored and worthy of the crowds it has drawn on Despot Day, the annual event celebrating the release of Enlightened Despot stout and its variants.

Big beers warrant big plans. In May 2017, Lisa, the company's CEO, played hostess to then-governor Terry McAuliffe in announcing a major step for Lickinghole Creek—a $14 million project that included expanded

Bracing winter weather didn't deter some beer aficionados from standing in line for a special release at Lickinghole Creek Craft Brewery in Goochland County.

brewing space, a new taproom, and a separate production facility in Lynchburg. In August, however, the Lynchburg project took a back seat to one in Richmond's Shockoe Bottom. "We're concentrating on doing one thing at a time," said cofounder Farris Loutfi. A "demolition party" drew fans to the Franklin Street spot by the 17th Street Farmer's Market, where a small brewing system was envisioned as part of a restaurant-bar operation to be called Lickinghole Goodwater. Head brewer Jimmy Walsh, whose background includes a stint as head brewer at O'Connor Brewing Company in Norfolk and gigs at Southern Tier Brewing Company and Five & 20 Spirits in New York, oversees the brewing at both facilities.

Urban expansion has added a new facet to the business's original identity. Lickinghole led the pack in helping develop the legal framework to pair brewing and farming. The idea grew after Sean-Thomas (who left the brewery in 2017) started growing hops at the property, "before we had any inclination of having a brewery out here," he said. He'd discovered craft beer while a student at the University of Montana, started homebrewing, and experimented with cultivating hops. Cascade, Columbus, and a dozen other varieties have been grown at Lickinghole Creek, and the farm operation has over the years included pumpkins, six-row Thoroughbred barley, wheat, rye, berries, and fields of sunflowers (a big attraction on "pick your own" weekends).

The early pumpkin planting and other farming chores fell to Loutfi, a former schoolmate of Sean-Thomas's. Loutfi has also provided mechanical and troubleshooting savvy, is "the face of the tasting room, and is a personality many of our customers and clients seek out," according to Lisa. The legal aspect entailed working with Goochland County officials as they revamped zoning ordinances to establish a farm brewery designation, and in 2014 the Virginia General Assembly passed legislation putting farm breweries on a more equal footing with the state's wineries.

The Lickinghole name comes from an actual creek that winds through the area. Beer names such as Gentleman Farmer Ale (made with homegrown Cascade, Chinook, and Nugget hops) and Virginia Black Bear (another brawny imperial stout at 9.3 percent ABV) also draw from the bucolic setting. And not all the beers are brawny—Magic Beaver Belgian-style Pale Ale and Pony Pasture Pilsner are in the quaffable neighborhood of 5.5 percent ABV.

Lickinghole Creek's goal of providing a "taste of place" has guided not only the brewing of beer but also sharing the experience of the natural world. As Lisa puts it, the vision was "a dream of creating a viable agricultural business model that would encourage the conservation of open space, wildlife habitat, promote agriculture, and encourage the public to embrace and play in the outdoors."

Try this: I've stood in line and waded through crowds for Enlightened Despot, and the beer is worth the effort. Lickinghole Creek has a knack for producing outstanding Russian imperial stouts, and this one has all of the dark coffee-chocolate grainy goodness that you look for in the style, plus the added vanilla notes from bourbon barrel-aging.

CHAPTER 9

Diverse Pockets Mark Tidewater

The arrival of San Diego's Green Flash brewery in 2016 made a splash in Virginia Beach, but it was the small breweries in the region that created the wave in the first place and sustained it after Green Flash closed in 2018. St. George brought English-style ales to Hampton in 1998, and Williamsburg's Alewerks and Virginia Beer Company have gained notice not only for cutting-edge brews but also for historic recipes developed in collaboration with the Colonial Williamsburg Foundation. O'Connor brought an innovative approach by creating an IPA with agave nectar, now its flagship El Guapo. Smartmouth proved its mettle by winning Best of Show among Virginia beers with Safety Dance Pilsner in 2017. A few paces away, Benchtop brewery dipped its buckets into the Atlantic Ocean to give its gose just the right saltwater tang. In Virginia Beach, Wasserhund hangs ten with its beers and hangs surfboards from the taproom ceiling.

Alewerks Brewing Company

If you think Virginia's craft beer scene is getting competitive, try being a hungry musician in Nashville. Geoff Logan and his bandmates in Rainmarket tried to make their mark in Tennessee's music mecca, but the dream never materialized.

"It's a cutthroat industry," Logan said. "The musicians there are very professional, hardworking, and organized. I guess Nashville was a swift kick in the rear for me in many ways. It taught me that if you want to succeed, you better work tremendously hard, have a great team around you, and never ever be bashful."

The lessons learned in the school of hard knocks now serve Logan in his position as brewmaster and managing director of Alewerks Brewing Company in York County. The brewing community also is known for being more collaborative than cutthroat, and that has helped the brewery grow, both creatively and commercially.

A staple in the Williamsburg area since 2006, when it moved into the spot vacated by the Williamsburg Brewing Company on Ewell Road, Alewerks has achieved acclaim on several fronts. Its Bitter Valentine Double IPA is rated outstanding by *BeerAdvocate* magazine and creates a buzz among hopheads only to be outdone by its bitterer half, Bitterest Valentine. On a different note, Alewerks has collaborated with Frank Clark, master of historic foodways for the Colonial Williamsburg Foundation, on several beers based on historic recipes. Old Stitch Brown Ale, based on a 1737 brew and named after a slang term for the devil, was judged best in its division at the 2014 U.S. Beer Tasting Championships and is a fixture at Chowning's and other colonial taverns in town. Between those bookends, the mild-mannered Weekend Lager won a gold medal at the 2017 Virginia Craft Beer Cup.

The business side of things took a step forward with the 2017 opening of a satellite tasting room, equipped with a three-and-a-half-barrel brewing system, in the nearby Williamsburg Premium Outlets complex. "This expansion allows us to reach an audience that might not gravitate toward Alewerks or craft beer," according to Logan. "The system is a long-awaited playground for us as brewers."

Beers at the mother ship are brewed on a twenty-five barrel Alan Pugsley system (Pugsley is cofounder and original brewmaster at Shipyard Brewing Company in Maine). Alewerks' annual production in 2017 was targeted at just under six thousand barrels, with distribution mostly in parts of Virginia and North Carolina. Barrel-aging and kettle-souring techniques have become tools to expand the brand's portfolio.

The forays into historic styles distinguish Alewerks from much of the craft-brewing crowd. The efforts combine Clark's knowledge of beer history with Logan's brewing skills. Dear Old Mum Spiced Ale, Wetherburn Tavern Bristol Ale, Toby's Triple Threads Porter (playing off the "three threads" nickname for porter), and Old Stitch evoke the flavors and brewing processes of yesteryear. "For brewing strong brown ale called stitch, this is mostly the first runnings of the malt but yet a longer length than is drawn off for stout," Clark said in a 2014 interview in *Williamsburg Yorktown Daily*. "It was a weaker version of what the manual calls a brown stout beer that was probably 8 percent alcohol. Mixing beers was very common during this time period and is how porter got its start."

Crafting bits of history was not a goal when Logan started brewing. A Delaware native, he began his rock exploits with Norfolk's Rainmarket shortly after graduating from West Virginia University with a degree in music. When the band's Nashville effort failed and hopes of a career in music paled, Logan's brother introduced him to homebrewing. "I liked beer, and I started tinkering around with Mr. Beer kits," Logan recalled. In 2007, after being hired at Alewerks, he received formal training through the American Brewers Guild in Vermont. "I've been brewing like crazy ever since."

Try this: Bitter Valentine DIPA and the historic beers get all of the attention, so I suggest a less celebrated seasonal, Alewerks Berliner. It's a Berliner weisse, a German style dubbed the "Champagne of the North" by Napoleon's troops when they spent a long weekend in Berlin. It's tart (*Lactobacillus* kettle-souring), crisp (loads of wheat in the grain bill), and easy-drinking (4 percent ABV) with tropical and citrus notes. If you've ever spent a summer in Williamsburg, you know you need a refreshing beer like this to keep cool under your tricorn.

The Virginia Beer Company

Imagine you're a young painter and you've just opened a gallery showcasing your work. You've barely snipped the ribbon when in walk Michelangelo, Van Gogh, and Banksy, eager to check out your work—and not shy about sharing their opinions. Talk about butterflies!

That's how I would have felt the opening weekend of Virginia Beer Company if I'd been in the shoes of co-founders Robby Willey and Chris Smith and brewmaster Jonathan Newman. They had literally cut the ribbon the afternoon of March 18, 2016, and that evening several of the biggest names in beer, visiting speakers at a conference on the history of beer, strolled in to toast and taste. The group included Mitch Steele, former head brewer of Stone Brewing and author of a book—THE book—on IPAs; Stan Hieronymus, author of THE book on hops; and Randy Mosher, author of THE book on tasting beer, giving their expert analysis of the Free Verse IPA and others. As I recall, the consensus was thumbs-up.

Since then, Virginia Beer Company has become THE brewery in Williamsburg. (Okay, so it's just a hair outside the city line, making it and Alewerks THE breweries in York County.) Willey, Smith, and Newman have carved out a reputation for solid beers and an adventurous spirit. Free Verse anchors the hoppy side of the year-round offerings, which include Saving Daylight Citrus Wheat, Elbow Patches Oatmeal Stout, and Wrenish Rye, a dry-hopped amber ale. On the wild side, they've brewed a saison fermented with *Brettanomyces* in a wine barrel and a Polish-style Piwo Grodziskie using peaches. Given the colonial-era surroundings, it's little surprise the brewery has been involved in several projects using historic recipes.

Head brewer Jonathan Newman of The Virginia Beer Company (*at left*), together with Paige Newman of the Virginia Historical Society and Frank Clark, master of historic foodways for the Colonial Williamsburg Foundation, collaborated on a colonial-era molasses beer recipe.

A collaboration with Frank Clark (the aforementioned master of historic foodways for Colonial Williamsburg) and the Virginia Historical Society yielded a plantation-era molasses ale, and VBC joined with Center of the Universe Brewing Company to produce a lemon persimmon wheat beer for the society's BrewHaHa festival.

In addition to history, the brewery plays off the co-founders' connection to their alma mater. Willey and Smith became friends at the College of William and Mary, and though neither stayed in Williamsburg after graduating, both found the pull of the area irresistible when searching for a brewery site. A former auto body shop on Second Street suited their needs, and they installed a five-barrel pilot setup and a thirty-barrel system for larger batches. "With both systems, we're essentially two breweries in one place. It allows me to experiment a lot while brewing large batches," Newman noted. A former high school English teacher, he worked at SweetWater Brewing Company in Atlanta and Jackalope Brewing Company in Nashville before joining Willey and Smith in Virginia.

Even before opening the brewery doors, the trio hooked up with Geoff Logan, brewer at Alewerks Brewing Company, to produce Red Rye IPA, the first beer to carry the Virginia Beer Company name. Newman and Logan also shared the stage as part of an "experts" panel for the 2017 BrewHaHa. Being involved in the community extends beyond the brewers' circle for Willey and Smith; both volunteer for their alma mater, and some of the beer names include clever references to William and Mary (Wrenish refers to the historic Wren Building, and Elbow Patches hints at stereotypical professorial attire). "[William and Mary] is where Chris and I met, and it's where we established our love of beer," Willey recalled. "The community and William and Mary have done a lot for us, so we decided we wanted to open a business that hopefully brings a lot of attention to the community in return."

One of the brewery's more unusual outreach efforts has been hosting a "Beer for Boobs" night to benefit Beyond Boobs, a support group aimed at helping young women dealing with breast cancer. Since I have a daughter who has dealt with breast cancer, I can't think of a better reason to hoist a pint glass.

Try this: I'm going to suggest Wrenish Rye for one simple reason—I spent many an afternoon in the Wren Building, trying to stay awake during classes such as Sixteenth Century Poetry and Modern American Literature (Mark Twain would have said something wry about a rye beer). Spiciness from the German rye works with fruit aromas and flavors of Simcoe and Jarrylo hops. It's a beautiful amber color and easy-drinking at 39 IBUs and 6 percent ABV.

St. George Brewing Company

Pick a metaphor or an image. A fiery dragon? A red cross on a medieval shield? A phoenix rising from the ashes? Horseshoes and hand grenades? All play into the fabric of Hampton's St. George Brewing Company.

The dragon is a natural association with Saint George, the patron saint of England. His legendary encounter with a fire-breathing, winged beast has inspired storytellers and artists, and it's the centerpiece of several St. George beers, including the Imperial Amber Bock and Imperial Stout. The shield and cross that represent the St. George brand also emphasize its primary focus on English-style ales.

The phoenix? St. George literally rose from the ashes of a fire on Christmas Eve 2000. The brewery had started as a brew-on-premises operation in Virginia Beach and moved to Hampton to crank up a full-scale commercial

St. George Brewing Company in Hampton started producing English-style ales in 1998.

operation. It was already earning medals and fans when the fire blazed. It left a smoking hulk of the brewery's Kecoughtan Road location but opened the door for a bigger site. "It was a blessing in disguise," said William Spence Jr., son of Bill Spence, owner and one of the founders. "It's one of those things. You fall into the briar patch. You never know where you're going to come out."

St. George was able to expand its product line from the original three beers—an English IPA, a porter, and a golden ale—with seasonals and lagers that reflect the contributions of brewmaster Andy Rathmann. He'd apprenticed in Germany after graduating from the master brewers program at the University of California–Davis, one of the premier programs in the country. St. George's portfolio includes a Märzen, pilsner, Vienna-style lager, and bock as a nod to the lager side of the brewing spectrum.

As far as horseshoes and hand grenades, that was Bill Spence's comment to me about coming close after St. George Summer Ale, an English bitter, won bronze Best in Show at the 2017 Virginia Craft Beer Cup. "It's like kissing your sister," he said with a smile as we spoke immediately after the awards ceremony (where Smartmouth won Best in Show with Safety Dance Pilsner). Spence's grousing was good-natured; the competition among Virginia's breweries has toughened as numbers have grown and quality has become more consistent—good things in Spence's eyes. "Look at where we've gone in the last ten years, particularly when you look at the West Coast [and] the number of major breweries that have made an East Coast base in North Carolina and Virginia. That's saying something for our two states, that we are now becoming the nexus of beer on the East Coast."

Not many breweries in the state can claim the long-term vision of St. George. Legend Brewing Company comes to mind, dating to 1993 in Manchester. The two veterans collaborated on one of the Richmond brewery's

Urban Legend Series beers, Teach's Oyster Stout. Named after the pirate Edward Teach (aka Blackbeard), the brew used oysters and provided a learning experience. "Andy and I, both seasoned brewers, were in fact swimming in uncharted waters here," said John Wampler, head brewer at Legend. The style, though, made sense for representing the Tidewater area and telling the story of a legendary figure.

A less briny stout, a Russian imperial, occupies a regular spot on the St. George taproom beer list, and is one of the brewery's big beers at 8.7 percent ABV. Only the Imperial Amber Bock, at 9 percent ABV, edges it out in alcohol content. Both showcase rich malt profiles, the stout with its coffee/chocolate signature flavor and the bock with some Munich caramel sweetness. Less extreme beers anchor the tap list's midsection, with St. George's focus on British styles apparent in its Nut Brown Ale and Summer Ale, both at 5 percent ABV. An award-winning Winter Scotch Ale (an 85-shilling wee heavy) uses peat-smoked malt for another taste of the United Kingdom.

As with many breweries in Virginia, St. George was facing the future in 2017 with plans for growth. Annual production stood at five thousand barrels, with distribution throughout the state and North Carolina and forays into Maryland and D.C. "We have additional tanks on order with a building expansion—production, tasting room, and beer garden—in the works for next year," Rathmann noted.

Try this: St. George is solidly grounded in both English and lager styles, so I'll suggest two. I'm a sucker for English bitters, having drunk my fair share on adventures in the UK. St. George Summer Ale does a good job of keeping the malt profile in balance so the flavor and bitterness of the East Kent Golding hops are accentuated (27 IBUs); at 5 percent ABV, it retains drinkability, a major feature of British pub beers. My favorite of all of the beers sampled, though, was the Imperial Bock. A rare style to find on craft brewery menus, it satisfied with a bold yet smooth malt presence (two-row with a bit of Munich) without too much sweetness. The alcohol content is 9 percent ABV; IBUs measure 28.

Green Flash Brewing Company

The sun-drenched canopy of crystalline blue sky over Virginia Beach showed nary a cloud on November 13, 2016, until a Navy prop plane laid a trail of vapor above a crowd gathered at Corporate Landing Business Park. The flyover was part of the town's toast to Green Flash Brewing Company, and even the weather seemed programmed to extend a warm welcome. City officials lauded the hard work and good fortune of landing the $20 million facility, and Green Flash cofounders Mike and Lisa Hinkley led participants through a "soul style" surfing move from the stage set for the occasion. Finally, Mayor Will Sessoms Jr. adroitly tapped a celebratory cask of West Coast IPA brewed with whole-cone Cascade and CTZ hops.

The launch added another star to Virginia's status as a beer-friendly state. Operating in California since 2002, Green Flash was the first prominent West Coast brewery to announce plans for an East Coast expansion in Virginia. Stone followed by selecting Richmond (and opening earlier in 2016); Deschutes and Ballast Point later pushed their pins in the Roanoke-area map.

Two years later, however, the brewery's star status would prove a flash in the pan. A sequence of events—beginning with the announcement of layoffs and distribution pull-backs in March 2018—ended with doors closing at Virginia Beach late that month. A sign saying "We are closed for business" was taped to the brewery's gate on March 26. The company was subsequently bought through a foreclosure sale by a newly created investor group, WPC IPA LLC, that included Mike Hinkley and other company officials. The Virginia Beach facility's brewing equipment was purchased by Atlanta-based New Realm Brewing, which in late April 2018 announced it would lease the building and open a brewery and taproom there. Mitch Steele, former head brewer with Stone, is one of the founders of New Realm.

In a memo to shareholders, Hinkley said that Comerica Bank, which was Green Flash's primary lender, would conduct the sale of the Virginia Beach brewery through a separate process. "After a general slowdown in the craft beer industry, coupled with intense competition and a slowdown of our business, we could not service the debt that we took on to build the Virginia Beach brewery, and in early 2018, the company defaulted on its loans with Comerica Bank," Hinkley wrote in a note to Green Flash shareholders. Additional details were unavailable as this book went to press.

The facility was designed to supply Green Flash accounts throughout the East to the Mississippi River. Production in the 58,000-square-foot facility was anticipated to reach 100,000 barrels at full capacity, using a system designed to precisely mirror the brewing setup at the home base in San Diego.

In 2017, its first and only year of competing in the Virginia Craft Beer Cup, Green Flash brought home three awards: second place for its Sea to Sea Lager, an unfiltered "Zwickel" lager using German and Czech hops; third place for GFB, a blonde ale with sessionable drinkability at 4.8 percent ABV; and third for flagship West Coast IPA, a double-barrel double IPA that clocks in at 95 IBUs.

Wasserhund Brewing Company

Creating identity is one of the biggest challenges in the burgeoning craft-beer era. Any fledgling brewery owner who doesn't have a clear vision of what he or she wants to be—whether it's the hippest spot in the hottest area, the friendliest staff with the friendliest beers, or the quirkiest taproom with the most extreme brews—runs the risk of becoming just another tap on the wall.

Wasserhund knows its nature. Take classic German styles, brew them well, mix in some hoppy American ales, brew them equally well, have fun with some one-offs and seasonals, serve them in a cozy, unpretentious setting with a local beach-dog theme (including surfboards hanging from the ceiling), and staff the place with folks who actually love beer. Add pizza.

From the Virginia Beach brewery's name (Wasserhund means "water dog") to the array of lagers, the main influence is German. Credit that to a trip that cofounders Aaron and Christine Holley took to Bavaria in 2012. They'd already been bitten by the beer bug. "We started homebrewing in 2010 in our teeny apartment in Northern Virginia," Christine recalled. "It was something to do in our free time as a couple. It kind of escalated pretty quickly."

At Oktoberfest in Munich, another bug bit—a love of lagers. Re-creating those beers became Aaron's passion in his homebrewing. "I kept working at it, trying to figure out what they did. A lager is a little more difficult to make than an ale," he observed.

Indeed. Brewer after brewer will testify to that. There's no hiding behind pungent hops or robust malts. Flaws in the process become conspicuous in the glass. Which is why finding such an assortment of well-made German lagers and ales makes Wasserhund a special destination.

Purebred Pilsner, Lapdog Lager, Black Forest Lager (a schwarzbier), and one-offs such as White Shepherd (a helles bock infused with chardonnay grapes) anchor the lager lineup, showing both a grasp of traditional styles and a sense of adventure. On the ale side, German Shepheweizen, unfiltered and appropriately imbued with the trademark clove/banana phenolics, and Atta Boy Altbier, smooth and fruity, expand the offerings. During my visit in September 2017, I was told I'd missed the Vienna Lager but was able to sample the Oktoberfest, a fitting malty salute to the Märzen seasonal.

As the beer names indicate, there's a playful spirit at Wasserhund. "Our name was inspired by our purebred German shepherd, Hertz. Our mutt, Hooper, is the inspiration behind the Haywire Husky (coffee lager) beer," Christine said in an email. Dog-related images abound, the bar displays bottle caps from around the craft beer universe, and the hanging surfboards look well-used. The dog theme carries over to the pizzas and other fare. Kibbles features crispy baked pepperoni slices; Puppy Tails are cheesy pepperonis twisted in dough and baked.

The taproom in the Hilltop neighborhood has that chummy feel of Munich's renowned Hofbrau beer hall, where long tables encourage strangers to make acquaintances over brimming liters. At Wasserhund, two twelve-foot tables evoke the same atmosphere. "It's our way of bringing Germany to Virginia Beach," Christine said.

Try this: A well-made altbier is a treat to behold, and Wasserhund's Atta Boy hits the spot. Copper in color with a lovely off-white head, the alt has enough fruity esters to distinguish its ale heritage but still captures that distinctive Munich-Vienna lager malt flavor. The hops are present but understated at 35 IBUs. Alcohol content is 5.9 percent by volume. If it's on tap and you're in the mood for something bigger, try the Haagen Dog Stout, a silver medal winner at the 2017 Virginia Craft Beer Cup.

O'Connor Brewing Company

When Kevin O'Connor and his crew brewed their first batch of beer on St. Patrick's Day in 2010, the recipe was for a traditional pale ale called Norfolk Canyon. Several other straightforward offerings followed—solid beers that attracted a following but nothing outside of the box.

"We were making everyday beers—red ales, pale ales.

Once we got going, people were saying, 'When are you going to make an IPA?'" O'Connor recalled. "So instead of making a traditional IPA, we made Great Dismal first." Great Dismal, named for the nearby swamp, is a black IPA that according to O'Connor "looks like a stout, drinks like an IPA," with 65 IBUs for plenty of hop zing to balance the full-bodied malt character.

Though popular, Great Dismal didn't hit the sweet spot for hopheads. "People were like 'When are you going to make a real IPA?'" O'Connor said, talking above the clatter of bottles moving through the filling line at the facility in Norfolk's Ghent district. Traditional IPAs are a dime a twelve-pack. O'Connor and his brewers wanted something different. They hit the mark with an ingredient O'Connor uses every day in his cup of morning joe—agave nectar. Sweeter and less viscous than honey, agave stood out in test batches and led to the creation of El Guapo Agave IPA. The medium body, citrus nose, hops presence (70 IBUs), and drinkability have made it a multiple award winner and a hit with hopheads. It accounted for about 60 percent of O'Connor's sales in 2016. "It's taken on a life of its own," O'Connor noted. "We go through a lot of agave. I wouldn't be surprised if we're one of the biggest buyers of agave, especially on the East Coast."

O'Connor is definitely the biggest brewer in Norfolk, cranking out roughly twelve thousand-plus barrels for distribution throughout Virginia and North Carolina's Outer Banks with plans for expansion. The portfolio of beers includes Red Nun, a traditional red/amber ale that's won medals in state and international competitions; ODIS Dry Irish Stout, another medal-winner that features roasted malt and coffee notes and a sessionable 4.5 percent ABV; Double Footer, a double-dry-hopped double IPA with supporting malt backbone; four highly quaffable saisons in the "Endless" series; Ibrik, a richly roasted 10-percent-ABV imperial stout named for the pots used to make Turkish

O'Connor's El Guapo Agave IPA accounted for about 60 percent of the brewery's sales in 2016.

coffee; and Winter Pecan Porter, which uses locally sourced pecans for a toasted nut character.

Speaking of locally sourced, O'Connor has deep roots in Norfolk. Born and raised in the area, he worked for his father in an auto parts business until the brewing bug bit hard. He had homebrewed while in college, and then fed his passion at the former Steamship Brewing Company. "That was my first brewing job. I loved it. I didn't mind getting up early in the morning. I didn't mind working twelve-, thirteen-hour days. It was just so much fun." Now his father works in the brewery's office as chief financial officer.

The company outgrew the original location and now fills a thirty-five-thousand-square-foot space on 24th Street that combines production brewing with several tasting areas—a cozy taproom; an expansive indoor area with tables and a stage for live music; an outdoor garden with umbrellas and games. Yoga enthusiasts swarm the brewery on Sunday mornings; military personnel receive special discounts on Mondays; record aficionados spin discs on vinyl nights; cyclists brake for post-pedaling pints; and food trucks circle their chuck wagons to provide toothsome fare.

All of those amenities and programs are part of O'Connor's emphasis on filling seats at the site. Senior status among the area brewers affords him a broad perspective on the changing landscape, and one of the trends—he calls it "Rotation Nation"—is for taps in restaurants and bars to turn over so quickly that flagships such as El Guapo and Great Dismal aren't ensured a spot. Still, he applauds the beer-loving culture that is evolving in Norfolk and surrounding areas. "Reaver Beach is doing a great job with their sour program," he observed. "Commonwealth is doing a great job. And then the smaller guys like Pleasure House and Big Ugly, Young Veterans, Back Bay—they're all doing great stuff."

He and his crew still want to think outside the box. Barrel-aging has a niche, and a wild yeast program figures in the future. That said, O'Connor sees the brewing pendulum swinging away from some of the extremes. "I really think we're going to see trending back into traditional beers," he concluded. "A good classic pilsner—I think we're going to start seeing more of that. Those beers are extremely hard to make because you can't hide any imperfections. You can make imperial IPAs, and you can hide an elephant in them and nobody's going to know."

Try this: Actually, try these—the two IPAs that wave the flag for O'Connor's excellent brewing. Great Dismal boasts roasted richness (a hint of coffee?) that you don't find often in IPAs, and O'Connor manages to achieve an interesting balance with the hops (a tang of grapefruit?). Hold it to the light and admire the glints of red in the darkness. As for El Guapo, you'd never guess this was 7.5 percent ABV. The agave nectar smoothes out the hop presence slightly. Check out the nose—floral, citrus, and potent.

Smartmouth Brewing Company

The Best in Show award of the Virginia Craft Beer Cup is one of the most unusual and ungainly trophies around. Rather than being an elegant example of gleaming statuary, it consists of two pieces of a beer keg connected by a metal plank. Picture the prize lamp in the movie *A Christmas Story*.

That said, the award is a coveted symbol among the state's brewers. Until 2017, only three breweries—Devils Backbone, The Answer, and James River—had taken it home since the competition's inception in 2012. At this writing, it rests against a wall on the far side of the bar in Smartmouth's taproom in Norfolk, next to seven framed displays of medals won in various judgings. It's a modest testament to a high standard, one that has guided Smartmouth since day one.

Smartmouth's launch in 2012 coincided with the change in state law that allowed retail sales of beer at breweries. Opportunity called to Porter Hardy IV, a business lawyer who grew up in Virginia Beach. Initial production included Notch 9 Double IPA, an 88-IBU turbo-hopped citrus aroma bomb (the name refers to a "turn-it-up-to-eleven" equivalent on a train's throttle), and Alter Ego Saison, a pepper-and-spice Belgian farmhouse ale. Both gained immediate acclaim, the saison with a medal at the Virginia competition, Notch 9 with a bronze at the Great American Beer Festival.

It was Safety Dance Pilsner, however, that brought the Best in Show trophy to Raleigh Avenue. The beer has special meaning for Hardy. The style evokes the lagers that drew him to flavorful beer during a semester abroad in Hamburg. It also is a style that tests brewing skills. "There's really nowhere to hide; there's no dark malt, not a whole lot of malt to cover up brewing mistakes," Hardy observed. In addition, it was a recipe that got a makeover

Smartmouth founder Porter Hardy IV (*center*), head brewer Jimmy Loughran, and packaging manager Sarah Johnson celebrate winning the 2017 Best in Show award at the Virginia Craft Beer Cup.

because the Smartmouth team wasn't satisfied. "Jimmy [Loughran, head brewer] and I and Chris Neikirk [co-founder] all sat down and did a blind taste test of Safety Dance alongside of other pilsners we really respect. It was not where we wanted it to be. We made some thought-out changes."

Other changes were under way in 2017. A second

facility, named the Smartmouth Pilot House, took shape in a 9,457-square-foot space in a former post office in Virginia Beach. The brewing system, though smaller than the twenty-barrel setup at the home base, enabled increased production, which stood at roughly 4,500 barrels in 2017. In addition, the "pilot" system opened creative possibilities, including barrel-aging. "It's our playground, our experimental station," Hardy said. "This will give us flexibility to just have an idea, let our brewers experiment more and try a variety of styles or twists on styles that we haven't ever made before."

The eight beers available in the Norfolk taproom during my most recent visit in September 2017 reflected Smartmouth's philosophy of "no gimmicks, no funny business, just an appreciation for well-crafted beer." Cowcatcher Milk Stout (rich with roasted coffee notes) and Golden Standard Golden Ale (fermented with Belgian Trappist yeast) caught my attention, but it was the Cargo Schwarzbier that captured my fancy. This black lager is not a staple of many breweries, so savoring a sample that was smooth, complex, and sessionable (5.2 percent ABV) brought a smile to my palate.

Try this: If the schwarzbier is available, ask for a sample; it's a limited release, however, so odds are low. Notch 9 DIPA is a sure bet. It's not the dankest of the doubles, but the citrus-grapefruit aroma from dry-hopping sets you up for the rich hop flavor (Centennial, Columbus, Falconers Flight, and Simcoe are used in the brew). The blend of pilsner, Carapils, and crystal malts gives balancing sweetness. Pay heed to the alcohol content (9.1 percent ABV); this is not a session beer.

Benchtop Brewing

Eric Tennant likes to describe the philosophy of Benchtop's brewing as "hop forward" but not mouth-blastingly bitter. You might be tempted to call one of his beers "pickle forward," but that would be confusing a process with an ingredient.

Quick Pickle Carrot Cucumber Gose represents the adventurous approach Tennant takes with his brews and attests to his culinary background. "The name is based on the culinary technique of quick pickling," he noted. "This is the processing of rapidly pickling veggies in a sour, sweet, and salty solution. That is essentially what I am doing in the fermenter with my kettle-soured gose. However, I have had quite a few people think that I named it that because it has pickle juice or is meant to taste like pickles. That's not the case."

Exploring such flavors has earned Benchtop top marks from palate-savvy folks. Trial of Dmitri, an interpretation of Slavic kvass using local beets, rye bread, and other ingredients, won a gold medal in the specialty beer category of the 2017 Virginia Craft Beer Cup competition.

More indicative of Benchtop's bread-and-butter brews are the juicy, flavorful IPAs and double IPAs on tap at the taproom on Boissevain Avenue (a brisk walk from Smartmouth, if you don't mind a little jaunt). Proven Theory, the flagship IPA, is double-dry-hopped with Galaxy hops, yielding an intense citrus aroma and fruity flavor. Juicy Thoughts DIPA uses Citra and Simcoe hops for a brew that's surprisingly accessible, in terms of bitterness. It led to a discussion with taproom manager Dale Price about the difference between numbers, as in IBUs, and perceived bitterness, as in what your senses tell you.

Tennant's chops in sensory evaluation have been well-honed through his degree in food science and his professional experience in the food industry. A native of North Carolina, he graduated from N.C. State and worked in quality control and research/development for food companies such as Smithfield and Alamance. While living in Wisconsin, he wandered down the rabbit hole of craft beer, took up homebrewing, won some awards, and began researching the potential for his own brewery. The business compass pointed to Norfolk, and a Kickstarter campaign helped him finance a seven-barrel system. Doors opened in December 2016.

From the get-go, Benchtop showed an edgy and local approach. In order to get that sea-salt quality for Mermaid's Scorn Gose, for example, Tennant drove his pickup to the beach and loaded the back with buckets of good ol' Atlantic Ocean water. Oysters used in the brew also were collected personally from local spots. Virginia-grown wheat and barley malts formed the grain base, and coriander and lemon zest added zing. *Lactobacillus* bacteria added in the kettle provided the souring agent for this historic German style, which he and other craft brewers have revived from near-extinction. "People who haven't heard of it might be a little weirded out," Tennant observed. Using local ingredients "really captures the essence of this area."

The tasting room also captures a spirit of down-home amiability. Price greets people as if each were a favorite cousin. A chalkboard bears beer names and details drawn in flourishes of vibrant colors. Planks of repurposed wood line the wall behind the taps. And an in-progress mural depicts a rural scene of meadows, ridges, and a weathered barn; tanks and lab equipment will be added. "The idea is that it will really capture our style, which is a blend of scientific precision and a farm-to-glass style that really allows us to utilize many local ingredients," explained Tennant.

Weirding people out is not Tennant's goal. Brewing balanced, interesting beer is. "Some people want to taste the malt, and other people don't want to taste the malt at all," he noted. "A lot of people probably measure craft brewers based on their hoppy beers . . . but it takes a bit of skill to get really good hop flavor and not have it be harsh."

Benchtop was on pace to produce up to one thousand barrels its first year, with Proven Theory IPA and Hazing Face Pale Ale leading distribution in the Tidewater region.

Tanks were added late in the year to increase capacity, and a canning program put a ribbon on 2017.

Try this: Proven Theory IPA illustrates the art of loading hop flavor and aroma into a beer without overdoing the bitterness. Dale Price, the man behind the bar, told me the bittering hops were Citra and Mosaic, but the spotlight is on double-dry-hopping with Galaxy, an Australian varietal high in alpha acids known for notes of passion fruit, citrus, and peach in its profile. Benchtop's version is fragrant and full-bodied while still being accessible at 7 percent ABV (IBUs were not available and, frankly, not pertinent). I also highly recommend the Chelsea-Tidewater Grisette, made with rye and wheat, plus some oats for smoothness. It's a Belgian style you don't find in many taprooms.

CHAPTER 10

Charlottesville Builds on Early Success

The Charlottesville region deserves a special spot in Virginia's beer lore. Home of the first brewpub in the state as well as the first beer tourism trail, the area began making its mark in the modern surge of craft brewing well ahead of the rest of the commonwealth.

Some of that is due to the trail blazed by vineyards in Albemarle and Nelson counties. They created models for developing destinations that catered to culinary explorers (aka "foodies")—people eager to experience unique tastes in pleasant places. When Taylor and Mandi Smack left South Street Brewery in 2006 to embark on their own entrepreneurial path, Blue Mountain was envisioned as a brewery firmly rooted in agricultural tradition. "The sign said Blue Mountain Brewery and Hop Farm. And that was part of our marketing—a farm brewery, a rural thing," recalled Taylor.

Starr Hill and South Street were already thriving, and when Devils Backbone pitched its tent by the South Fork of the Rockfish River—on one hundred acres at the base of Wintergreen resort—a light bulb flickered on in the mind of Maureen Kelley, economic development officer for Nelson County: connect the dots and promote these budding businesses and their mountainous setting. After all, Charlottesville routinely finds itself on lists of top places to live; why not promote it as one of the top places to find craft beer? As Wild Wolf sprouted in Nellysford and the Blue Mountain Barrel House rose in Arrington, they were added to the string, and the Brew Ridge Trail became a model for subsequent endeavors around the state.

That tells only part of the story. The change in state law in 2012 allowing breweries to sell beer on-site without having to provide food spurred growth in Charlottesville as well as elsewhere. Champion, Three Notch'd, and C'Ville-ian (now closed) breweries opened in a brief span, followed by Pro Re Nata, Random Row, Wood Ridge Farm Brewery, and, in 2017, Reason and Hardywood Park, a satellite of its Richmond operation. Broaden the lens, and you'll see breweries across the map, from charming Bedford County to the horse country outside of Waynesboro. Here's a rundown of selected sites, beginning within the city limits.

South Street Brewery

The grandfather of Charlottesville's existing breweries also has served as a bit of a godfather to its offspring. Jacque Landry, the original brewer, came out of a consulting gig in 2016 to sign on with Basic City in Waynesboro. Taylor Smack began his brewing career as an intern at South Street; in 2014, he and Mandi, his wife, came full circle by purchasing the brewpub. Apparently an offer was made that couldn't be refused.

The scene was percolating when restaurateur Duffy Papas joined with Fred Greenewalt to open South Street in 1998. Blue Ridge Brewing Company had broken ground as the state's first brewpub when it opened on West Main Street in 1987. Monticello Brewing Company offered a brew-on-premises operation on Grady Avenue. Papas and Greenewalt saw opportunity in a former seafood restaurant on South Street near the Downtown Mall. Landry brought valuable experience from brewing in Colorado, and a seven-barrel system found a snug fit into the building, a one-time grain warehouse dating to the 1800s.

The spot became a magnet for students and local

residents. The stable of beers included Satan's Pony, a malty amber; Absolution, an American strong ale; and J.P. Ale (a pale ale named after Charlottesville's Jefferson Park Avenue, locally known as JPA). Change came as the years passed. Papas left, and Landry became part-owner. They contracted with Taylor Smack to produce South Street beers for distribution. In July 2014, Papas and Landry quietly let it be known that they were closing; the Smacks lost no time in purchasing the business.

A clever renovation added fresh touches while maintaining the charm of the space—lots of brick with an open fireplace and the brew tanks visible through glass behind the bar. The menu also found new breadth and reflects an upscale comfort-food orientation.

The beer list reflects a mixture of the familiar and the adventurous. Satan's Pony is a regular; Absolution surfaces seasonally. But Mitch Hamilton, South Street's brewer, has made his mark with a range of styles. An Alabama native and graduate of the College of William and Mary, Hamilton spent time at SweetWater Brewing Company in Atlanta before landing at Blue Mountain in Afton, and then transitioning to South Street. His Bar Hopper, an aromatic West Coast–style IPA, and Acoustic Kitty, an 82-IBU double IPA, appeal to hopheads, while My Personal Helles, a flavorful Munich-style helles lager, and Slippery When Wit, a hybrid gose-witbier offering, show the breadth of Hamilton's brewing skills. Slippery When Wit won a medal at the 2016 Great American Beer Festival, as did Twisted Gourd. At the 2017 Virginia Craft Beer Cup, South Street's Virginia Lager and Astrognomer IPA took home medals.

Not all of the recipes are his, but Hamilton has fairly free rein in creating beers for six of the twelve taps, a luxury he appreciates after having little creative input at the far larger SweetWater operation. For Taylor Smack, it's a measure of trust. "I say, 'Brew what you know we need and come up with the other stuff—maybe let's talk about it, maybe let's not.' Sometimes I walk in here and it's like 'I've never heard of that beer.'"

Try this: Satan's Pony has earned its reputation as one of Charlottesville's iconic beers, and the ale has gained a wider audience since it became available in bottles. Highly drinkable at 5.3 percent ABV and 12 IBUs, it is brewed with seven malts to give a slight toasted character and a rich amber color; Centennial hops provide just enough bitterness to balance the sweetness. A barrel-aged imperial version ups the ante significantly to 9 percent ABV, putting the beer in the Scotch ale bracket with an oak-bourbon nose and flavor.

Three Notch'd Brewing Company

Every Thursday, back in the infancy of Three Notch'd Brewery in Charlottesville, Dave Warwick would stand on a chair at the original Grady Avenue location, call for everyone's attention, and announce the details of a new beer on tap. The bustle and chatter in the tasting room would subside as he raised his voice, raised a glass, and introduced the moment's marquee brew. Nine times out of ten, it would be a collaboration, whether with another brewery, a worthy charity, or a savvy homebrewer.

Warwick, who has been brewmaster since Three Notch'd pitched its first yeast in 2013, embodies that collaborative spirit of the brewery and its Tap That Thursday Beer Release tradition, which continues now at the Craft Kitchen and Brewery in Ix Art Park. A big bear of a guy—former football lineman and rugby stalwart—he exudes a warm and welcoming presence, an inclusive feeling that puts a face on the driving force of the business.

"My philosophy has always been that a beer is better shared with friends," explained Warwick. "I heard a friend

One of the traditions of Tap That Thursday at Three Notch'd in Charlottesville has been head brewer Dave Warwick's proposing a toast to the latest collaboration.

say that it's better for eight people to each have one beer than for one person to have eight beers. Sharing beer is better with friends, and I think brewing is too."

The result is a continual mix of something new and different alongside the brewery's flagship beers. As a change of pace from the best-selling 40 Mile IPA, say, you could have a maibock courtesy of Charlottesville's Brew Betties group. Or Fandom of the Hopera, an imperial red ale loaded with Summit and other hops brewed in collaboration with David Hunter's Fans of Virginia Craft Breweries group.

"We've brewed some amazing collaborations here that I would have never dreamed of myself, so it takes the load off of my plate of having to come up with all the recipes myself," said Warwick. "I'm lucky enough to have inspiration from the whole town to help me out."

The collaborative theme has played out in the satellite

operations that Three Notch'd established in Harrisonburg and Richmond. Both feature smaller brewing systems—required under state law—and a steady flow of beers fashioned through partnerships and community outreach.

The business itself started as a concept broached over beers among three friends—George Kastendike, Scott Roth, and Derek Naughton. Roth had opened McGrady's Irish Pub in 2006, and his restaurant experience, combined with Kastendike's business aptitude and Naughton's social networking, provided the foundation for their idea of starting a brewery in the heart of the city. They lacked a brewer, however, until they ran into Warwick at the Virginia Craft Brewers Fest in August 2012. His background of brewing with Rock Bottom at locations in Colorado and Northern Virginia impressed them. Their shared love of hoppy beers sealed the deal. "One of the things we told him was that we wanted to do our best to own the IPA category," Kastendike recalled.

That's a tough target. IPAs are the country's most popular style, and excellent versions abound. But Three Notch'd hit its three-year production goal within seven months of opening in August 2013. Fans immediately took to 40 Mile IPA, named for Jack Jouett's famous ride to warn Governor Thomas Jefferson and other members of the Virginia legislature (who had fled from Richmond to Charlottesville) of approaching British soldiers led by Banastre Tarleton. Its four-hop profile features El Dorado for a tropical fruit aroma and flavor and a 50 IBU zing. Other beers also made their mark. At the 2014 Great American Beer Festival in Denver, Hydraulion Red, an Irish-style red ale, won a bronze medal; the following year, judges awarded it a silver in the Virginia Craft Brewers Cup competition. The name is a nod to the fire company started in 1828 by University of Virginia students. Many of the other beers—No Veto English Brown Ale (a three-time medal winner in the Virginia Cup), The Ghost of the 43rd American Pale Ale (another state medal winner), and Brother Barnabas Belgian Tripel Ale—have historical or personal connections.

The business created a separate entity for self-distribution, allowing Three Notch'd brands to build markets around the state. One of the biggest steps, however, came at home—a full-size restaurant and brewery overlooking IX Art Park, available for viewing just in time for Charlottesville's inaugural hosting of the Virginia Craft Brewers Fest in 2017. The twenty-barrel brewing system was moved from the original location on Grady Avenue, additional tanks boosted production, and a three-barrel pilot setup enhanced creative capabilities. The tanks are visible through glass panels in the 6,800-square-foot restaurant space, which includes an area for private events and a poured-concrete bar with more than forty taps. The new facility came as an extension not only of the company's business goals but also of its role within the community.

"We love the city, we love our families growing up here and we saw an opportunity to build something that would allow us to interact with it very tightly," Kastendike concluded.

Try this: What are you in the mood for? Something hoppy? 40 Mile IPA, Minute Man New England Style IPA, or Killer Angel Double IPA can scratch that itch (the last of these features six hops in the boil and two more, Centennial and Citra, in dry-hopping additions for 87 IBUs and 8.7 percent ABV). That said, I heartily recommend No Veto English Brown Ale for its nutty-toffee-chocolate malt character. At 5 percent ABV and only 30 IBUs, it is an accessible, flavorful beer worthy of its association with Patrick Henry, who argued in a Virginia court against the Crown's right to veto colonial laws.

Champion Brewing Company

Hunter Smith chose to name his brewery's flagship IPA after a missile; turns out that has been an apt symbol for the company's growth. Opening in late 2012 with a three-barrel system next to the tasting room on Sixth Street in Charlottesville, Champion soon expanded production with a thirty-barrel outpost called the Missile Factory in the city's Belmont neighborhood. Distribution grew, as did Champion's business presence. In January 2017, a brewpub was launched in a former bank building on the corner of Fourth and Grace streets in downtown Richmond. And the following month saw the doors open on Charlottesville's Downtown Mall for Brasserie Saison, which emphasizes locally made Belgian-style beers paired with Belgian cuisine. Following that, Smith announced he was eyeing a historic church in Norfolk for yet another brewing spot; that project proved unfeasible because of the renovation estimates.

Smith's eye for opportunity comes from seeing possibilities where few or none seem to exist. Even in 2012, though the area had well-established breweries in Starr Hill, Devils Backbone, and Wild Wolf, Smith sensed that "people were looking around for 'What's next? What's new? What haven't I had before?'"

Most people—including me—hadn't had a gose, one of the beers in Champion's initial lineup. That German style calls for sea salt to provide an understated tartness, comparable to a squeeze of lemon in a glass of iced tea. Also on that 2012 menu was a Berliner weisse, another German style that uses wheat and achieves a mild sourness and tartness accompanied by a light, fruity flavor.

Smith saw another "hole in the market" that spurred his idea for Brasserie Saison, launched with restaurateur Wilson Richey. "We had all this great food in the area, but beer food was greatly underserved. It was all pizza and wings and burgers, great American traditions. . . . But there are some great Belgian traditions that we just don't have," Richey observed. Oysters on the half shell, steamed mussels, duck sausage, and dishes with brussels sprouts share the menu with three interpretations of saisons, a Belgian-style dubbel, and Champion mainstays such as Shower Beer and, yes, Missile IPA.

Music has played another role in shaping the brews at Champion. A Charlottesville native, Smith studied music at Northeastern University and spent time touring as a punk rocker and working in a recording studio in Boston. He's kept it loud and proud with beers based on collaborations with bands: NOFX and Stickin' in My IPA (a West Coast–style rye IPA) and The Hold Steady and Positive Jam, a spring ale made with coriander and lavender.

The addition of brewer Levi Duncan, a veteran of Starr Hill and elsewhere, in March 2014 was a booster rocket for the Missile team. At the 2015 Virginia Craft Brewers Fest, Champion garnered three medals. At the Great American Beer Festival in Denver the following month, Shower Beer won a coveted gold medal and a nod from *Men's Journal* magazine as one of "20 Great American Beer Fest Winners You Never Heard Of." With expanded distribution and new sites open in 2017, Champion appeared ready to move off the "never heard of" list.

Try this: Champion offers a bevy of flavorful beers, but one close to my heart is Face Eater Gose. For one, its tart tang and sour notes hit my sweet spot, especially if my palate is a little weary from the hoppy beers I often tend to favor. In addition, the modest ABV (5 percent), light color, wheat zest, hint of fruit, and salty sass make it a great warm-weather beverage (and of course the beer carries the name of a band).

Random Row Brewing Company

The changes occurring in the American beer scene play out in many ways, but none more conspicuously than in brewery tasting rooms. Families gather, children romp, and grownups chat, all in an atmosphere of conviviality.

Random Row's grand opening in Charlottesville showcased one of its prime features—a family-friendly environment.

And while the adults are savoring tasty beverages, you can bet the kids are watching. Every tip of a pint is a potential lesson in responsible drinking.

It's a model that's existed in Europe for decades, and it's one that Random Row aspires to emulate. "Our goal here is to be not just a brewery but a gathering place, where people can talk about what they did during the day and the kids can be running around," noted Kevin McElroy, head brewer and cofounder.

Bingo night proves his point. The monthly event draws big crowds and raises money for area charities, both through proceeds from the game and donations of a buck a pint from the brewery. "We're raising something like $500 each month," he said. "We do things like that to give back to the community."

The business's name and logo reflect local ties as well. Random Row was an adjacent historic area, and the rough-hewn edges of the logo are a tip of the hat to the King Lumber Company that years ago filled the property with the smell of fresh-sawed wood.

Now you're more likely to whiff the aroma of barley and hops coming from McElroy's ten-barrel brewing system, visible behind the bar. Method IPA, a West Coast version of the hoppy standard, and The Hill Lager, a German-style golden lager, are the flagships and probably will be the first beers distributed. Production in the first year totaled about three hundred and fifty barrels, so McElroy plans to keep distribution limited to kegs in the immediate region. "We're small, and our goal is to stay small. I want this to be the kind of place where people come in, see me, and know who I am."

His brewing philosophy is to make accessible beers. "Whatever beer I make I want someone to sit down and be able to have two pints of it." The fourteen taps also include some rare and complex brews; several one-barrel fermenters allow him to spin off smaller batches. Hibiscus Saison graced the early fall beer menu, and Yes You Can, a tart IPA kettle-soured with *Lactobacillus,* provided tangy refreshment in warm weather. The most popular beer, McElroy observed, has been a grapefruit version of Method IPA that includes zest from grapefruit and orange peels, a chore he does by hand. "It's a labor of love, but people love it so I'll keep doing it as long as they want it."

The brewery's birth on Preston Avenue in September 2016 grew from the combined resources of Bob Thiele, Bradley Kipp, and McElroy—Thiele as investor (and as executive chairman), Kipp as business manager, and McElroy as brewer. A homebrewer for six years previously, McElroy had impressed friends with his beers. In his first-ever contest, he won silver Best in Show in the 2013 Dominion Cup statewide homebrew competition. Going pro seemed logical.

Kipp and Thiele also have families, giving added impetus to creating a tasting room comfortable for young and old alike. One whole wall is covered with chalkboard paint, giving kids artistic license to draw turtles and such—or just scribble and scrawl. Wood and metal combine in the furnishings for a modern industrial theme. And the family connection extends one step further. Keagan Imperial Stout, a winter seasonal, is named after McElroy's daughter, who is named after Keagan's Irish Pub, the McElroys' favorite haunt when they lived in Virginia Beach. Their son Jameson? You can figure that out.

Try this: The flagships, Method IPA and The Hill Lager, are sure bets. But I'm going to steer you to Not Yours Maibock. I have a weakness for bocks—their malty sweetness, the clean lager finish, and the full-bodied mouthfeel. Maibocks are the lightest of the family, and Random Row makes their brew work. German law prescribes that no bock should be lower than 6.3 percent ABV, and this version hits that on the head.

Reason Beer

When Reason Beer debuted its inaugural releases in July 2017, the dominant style among breweries in the United States was India pale ale. That single style accounted for 25 percent of the market's dollar share, well above the seasonal category. To quench that thirst, brewery after brewery offers at least one IPA, often two and a double IPA to boot.

Not Reason. No IPA was among its first four releases. And it's not because of any fear and loathing of hoppy brews. "IPA is probably my favorite style," said Mark Fulton, Reason's head brewer. "We've heard from sales reps, they go into a meeting and people say, 'Reason—those are those guys who hate IPAs.' And it's really not true." (Indeed, Reason included IPAs among later taproom offerings.)

As we spoke in the production area of Reason's facility

off U.S. 29 North, yeast bubbled with a steady blip-blip in a sixty-barrel fermenter filled with Reason Pale Ale. Fulton poured me a sample, and the understated hop character makes a point that holds true with Reason's other ales—Blonde, Saison, and Black. All sport relatively low alcohol levels—5 percent or under ABV—and feature blends of ingredients that defy immediate pinpointing, like combining German noble hops—Hallertauer and Tettnanger—with American heavyweights such as Citra, Mosaic, and Amarillo for a unique profile.

"My dream come true is when it's not obvious which hops are in the beer," Fulton said. "I've found that playing with different base malts—and playing with hops that might not be expected—you can actually produce a total flavor profile that's not expected. . . . I like to blend it so it's not just the malt, and not just the hops, but that you really like the flavor of this beer."

Fulton wore a T-shirt from Maine Beer Company, whose signature beers include Lunch, an IPA, and Dinner, a double IPA. He worked there, moving up the ladder to become director of brewery operations, after starting his professional career with Sebago Brewing Company in Portland, Maine. His brewing roots, however, go back to the foundation of Reason's existence—his friendship with cofounders Patrick Adair and Jeff Raileanu.

The three became buddies as elementary schoolchildren in Charlottesville after meeting at their church's youth group. All went to high school in the area; after graduating, Fulton and Adair attended UVA while Raileanu went south to Duke. Adair was the first to venture into homebrewing while he and Fulton were sharing an apartment in Pittsburgh. Fulton caught the bug, too, and soon was the go-to guy for brewing tips. They and Raileanu, also a brewing hobbyist, toyed around with the idea of starting a brewery for years, but dreams didn't gel until January 2016. They discussed various locations around the country—Adair lives in California, Raileanu in Washington, D.C.—and liked the opportunity Charlottesville presented. Plus there was the pull of family and other familiars. "This is home for us," said Fulton. "My parents live here, my wife's parents live in Richmond. . . . We were [in Maine] for six years, and we have a daughter now. It made sense."

While Fulton oversees the brewing operation, Adair manages sales and marketing, and Raileanu handles the finances. Adair's experience as a TV set designer in Hollywood played into decisions about the taproom—reclaimed wood for the bar—and packaging. You won't find Reason in cans. "A lot of people love cans, for when they're camping or outdoors," Adair said. "But we really like the presentation of the bottles."

The initial production target was one thousand barrels a year with an eventual capacity of ten thousand barrels. In addition to the four flagships, one-offs and test brews will be possible on a one-barrel pilot system that Fulton has been using for years to develop recipes. "During recipe development, I was trying to find a way that I could deliver complex, interesting hop flavor and aroma without having to also deliver higher ABV, higher bitterness, and more of a lingering aftertaste. It's not simple; it's not impossible, but we committed ourselves to trying to find a way to do that."

Try this: Reason Black got the highest marks from several folks I talked with at Reason's release at Beer Run in Charlottesville, and I agreed. The complexity of the malt character—lots of roast without being overbearing—and the refreshing fruity hop aroma give it layers and depth with low ABV (5 percent) accessibility. Steaks and burgers are natural pairing selections, and the Reason guys say it "goes remarkably well with raw oysters."

Starr Hill Brewery

Few breweries have faced the challenges that confronted Starr Hill in early 2015. Mark Thompson, the face and co-founder of the company, had announced his retirement. Beer recipes and branding needed freshening. And Devils Backbone to the south had eclipsed Starr Hill's status as the state's top craft beer producer. Over the ensuing two years, Starr Hill took steps to embrace major change without losing identity. Redesigned packaging found favor in the marketplace, as did the brighter hopification of flagship Northern Lights IPA. Production grew and festivals flourished; by the fall of 2017, Starr Hill was celebrating the opening of a second brewing location in Roanoke, all without losing its niche—brewing beers to drink when the band starts to play.

"Starr Hill's identity, from the Charlottesville Music Hall to pouring beer at the first FloydFest, is deeply rooted in live music," said Jack Goodall, marketing manager, when the Roanoke location was announced. Starr Hill's original location on West Main Street in Charlottesville featured an upstairs music venue known for rocking the town. The Roanoke spot, on South Jefferson Street within view of the Mill Mountain Star (the source of Roanoke's nickname, "Star City of the South"), opened with twenty-three beers on tap and a setting designed to amplify the brewery's musical bent (a colorful mural shows a local musician wearing a paisley vest playing an acoustic guitar). In addition, a five-barrel pilot system adds to its recipe development potential with experimental, small-batch brews. "This is set up to allow us to do kettle souring and some other things," said Allie Hochman, manager of retail operations. Brewmaster Robbie O'Cain is handling the initial batches, then members of Starr Hill's brewing team will rotate to Roanoke with their own recipes.

Keeping up with the latest technology has been a significant factor in O'Cain's approach. A process called "hop bursting," where massive amounts of hops are added late in the boil to emphasize flavor and aroma rather than bitterness, was used in the 2015 redesign of Northern Lights IPA and in the 2017 revamping of Grateful Pale Ale. A hop cannon, which injects fresh hops into fermented batches to enhance aroma, and a centrifuge, which uses centrifugal force to separate out hop residue and other particulates to clarify beer without stripping flavor, have been important tools in Starr Hill's shop. Grateful's new recipe emphasized fuller body as well as fruitier hop aroma by adding Carafoam malt and torrified wheat to the grain bill.

A native of North Carolina, O'Cain came to Starr Hill in 2011 after years of homebrewing and studies through Siebel Institute's World Brewing Academy Master Brewer Program and at Doemens Academy in Munich. He soon was producing award-winning beers in Whiter Shade of Pale Ale, a gold medal winner at the 2014 World Beer Cup, and King of Hop Imperial IPA, named best IPA in the state at that year's Virginia Craft Brewers Cup competition. The popularity of IPAs also served as a springboard for Starr Hill's IPA JamBEERee event, held at the Crozet facility as a showcase for hoppy brews from around the region.

IPAs aside, part of Starr Hill's appeal is its stylistic breadth, from Snow Blind Doppelbock, malty and hefty at 7.7 percent ABV, to Basketcase, an American helles lager, which uses Cascade hops to distinguish it from the classic German version. Throw in a Scotch ale, a Berliner weisse, a double-chocolate stout, a German-style pilsner, a barleywine, and collaborative ventures such as Ménage à VA (a collaboration with O'Connor and Fair Winds breweries released at the 2017 Craft Brewers Conference in Washington, D.C.), and you get a sense of Starr Hill's range.

Part of Starr Hill's identity also is its veteran status.

Since opening in 1999 with Mark Thompson at the helm, it has seen many breweries come and go, with South Street in Charlottesville and Legend in Richmond among the senior elite survivors. For years, Starr Hill held the high ground for volume of production among the state's craft breweries, and when Devils Backbone was acquired by Anheuser-Busch InBev in 2016 (removing it from craft brewery status), Starr Hill again became Virginia's leader. Output in 2016 was twenty-eight thousand barrels per year, up from twenty-five thousand in 2015, the year of Thompson's departure; distribution ranged throughout the mid-Atlantic and Southeast regions, reaching well into Alabama. In addition to the Roanoke expansion, in 2017 Starr Hill opened a craft beer bar in Norfolk's Waterside district.

Try this: Normally I would say Reviver Red IPA, which uses five hops, including Citra, Simcoe, and Mosaic, and four malts, including chocolate. It is a lovely garnet color and hits a sweet spot in the grain-hops blend while retaining drinkability at 6.2 percent ABV. But I can't resist recommending Snow Blind Doppelbock, a style I love and don't see enough of. It evokes the "liquid bread" association with bold malty character and appropriate alcohol content (7.7 percent ABV). What better for listening to a Bach concerto on a blustery day?

Blue Mountain Brewery, Blue Mountain Barrel House

Before barrel-aging beers was a trend, Taylor Smack was in Chicago learning how to unlock the secrets of bourbon casks. Before farm breweries became a trend, he and Mandi, his wife, were in Nelson County modeling their new brewpub after the rural appeal of vineyards. Before hops became a staple of nearly every brewery with a half-acre to spare, the Smacks partnered with hops guru Stan Driver to grow Cascade at two locations. And well before

Taylor Smack's barrel-aging program at Blue Mountain Barrel House draws on his years at Goose Island in Chicago.

lupulin powder became all the rage in bittering beers . . . well, you can guess.

It's not like he wakes up every morning thinking, "What new terrain can I pioneer today?" But Taylor seems to have a knack for knowing where the current is headed. Back when Virginia counted fewer than twoscore breweries, the sight of grain silos going up in the shadow of Afton Mountain raised local eyebrows. "When we started building, people made fun of us a little bit. Every other person would stop and say, 'What are you building here? Looks like a boat garage.'"

Now there's no mistaking Blue Mountain's presence. Since opening in October 2007, the restaurant has gone through several expansions and now seats nearly seven hundred people. The taps have doubled to ten, offering staples from the early days—Kölsch 151, Full Nelson Virginia Pale Ale, Blue Mountain Lager—as well as seasonals and special brews such as Maggie Maibock and Mandolin Belgian Ale. Most are brewed on-site, others at the Blue Mountain Barrel House in Arrington.

The latter has its own tasting room but largely serves as a production facility, enabling Blue Mountain to target more than sixteen thousand barrels of beer produced in 2017 (that includes South Street beers). A switch in distributors in the Richmond area showed a spike in sales there, and a change in yeast used in the flagship Full Nelson kept the Smacks on the cutting edge.

"We now ferment it with the New England ale yeast strain, the Alchemist strain," Taylor said, referring to Vermont's Alchemist Brewery, maker of the popular Heady Topper Double IPA. "It was a risky move. We didn't want to talk about it because we didn't want some kind of 'New Coke' backlash. We tested a batch. I loved it so much that I said, 'I'm OK with change as long as it's change for the better. Let's just put it out there and see what people do.'"

The response was enthusiastic, breathing new energy into a veteran brew. It's not the first time Taylor has turned risk into reward. Getting into brewing at all was a step off the beaten path. A Lynchburg native and Hampden-Sydney College grad, he was working at a mind-numbing job in Charlottesville when he began volunteering at South Street Brewery. He soon felt the call of professional brewing and enrolled at the Siebel Institute of Technology in Chicago, one of the nation's premier brewing school. Fortune smiled when he landed a job in Chicago as head brewer at two brewpubs of Goose Island Beer Company, then a craft beer pioneer in barrel-aging and style development. "My whole career has been guided by Goose Island," Taylor noted. "Everything I saw there was so far ahead of what other people were doing in the country."

He also met Mandi there, and the two moved back to Charlottesville and were married in 2004. Taylor returned to South Street as a brewer; Mandi worked as a hostess and server (her day job was as comptroller for two local publications). A dream of starting their own business came to fruition when they and cofounder Matt Nucci staked their future on a postcard setting in Nelson County for the site of Blue Mountain. This was 2006, a time when the initial wave of microbreweries had ebbed, before farm breweries, and well before a 2012 Virginia law would light the fuse for a craft beer explosion. "Some of our first customers that came in pretty much laughed in our faces and said this isn't going to work," Mandi recalled.

The last laugh is theirs. Not only has the business blossomed but the beers also have won critical acclaim. Blue Mountain's Blue Reserve ale, a Belgian-style IPA made with fresh homegrown hops, has won medals at the World Beer Cup and the Great American Beer Festival. In 2010 and 2011, Blue Mountain received back-to-back golds at the GABF, the only Virginia brewery to do so at the time. And at the 2016 GABF, the 13.Five Ofest won silver and South Street's Twisted Gourd and Slippery When Wit took home silver and bronze medals, respectively.

Though the schedule can get hectic balancing business demands with family obligations, the Smacks' success fulfills a wish dating to the earliest days of their relationship. "Ever since we first met in Chicago, we had been talking about doing a business together," Taylor said. Mandi smiled and added, "I think on our first date we ended up talking about a Laundromat brewery."

Try these: Full Nelson Virginia Pale Ale straddles styles—with 60 IBUs, the hop profile rubs shoulders with IPAs, but the accent is more on hop flavor and aroma than bitterness. The switch from standard California ale yeast to New England yeast adds some of the fruity, juicy qualities characteristic of those beers. For something completely different, turn to Dark Hollow. This imperial stout has the usual notes of vanilla you get from oak bourbon-barrel aging, but what will blow you away are the elegance, smoothness, and complexity of the roasted malts—layers of chocolate and coffee dominate with a bit of boozy quality (10 percent ABV). If you like big beers, this one packs plenty of flavor.

Wild Wolf Brewing Company

When Mary Wolf and her son, Danny, opened a homebrew shop in Nellysford in 2010, people would often come in and express highly judgmental opinions about various beers. She knew enough about beer to know that those critics didn't know much. These days, she finds a higher level of sophistication in beer drinkers' comments. "Consumers are becoming much more educated and discerning. And I think that's a good thing. I love to see people that understand great beer," she said.

Making great beer batch after batch, can after can, requires the attention to detail that only science can bring. To that end, Mary and Danny, who heads up the brewing side, decided to invest $75,000 in 2017 to equip a lab, a big step toward ensuring high quality. "Nothing will leave this building unless it's been tested," according to Mary. "Over the next several years, quality control will make or break people."

If anything breaks Wild Wolf—and that's highly unlikely,

given its steady growth and diverse business—it will be keeping up with demand. That too seems unlikely, considering the addition of fermentation tanks to the fifteen-barrel system, construction of a three-thousand-square-foot packaging building and a two-thousand-square-foot cooler. Annual production stood at roughly four and a half thousand barrels in 2017 with capacity for another thousand before additional tanks are needed.

Blonde Hunny, a Belgian-style blonde ale brewed with wheat and orange blossom honey, leads the pack in terms of Wild Wolf sales, which extend throughout Virginia, Washington, D.C., and West Virginia. To Mary's surprise, drinkers in the Mountain State actually favor Primal Instinct IPA, the brewery's second-best seller. At 95 IBUs, it feeds a hophead's yen for bitterness, plus it has a distinct "taste of place"—every batch includes Cascade hops grown on the property.

That's part of the philosophy that inspires the beer, the restaurant's cuisine, and the brewing process. Using local products and sustainable practices has led to awards for both food and beer. Mary is particularly proud that the business was designated the Green Brewery of the Year by the Virginia Green Travel Alliance in 2015 and 2016. Part of the effort includes going largely with cans rather than bottles (cans account for about 70 percent of the non-keg packaging). The rationale is that cans are lighter, which requires less fuel in shipping, are easier to recycle, and actually protect the beer better from light exposure that could produce the skunk factor.

Conserving and protecting their water is another passion. It's so free of ions and minerals that Mary describes it as "perfect" for brewing. "When Danny saw the test results for the first time, he nearly cried," she recalled. "He insisted that it be tested again, and it came out the same."

Mary has a certain disbelief herself when she thinks about the evolution of Wild Wolf. She and her husband came to the Wintergreen area from Northern Virginia, where she worked as an executive for AOL. She favored wine over beer, and her activity list focused on golf, bridge, hiking, and relaxing. "If you had asked me when I retired from AOL if in ten years I'd be running a brewery, I'd ask you, 'What's wrong with you?'" she chuckled.

Danny had followed a passion for making beer and had just returned from brewing school at the Siebel Institute of Technology in Chicago. The initial homebrew shop led to a small brewing operation, which led to relocating to a historic schoolhouse nearby, which led to building a three-hundred-seat restaurant, a bar with a big-screen TV, a wedding and event center, and a company store.

The beer menu has expanded as well. While Blonde Hunny, Czeched Out Pils, and Whoa Nelly, a Scottish ale, anchor the easy-drinking side, Four Paws, a Belgian quadrupel (12 percent ABV), and Wolfinstein, a Russian imperial stout (13.3 percent ABV), float the boat for extreme beer lovers. The popularity of Primal Instinct has spawned cousins such as Primal Urge (sessionable at 4.9 percent ABV), Primal Passion (brewed with five malts and fermented with passion fruit), and Prime-Apple Express (a 95-IBU New England–style IPA).

The complexity, drinkability, creativity, and diversity of those and other beers have made Mary give up her wine-drinking ways. She and her husband had a cellar of some three thousand bottles. "But I don't drink wine anymore," she said. "I just have fallen head over heels in love with beer."

Try this: At the end of our conversation in September 2017, Mary Wolf asked me to compare Primal Instinct IPA with Bell's Two Hearted Ale, one of my go-to beers and a national favorite (voted the nation's top beer by readers of *Zymurgy* magazine in 2017). The results of my taste test are between her and me (she asked for candid feedback in a continual effort to be brewing the best beer possible),

The Hops in the Park festival at historic Henricus in Chesterfield County combines history and craft beers made with Virginia ingredients.

The Peter Stumpf brewery at Harrison and Clay streets in Richmond evolved into Home Brewing Company, maker of Richbrau beer.

A collection of colorful and historic cans adds to the flavor of Barrel Oak Farm Taphouse's tasting room near Delaplane.

The 2017 Virginia Craft Brewers Fest was held for the first time in Charlottesville, drawing thousands of beer lovers to IX Art Park.

Glasses from Corcoran brewery hint at the merger with Round Hill's B Chord Brewing, where musicians are a regular feature in the taproom.

A bustling tasting room is common at Parkway, which opened its doors in Salem in January 2013.

German and English styles are the backbone of Black Hoof Brewing Company in Leesburg (*above left*); the Oozlefinch Craft Brewery in Fort Monroe boasts one of the more curious legends regarding its name (*above right*).

David Downes (*left*), founder of the Virginia Beer Museum in Front Royal, watches as Judge H. David O'Donnell cuts the ribbon on the museum's opening day in September 2016.

Jeramy Biggie's passion for barrel-aged and sour beers has made Commonwealth Brewing Company a destination for aficionados in the Chic's Beach area of Virginia Beach.

The Blue Mountain Barrel House in Nelson County has a postcard setting well suited to playing cornhole and imbibing award-winning beers.

Izzy Kane (*left*) helps keep the beers flowing at the Final Gravity Brewing Company's second anniversary celebration in Richmond.

Murals depicting conviviality, colonial-era brewing, and modern brew houses brighten the walls inside and outside Spencer Devon Brewing in Fredericksburg.

Hikers on the Appalachian Trail can wet their whistles and unlace their boots at the Damascus Brewery (*above left*); Craig Nargi, owner of Stable Craft Brewing outside Waynesboro (*at left*), talks with head brewer Christopher Fann (*above right*).

Aslin Beer Company in Herndon draws lines and crowds for their releases and celebrations, such as their first anniversary party in September 2016.

Flights of beer and a football game provide a good time in Starr Hill's Crozet tasting room.

Jeremy Wirtes, Adam Worcester, and Scott Jones (*left to right*) opened the second location of Triple Crossing Brewing in Richmond's Fulton Hill area in December 2016.

Benchtop's colorful and flavorful beers are made with local ingredients, including water from the Atlantic Ocean for its salty gose (*above left*); the sign on the wall—RECYCLE BEER HERE—speaks for itself at Studio Brew in Bristol (*above right*).

but I suggest the same fun here. Robust aromatics and notes of tropical citrus and resinous pine in the flavor profile are qualities to look for in Primal Instinct (remember, each batch has homegrown Cascade hops). At 7.4 percent ABV and 95 IBUs, it's a hunny.

Devils Backbone Brewing Company

Steve Crandall grew up in the suburbs of Fairfax County. The outdoors called him—he played by Accotink Creek and as a boy trapped there with friends. Later, hunting became a passion. "I have a picture of me at four years old with a coonskin cap and a six-shooter on," he said. "And nobody in my family hunted. It was just my DNA. Children, when they are born, may just go off in a certain direction, and that was me."

Trophies of deer, bear, sheep, and other hunting exploits deck the walls and halls at the Devils Backbone Basecamp Brewpub & Meadows lodge in Nelson County. The DNA hasn't changed, nor the inclination to go off in a certain direction. The acquisition of the company by Anheuser-Busch InBev in 2016 put Virginia's largest homegrown brewery on a different path, removing it from the craft brewery category and stirring heated opinions among beer aficionados.

"It's been a bit of a roller coaster," Steve concluded a year later. We sat outside with Heidi, his wife and the company's vice president of branding, and Hayes Humphreys, chief operating officer. It was a beautiful September day, cool and brilliant, the mountains lush with green in the last weeks before Virginia would put on its coat of many colors. Sounds of hammering and sawing, men working and projects progressing created an atmosphere of growth and change. And though the conversation carried an occasional twinge from the acrimony generated by the acquisition, the Crandalls exuded optimism and energy. Being "beer positive" is one of their core values. "There may be some things that we wouldn't do or that we don't agree with, but at the end of the day, we're all about craft beer in Virginia and supporting that industry," explained Steve.

Vienna Lager is still the backbone of the business, accounting for roughly 70 percent of the eighty thousand barrels produced annually. Plans are underway to produce it at AB's Williamsburg facility. Whether you call it a craft beer or not, Vienna Lager is special, a testament to the acumen of brewmaster Jason Oliver. It's an attractive beer, a light copper in the glass with a whitetail head. It goes down easy (5.3 percent ABV) and doesn't require a geeky analysis, but if you pay attention, the caramel and toasted quality of Munich and Vienna malts unfolds in your mouth with Northern Brewer and Saaz hops creating a delicate balance. It's won more medals than I have time to count.

The Crandalls anticipate that having it produced offsite will provide on-site flexibility in creating new beers and perhaps doing some cross-brewing with others in AB's High End division. There's expansion in the works overseas as well with the American IPA brewed for the UK market.

The changes in the past year are myriad. Some are readily visible at the Basecamp—an office building and distillery under construction; a rustic "Shanty" with rare beers, fine spirits, and cigars; nursery structures where gourds, herbs, and produce grow. The campground also sports upgrades—more sites and amenities. At the Outpost in Lexington, the business's main production facility, a fifty-two-thousand-square-foot packaging and shipping facility is being built, plus an eleven-thousand-square-foot cooler is online.

Some changes you don't see, like improvements in safety. The staff includes a dedicated safety manager, and putting in a new centrifuge filter was an early order of business. The list continues—improvements in kegging and labeling, new hires in the sales force, and better benefits and pay for employees.

And then there's what Steve calls "The Jason Oliver Project." Oliver takes me behind the bar at the Basecamp to show an open fermenter, wooden foeders, an ozone generator for disinfecting and sanitizing, horizontal lagering tanks, and more. "I love horizontal lagering tanks," Oliver said. "Different techniques give you different beers." There's even a setup for producing kombucha-beer hybrids.

Things have come a long way since Steve had a flashing-lightbulb beer moment years ago— Weihenstephaner hefeweizen on a ski trip in Italy—"It touched my lips, and I had an absolute epiphany," he said at a *Brewbound* business forum. Steve, a building contractor by trade, and Heidi began exploring beer hotspots such as Oregon and Colorado for potential brewery sites. The mountains and meadows of Nelson County, with Wintergreen resort nearby, proved ideal, and the Basecamp Brewpub & Meadows took shape on one hundred acres; doors opened in 2008.

Oliver, a Maryland native, had come to Devils Backbone with one condition. "I told Steve: 'I'll take the job, just don't tell me what to brew,'" he laughed. He'd been through the master brewing program at the University of California–Davis and served stints at The Wharf Rat in Baltimore and two other breweries in the D.C. metro area. Lagers became his love, and an 8.5-barrel Miyaki system made especially for brewing German-style beers set the hook for joining the Devils Backbone crew. The initial core beers were Gold Leaf Lager, an American helles; Eight Point IPA, rich with citrus and pine notes; a weiss beer now called Trail Angel; and Vienna Lager. Oliver put a lot of thought and study into developing Vienna Lager before it hit the tanks. "I wouldn't have foreseen the success that it has," he said.

Winning a medal at the Great American Beer Festival in Denver is nothing new for the Devils Backbone crew, but the thrill is never gone.

That success led to others. The brewery was named tops in the country at the Great American Beer Festival three consecutive years—first as small brewpub, then small brewing company, then again in the mid-size brewing company category. Devils Backbone also was awarded Champion Brewpub and Brewmaster at the 2010 World Beer Cup. Business grew 278 percent between 2010 and 2013, leading to construction of the Outpost in Lexington. Three years running Devils Backbone beers won Best in Show at the Virginia Craft Brewers Fest, which it hosted before the AB acquisition.

The decision to sell to AB was made on a business basis, and it led to a substantial investment that put those hammers and saws to work. Heidi's touch is apparent throughout. She knows every plant in the nursery. The Shanty has a European tavern feel with a woodstove, local antiques, and repurposed wood creating a cozy man-cave space. The distillery parallels the big-beam construction of the lodge.

A huge stone fireplace dominates the lounge area, and the bar is topped with live-edge wood.

Time has smoothed the edges of some of the initial hostility that arose when the acquisition was announced. "I find more people defending us when somebody throws a barb at us now," Steve said. "We chose to use a business solution to grow our business."

And he'd like to see a more inclusive, more beer-positive attitude statewide. "I think the slogan in Virginia shouldn't be 'Virginia is for Craft Beer Lovers.' It should be 'Virginia is for Beer Lovers,'" he concluded. "It should be about everybody."

Try this: I'm assuming you've had Devils Backbone Vienna Lager, so I'm suggesting the Black Lager. A schwarzbier (literally, "black beer"), this is another multiple award winner (including gold at the 2016 World Beer Cup) and showcases Jason Oliver's magic touch with lagers. It delivers on the promise of dark, roasty malts, but you don't get that bite that often accompanies dark ales (imperial stouts, robust porters). The finish is clean; the ABV is 5.1 percent, so it's not relegated to the winter sipper group.

CHAPTER 11

Roanoke Comes of Age

As with Virginia Beach and Richmond, the Roanoke area proved fertile territory for attracting big West Coast breweries. Following the footsteps of Green Flash and Stone, Deschutes of Oregon and Ballast Point of California announced plans for production facilities in the shadow of Mill Mountain.

Ease of transportation, economic support from state and local governments, the beauty of the Blue Ridge Mountains, and a city on the move played into the big brewers' decisions. But as with other parts of the state, a vibrant culture of local breweries and vocal beer lovers factored into the equation. Destinations such as Parkway in Salem, Big Lick and Soaring Ridge in Roanoke's urban core, Twin Creeks in Vinton, and Chaos Mountain near Boones Mill have kept the scene buzzing in the immediate Roanoke area, while to the southwest Wolf Hills in Abingdon, Bristol Station and Studio Brew in Bristol, and Damascus in, well, Damascus, have waved the craft beer flag with admirable vigor. Even Bedford, nestled at the foot of the Peaks of Otter, became a beer destination with the opening of Beale's Beer in 2017.

The Star City will certainly shine brighter when both Deschutes and Ballast Point are brewing locally. The former opened a downtown taproom after announcing in 2016 plans to spend $85 million on a 150,000-barrel plant off U.S. 460, with construction set to begin in 2019. The latter invested $48 million in a 259,000-square-foot vacant warehouse in nearby Botetourt County and opened a hip tasting room and restaurant with an incredible view in the spring of 2017 (on-site brewing began that August). Here's a more detailed look at some of the region's existing breweries.

Deschutes Brewery

Deschutes didn't really choose Roanoke as the site for its East Coast facility; it was more like the residents of the Star City gave the Oregon folks a huge bear hug and never let go. A four-year courtship that began in January 2012 included hikes, bike outings, a dinner at the governor's Executive Mansion featuring Grateful Dead music, and a social media campaign that surprised even Roanokers for its warmth and effusive support. When the news was announced on March 22, 2016, that Roanoke had been selected, a downtown crowd of people erupted in cheers and shouts.

As plans for the main brewery began taking shape on a forty-nine-acre parcel in an industrial park near Blue Hills Golf Club, Deschutes kept the excitement flowing with its taproom in the heart of the historic city center. A line of some two hundred people formed hours before doors opened on August 28, 2017, and founder Gary Fish was on hand to hoist the first pint.

The debut of the first Virginia-brewed beer, however, came during a quiet Sunday afternoon in mid-September. I'd struck up a conversation with Johnny Camacho, a young playwright from Brooklyn who was working behind the bar. When he mentioned that the first on-site batch was maturing in the twenty-gallon pilot system at the taproom, I suggested the possibility of getting a taste. "You're the very first person outside of the Deschutes family to have this," he said, handing me a small plastic cup with a hazy, fruity IPA. Deschutes—delicious.

While I was making history, other patrons were choosing from a dozen beers listed on the screen behind the bar. The options ranged from a 12-percent-ABV Reserve Series

Black Butte XXIX Imperial Porter, brewed to celebrate the company's twenty-ninth anniversary, to a 7.2-percent-ABV saison brewed in collaboration with five local breweries—Chaos Mountain, Parkway, Soaring Ridge, Big Lick, and Flying Mouse. The hoppy side of the menu was anchored by the brewery's flagship, Fresh Squeezed IPA (6.4 percent ABV and 60 IBUs). The "pub exclusive" was Bachelor Bitter, a take on the English bitter style.

The 4,700-square-foot pub is bright with lots of big windows that offer views onto the shopping district; you also can find glimpses of the business's character on interior walls. Beside a mural-size photo of hop cones flowering on bines, three help-yourself canisters are filled with whole-leaf Cascade, Nugget, and Mosaic hops (the Pacific Northwest is a breadbasket of hops). A timeline outlines company history, beginning with Fish's opening the Deschutes Brewery and Public House in downtown Bend, Oregon, on June 27, 1988, with three beers—Black Butte Porter, Cascade Golden Ale, and Bachelor Bitter.

Production that first year was 714 barrels, a far cry from the 150,000 barrels that Deschutes, eighth on the craft beer volume list, anticipates producing at Roanoke's facility when full-scale brewing begins. When that might happen became a question mark, however, after Deschutes announced in April 2018 that it was pausing production plans. Still, it showed its commitment to building the East Coast facility by purchasing outright the acreage for the site. As with Ballast Point's plant in Daleville and Stone's brewery in Richmond, landing the deal initially included some government sweeteners.

The most compelling inducement, however, was the feeling that Deschutes and Roanoke were kindred spirits. The company had explored numerous options—Asheville in North Carolina, Charleston in South Carolina, and even a brief exploratory probe in Albemarle County, Virginia. The Star City's outdoorsy nature, its bounty of excellent water, its history of ups and downs as a railroad town, and the genuine outpouring of enthusiasm proved the deciding factors. "We just felt like this place suited us best," Fish said when the deal was announced. "We think this fits our entrepreneurial spirit and our sense of community."

Try this: Fresh Squeezed IPA is a natural recommendation, given its flagship status. If you haven't had some, do so immediately. However, I'm going to steer you toward one of the originals, Bachelor Bitter, named after an Oregon skiing spot, Mount Bachelor. It's a style you don't see enough of in this country, though it's a staple in the UK. Don't think of "bitter" in the hopped-up West Coast IPA sense, though Bachelor Bitter, at 50 IBUs, is a bit hoppier than traditional versions. Bachelor offers smooth malthops balance with sessionable drinkability (5.2 percent ABV). East Kent Golding hops give it some true earthy English character (Galena and Willamette also figure in the hop profile); crystal malts provide caramelized notes in the flavor.

Big Lick Brewing Company

Before there was Roanoke, there was Big Lick. The current name has Native American roots, with Roanoke being an Algonquian word for shells used as money. Big Lick, established in 1852, gives a nod to geology—large outcroppings of salt that drew wildlife and people from hither and yon.

Instead of salt in your Big Lick beer in the form of perhaps a tangy gose, expect full-bodied variety in brews such as Bloody Brilliant English Porter, Get on the Good Foot Imperial Brown Ale, and Knock on Wood, a sour American ale fermented with wild yeast. The tap list when I visited the original taproom at 135 Salem Avenue also had three hoppy brews, including a black IPA juiced with blood red orange purée to give a citrus complement to the pine notes of the Amarillo and Citra hops. There was a bit of fun in Casey's Kölsch, which, according to the brewery's website, was named after local columnist Dan Casey because he "whined and moaned so much about being overlooked" after coworker and author Beth Macy had a beer named in her honor at Parkway. Those beers might not be on the tap list in future visits. Cofounders Bryan Summerson (head brewer) and Chuck Garst pride themselves on creativity, as evidenced in their slogan, "Rarely will we have the same beer twice."

Big Lick completed a significant expansion in October 2017. A production facility at 409 Salem Avenue downtown as part of The Lofts at West Station was fashioned to include a fifteen-barrel system in a 1,635-square-foot brewing area with a two-barrel pilot setup for test batches. The new site features an indoor tasting room with twenty-four taps and a 5,700-square-foot beer garden with fire pits and picnic tables. Once again, history has played a role—the barrel-roof structure was built in 1910 and served as a trucking depot. The brewing capacity is expected to increase fivefold and set the stage for Big Lick beer in cans. "We're going to keep doing what we are doing," said Summerson. "It's just going to be bigger."

Try this: By the time you read this, Big Lick will be in new digs, so this is a shot in the dark based on my visit to the original site in 2017 (the opening for the new site happened on deadline for this book). Let's hope a porter similar to Bloody Brilliant will be on tap. Brewed in the English tradition, the dark, malty ale lived up to its description of "irresistibly drinkable," with an accessible 5.5 percent ABV. The beer menu gives credit to David Wheeler, "who won the dark category at the Star City Throwdown homebrew competition. His recipe includes Maris Otter and several British dark malts."

Soaring Ridge Craft Brewers

There's a taste of place at Soaring Ridge that goes beyond the beer. The Shenandoah Avenue location snugs up to

Colorful banners, historic photos, and flavorful beers are attractions at Soaring Ridge brewery in Roanoke.

the railroad yards that are fundamental to Roanoke's past and present. Displays just inside the entrance chronicle the heyday of operations such as the Virginia Brewing Company and Robert Portner Brewing Company, both of which suffered when the state went dry in 1916 (see chapter 1). Photos of post-Prohibition resurgence chronicle the efforts of E. Cabell Tudor, president of the Virginia Brewing Company, and others. The Soaring Ridge taproom and beers do their part, though, to bring you up to speed on styles and flavors that make the craft beer boom so exciting. Light streams through bay doors facing the street, and banners draped above brewing vessels give color and character to the industrial setting.

The brewery has its own story of evolution, beginning as Big Daddy's Brewing Company in the Towers Shopping Center. In 2014, brewmaster Sean Osborne and his partners announced they were moving to the former Flowers Baking Company building on Shenandoah Avenue. They brought with them, among other beers, their Virginia

Creeper, a moderately hopped American-style pale ale named for the railroad track turned biking/hiking trail.

Other beers give a nod to outdoor activities and features. Night Hiker is a black IPA with 74 IBU zip from Falconer's Flight, Cascade, and East Kent Golding hops; Trail Head is a mildly malty nut-brown ale made with English hops; Tinker Creek, one of the flagship brands, is an easy-drinking (4 percent ABV) kölsch that pays homage to the style's roots with German malt and hops.

Try this: For me, it's a tossup between two beers derived from English styles. Trail Head Nut Brown Ale (6 percent ABV) combines English hops with a roasty, nutty malt presence to invoke favorites such as Samuel Smith's Nut Brown Ale. While porter is English in origin, Soaring Ridge's Twisted Stump has a more robust American take. For good reason, it's called an imperial porter; its higher alcohol (8.5 percent ABV, according to the brewery's website) is well above the 4 to 5.4 percent range of traditional English porter. The malts deliver big chocolate and caramel flavors, with notes of coffee; a bourbon barrel–aged version made with coconut was featured in January 2017.

Ballast Point Brewing Company

At 3:32 P.M. on August 23, 2017, the Ballast Point Virginia Facebook page posted a note saying, "First East Coast brew is in the books." Twenty-six days later, brewery officials were at the Executive Mansion in Richmond, joining then-governor Terry McAuliffe in a toast of the first Ballast Point Sculpin brewed at the Daleville site.

For McAuliffe, celebrating a brewery's debut in the Old Dominion is nothing new. He had announced a goal of visiting every brewery in the state before leaving office. For Virginia, welcoming a West Coast brewery was getting to be old hat as well. Ballast Point had followed Stone, Green Flash, and Deschutes into the state, though it beat Deschutes to the local brewing kettle.

Sculpin was an appropriate choice for the governor's glass. Though Ballast Point brews more than fifty styles of beer, this IPA is an icon among West Coast hoppy beers. The name comes from the sculpin fish, which has tasty meat but poisonous spikes—flavor with a sting. The beer has won medals everywhere from the California State Fair to the World Beer Cup (throw in some awards from Australian, Japanese, Danish, and Belgian beer judges as well). Sculpin and its school of offshoots—Grapefruit Sculpin, Pineapple Sculpin, Habanero Sculpin, and more—will be emphasized in Daleville's initial brewing. "However, we just recently completed our first batch of CA2VA, which is a new IPA brewed with some local ingredients that will be for sale in Virginia only," said James Fox, brewing manager at the Virginia site, in September 2017. Small-batch one-offs and seasonals also will be flowing through the tasting room taps.

That kind of variety is part of the draw to Ballast Point's $48 million Botetourt County location. Well, that and the view—on a clear day you can look out onto ridges of blue ringing the area. Once an auto parts factory, the 259,000-square-foot facility sports nearly one hundred taps in a 10,000-square-foot tasting room, bar, and dining area; an event space with ten more taps; a second level for savoring that view; and brewing systems with copper-plated kettles and stainless steel tanks expected to churn out 130,000 barrels of beer in the early going. The ultimate capacity could be one million barrels with full expansion.

That's more than a little drop in the growler for Ballast Point, which was listed as the eleventh-largest craft brewing operation in 2015. Late that year, it was purchased for $1 billion by Constellation Brands, a move that fueled growth but removed Ballast Point from the list of craft breweries, as defined by the Brewers Association (see chapter 3).

The price tag for Constellation's purchase raised some

Ballast Point's Daleville facility boasts beautiful views of the Blue Ridge Mountains outside Roanoke.

eyebrows, as did the package put together to bring the San Diego stalwart to Virginia in 2016. The deal included $1.4 million in tax incentives from Botetourt County, performance grants estimated at $650,000, a possible grant of $250,000 from a state fund, and waiving some permit fees. The state granted the county $2.4 million to make up for lost revenue.

The opening of the taproom in June 2017 inspired jubilation and praise. My visit the following month proved pleasant on every level, from the quality of the beers to the excellence of service. I had been to Ballast Point in San Diego in January 2015 and enjoyed the beers there; this was no letdown.

On a corporate level, though, the summer of 2017 carried some less than rosy news. In reporting Constellation Brands' earnings for the first quarter of fiscal year 2018 (up 8 percent overall in beer sales), CEO Rob Sands said in a news release that Ballast Point had "not performed up to expectations from a growth standpoint." The value of the brewery's trademarks was devalued by $87 million; industry analysts, however, remained positive about prospects. The earnings statement came out in June, before Virginia came online. The Daleville brewery has easy access to Interstate 81 and other arteries, allowing the brewery to help with distribution throughout the country and internationally while focusing primarily on getting fresh beer to the East Coast.

It was the freshest of Sculpin IPAs on the lips of McAuliffe and Ballast Point officials during the September session in Richmond. The gathering was devoted to celebrating fine beer, the addition of another partner to the state's scene, and the kinship among beer lovers. Interestingly, Ballast Point was started by two former college roommates in the back room of a homebrew shop in 1996—the same year that Stone started. Who could have guessed both businesses would call Virginia a second home someday?

Try this: Sculpin IPA is the logical recommendation, if you haven't consumed mass quantities already. It really is a beer that needs to be on your bucket list, largely for being a definitive version of the West Coast IPA style. You have to want the bite, though, at 70 IBUs. Look for apricot, mango, lemon, and peach flavors, according to the brewery's website; I get more citrus and pine. The mouthfeel is full-bodied, the bitterness lingering. The alcohol level is a little above sessionable at 7 percent ABV. The treat now is getting it fresh from a Virginia location.

Parkway Brewing Company

Before brewing became the prevailing passion of Mike "Keno" Snyder, music claimed the center of his soul. The North Carolina native played classical guitar and studied music composition at Virginia Commonwealth University in Richmond, where he later worked in studios as a sound engineer.

While at VCU he also met the woman he would marry,

Lezlie, and in 1999 the couple moved to Roanoke, her hometown, and started a family. Keno's love of cooking led to some homebrewing adventures and a stint in Colorado at Breckenridge Brewery. That experience convinced him to continue pursuing brewing, and in April 2010 he took a full-time gig as head brewer at Roanoke Railhouse Brewing Company (then the city's oldest craft brewery, operating from 2009 to 2016).

The yen to branch out led him to design a business plan with Ryan Worthington, then brewmaster at Roanoke Railhouse. But it was a twist of circumstance that led Keno to Parkway's current site in an industrial facility on Kessler Mill Road in Salem. "I just happened to be driving down the road and saw this building was for lease. I walked in and saw the floors and trench drains, and I said, 'Perfect!'"

The brewery opened in January 2013 with four beers, and the first to kick was Bridge Builder Blonde, an accessible Belgian-style ale with a wheat backbone and hints of clove, banana, and pear. "I didn't expect that to kick first," Keno said when I first talked with him shortly after the grand opening. He had put me to work the minute I walked in the door, flipping bottles in preparation for a run through the filling line.

Keno also didn't expect a strong market initially for IPAs, but Get Bent Mountain IPA, at 7.2 percent ABV with citrus notes characteristic of West Coast styles, has been a sales leader. Like many Parkway brews, this beer gives a nod to local points of reference; Bent Mountain overlooks the Blue Ridge Parkway a dozen miles south of Salem. Raven's Roost, the brewery's robust Baltic porter, is named for another scenic spot popular with climbers. Factory Girl Session IPA celebrates local author Beth Macy's first book, *Factory Man.*

Parkway went gung-ho from the get-go with a thirty-barrel brewing system, and sales doubled every year as distribution expanded throughout much of Virginia and neighboring states. The tasting room, initially with no wall between benches and brewing vessels, also was up-sized to include a glass partition, colorful murals, a stone fireplace, more benches, and outside amenities. And, of course, a spacious stage provides an inviting venue for area musicians.

The Parkway tap list has grown as well, and you can expect to see ten or so beers on the menu. You'll find big beers—Fortification Barleywine, aged twelve months in whiskey barrels (12.5 percent ABV), and Magella, a Belgian strong dark ale (11.1 percent ABV)—alongside less hefty offerings—Go Fest Yourself Saison Ale (6 percent ABV) and Bridge Builder Blonde (5.9 percent ABV).

Try this: Majestic Mullet Krispy Kölsch—the rednecky name belies the complexity of the kölsch style, often offered in breweries primarily as a gateway beer to open the door for mainstream drinkers to try a craft beer. This golden ale, however, has a rich grain bill, giving a bit of bread in the nose and the flavor, complemented by a floral hop aroma and funky yeast. This may not be the beer you write home about, but it is a notable offering for its drink-ability (6 percent ABV) and surprisingly big flavor.

Chaos Mountain Brewing

Getting to Chaos Mountain's tasting room requires a bit of a roller-coaster ride on the serpentine roads southwest of Roanoke, but as Wendy Hallock says, "We think it's worth the drive"—particularly when Virginia's fall foliage is in full spectacle, as the twists and dips around Cahas Mountain offer postcard views of the peaks and hollows that make this part of the state a rural treasure.

Once at the tasting room, soak in the classic rock (Clapton, Hendrix, even Jethro Tull), the bowling-alley expanse of space, the poster-size label art on the walls, and, of course, the beer. Sixteen or so brews are usually on tap, and the offerings range from the light-bodied Shine

Runner Czech-style pils to the ultra-intense Theory of Chaos, a Belgian strong ale that packs an 18-percent-ABV velvet wallop. "I think it has the highest ABV of any beer in Virginia," says Joe Hallock, Wendy's husband and co-owner of the business.

Belgians are Joe's favorite. He and Wendy have toured Belgium, and the spicy, fruity flavors of the beers there fit Joe's palate. "I was a wine drinker, and I love that Belgian beers have that same kind of flavor profile." The brewery's portfolio includes two of his recipes—the Trappist-inspired Agents of Chaos Belgian-style dark strong ale and the 4 Mad Chefs Belgian Quadrupel.

It is Scottish tradition rather than Belgian that shapes Chaos Mountain's flagship Squatch Ale, however. A "wee heavy" in the Scotch ale mold, it has powered the growth of the brewery into markets from Virginia Beach to Loudoun County. The annual volume from the thirty-barrel system (a seven-barrel system provides one-offs and seasonal small batches) was running around 2,400 barrels in 2017; more tanks are planned to expand the footprint.

It's Wendy's fingerprints you'll see on beers such as 4 Mad Chefs. A career in the food industry has fostered ties with some prominent professional foodies, and the Belgian quad featured collaboration among a fab four—John Schopp (owner of Center Stage Catering), Ted Pofelt (executive chef for the Jefferson Street restaurant group), Joseph Zeisler (head of Virginia Western Community College's culinary program), and Geoff Blount (a faculty member at the International Culinary Institute at Myrtle Beach and Callebaut Chocolate Ambassador).

The recipe for starting their craft brewery involved some tough ingredients. Joe experienced an extended illness that led him to sell his share of SleepSafe Beds, a company he had started that designs and builds protective beds for people with physical disabilities. He'd already been bitten by the homebrewing bug, thanks to a starter kit Wendy gave him for Christmas in 1996. The Hallocks decided the time was right to change direction, so they used a twenty-thousand-square-foot building already owned by the business to house brew kettles, tanks, and a bottling line. After a sojourn abroad to visit European brewing centers, the Hallocks got Chaos Mountain beers abubbling in 2014.

Medals followed almost immediately, at Microfestivus in Roanoke and the Virginia Craft Brewers Fest, where Cocoborealis (a triple chocolate stout) and Agents of Chaos received silver and gold, respectively. The tasting room also proved a magnet for beer lovers; Joe estimates it accounts for about 35 percent of annual revenue. Part of the appeal might be local references such as Shine Runner Pils (a nod to Franklin County's reputation as moonshine king), Squatch (Sasquatch is Virginia's version of Bigfoot), and the name of the brewery itself (a playful rendering of Cahas Mountain).

As with so many microbreweries, Chaos Mountain also has the charm of a small business run with family appeal—son Ben supervises bottling and packaging. His father's illness was a factor in Ben's leaving James Madison University to help at the brewery. "We've been through enough hardship that this was really just what we needed," Ben concluded. "I couldn't be happier with it."

Try this: A beer-wise friend of mine had a healthy taste of Squatch Ale and became a devotee of the Scotch ale style. It has the full-bodied mouthfeel and alcohol punch (7.5 percent ABV) you look for in a "wee heavy," thanks to a four-malt grain bill that puts the spotlight on roasted barley. Hops are in the background (25 IBUs), just enough to keep the sweetness at bay.

Wolf Hills Brewing Company

You're more likely to hear the rumble of a passing train than the howling of hungry wolves at Abingdon's signature brewery. Railroad tracks lie within bunting distance of the tasting room and brewery, so Wolf Hills patrons periodically have to raise their voices as well as their pint glasses. Still, the romance of the brewery's name—that wolves threatened Daniel Boone on an expedition in the area— lives in posters and logos on the walls and taps.

Those taps carry an appealing assortment of beers, including the popular White Blaze Honey Cream Ale (made with Appalachian honey) and Wolf's Den Double IPA (a 100-IBU zinger made with five hops). Those are two of seventeen options listed on a blackboard behind the bar, a gleaming wooden beauty made with boards taken from Troopers Alley, a notorious side street in town. "We're really proud of this bar," said server Jeni Marie Blackmon.

On a Saturday afternoon in December 2016, the brewery bustled with a mixed crowd of young millennials and seasoned veterans. A stage invited live music, but for the moment Tom Petty, the Beatles, and Jimi Hendrix provided the soundtrack. I sampled a flight of beers—

Jeni Marie Blackmon works in the taproom at Wolf Hills Brewing Company in Abingdon.

Wolf's Den DIPA, Appalachian Pale Lager, Creeper Trail Amber Ale, Stonewall Heights Stout, and Blackstrap Pecan Porter—and talked with Alex Werny, a brewer who has since left Wolf Hills, about some of the recipes. We focused on Auld Magnus Winter Warmer, a Belgian-style strong ale that uses ginger, cranberries, and orange peel and is aged for more than two months. It was the first Wolf Hills seasonal beer to be packaged in cans, he noted.

Brewing is done now on a seven-barrel system, a step up from the original one-barrel operation used by Chris Burcher, the founding head brewer. Burcher, a former biology professor and avid homebrewer, and three others started Wolf Hills as little more than a homebrew showcase in August 2009 in a rented house in Abingdon's Stonewall Heights. They upped their game and expanded into a historic icehouse providing six thousand square feet of space. "It's operating a lot more like a real business than being something we did just for fun," cofounder Cameron Bell said in a 2011 article.

Being in the vanguard of craft beer in the Abingdon area meant Burcher and others needed patience to bring patrons up to speed on the diverse possibilities of a small brewery. Burcher couldn't even find a double IPA locally when the business started, and now Wolf's Den DIPA is a hit. White Blaze Honey Cream Ale, however, is the top seller in Wolf Hills' distribution area, which stretches from Blacksburg south into Tennessee.

Being in a small rural area, without the population density and easy walking access of urban centers, has its challenges. Wolf Hills' annual production level, estimated at about one thousand barrels in 2017, is holding its own at best, Burcher said. The number of craft breweries has stiffened competition in retail outlets. "There's just no room to grow anymore in the marketplace."

John Wesley "Wes" Chastain now heads the brewing chores. A native of Florida, he had extensive experience with the Hops Restaurant Bar & Brewery chain before taking on brewing chores at the now-defunct Jefferson Street Brewing Company in Lynchburg. "I met him when I was first trying this idea out," Burcher recalled. "We started out with $15,000 and a lot of sweat equity. I'd like to see somebody beat that now."

Try this: It's a seasonal beer, but Auld Magnus is worth keeping an eye out for when it's available. The Belgian strong ale style means relatively high alcohol content, and this brew comes in at 8.5 percent ABV. The cranberries and orange peel give it a holiday flavor without the usual nutmeg, allspice, and cinnamon. Ginger also balances out the sweetness and combines well with the Belgian yeast.

A Bristol Pair

In downtown Bristol, it takes only a step to move from Virginia to Tennessee, and you'd hardly know the difference. For beer seekers, it takes a few more steps to move from one brewery to another, and you'd see a definite contrast.

Ken Monyak decided to take a no-frills, center-of-the-road approach when he opened Bristol Brewery (changed to **Bristol Station Brews & Taproom**) on Piedmont Avenue in July 2015. Craft beer had yet to create a substantial consumer base, so one of the first beers out of his tanks was BFW, aka Beer Flavored Water. The lager used rice as an adjunct (similar to another ubiquitous lager) and touted an easy-drinking 3.6 percent ABV. Not a beer aficionado's dream brew, but "it sold like gangbusters," Monyak said. Make no mistake, though—he shows his brewing chops with another lager, the full-bodied Bearded Goat Bock, and a couple of IPAs, particularly Double Loco Imperial IPA (80 IBUs, 8.7 percent ABV).

With a ten-barrel system, Monyak cranks out roughly six hundred barrels a year and targets distribution mostly in Southwest Virginia and a slice of Tennessee. Three brews—Bristol Helle Raiser, Vanilla Porter, and Barefoot

Blonde Ale—won medals at the Thirsty Orange Brew Extravaganza. Though he doesn't shy from creative approaches, he doesn't stray far from traditional offerings. "We're just now getting craft beer [in Bristol]," he said when I visited in late 2016. "There are not enough people here who are world travelers and understand what that means. But people can generally can find something they like."

It's a good leg-stretcher across Cumberland Square Park to get to **Studio Brew** on Moore Street, and the palate gets a good stretching there as well with fruit-infused Belgians, bourbon barrel–aged IPAs, and more. Erich Allen, master brewer and co-owner with his wife, Pamela, traded a career in photography for his beer job, and his approach reflects a consistent sensibility. "Our motto is 'Beer is an art, a very tasty art.' And to that end, everything we produce is with that theme in mind."

Located in a former historic fire museum, Studio Brew has an upscale ambience and clever menu (options are organized like a film—snacks under Opening Sequence, starters under Story Board, entrees under Main Action) that reflects the Allens' goal of creating a destination. Lively chatter feeds a buoyant atmosphere as you ponder selections—perhaps starting with Mex-I-Can Vienna Lager paired with Brewmaster's Bacon (brown sugar and Sriracha-rubbed bacon with beer reduction drizzle and Belgian arugula).

Erich was on hand at the 2016 Great American Beer Festival in Denver to pour beers. And while he won no awards that trip, Studio Brew came away with two golds at the 2017 Virginia Craft Beer Cup for The Ferguson, an oatmeal chocolate milk stout, and its bourbon barrel–aged cousin, and a gold as well for The Ferguson at the 2017 GABF.

Beale's Beer

The call letters of a Bedford radio station, WBLT, have long stood for "World's Best Little Town." The same phrase on a roadside sign for years greeted motorists as they entered Bedford's northeastern edge, and though it might sound like a corny slogan, don't sneer at it when you're around local folks. With the Peaks of Otter defining the western skyline, the National D-Day Memorial standing as a monument to wartime sacrifice and bravery, and a vibrant spirit of hometown pride among residents, Bedford has much to recommend it. The best, however, got just a bit better with the opening of Beale's brewery.

Housed in a historic building that saw prosperous times as a woolen mill and a furniture manufacturer, Beale's opened a thirty-barrel production facility with a restaurant and spacious taproom in June 2017. Its flagship beer, Beale's Gold, has several layers of meaning: the color of the easy-drinking German lager; the shot in the arm for the local economy (thirty jobs were created as part of $2.5 million in economic impact); and the reference to a long-standing legend about buried treasure in the hills of Montvale.

Opening weekend was a homecoming of sorts for head brewer James Frazer, who exuded giddiness as he led tours of the tanks and fermenters in the twelve-thousand-square-foot space. A Bedford native, he had built a reputation for adventurous brews at Trapezium Brewing Company in Petersburg, the initial brewing venture of entrepreneur Dave McCormack. Trapezium won two medals at the 2017 Virginia Craft Beer Cup, a gold for its Strawberry Blonde among fruit beers and a bronze for its brown ale in that category. "We're thinking Trapezium and Beale's will have a Superman and Clark Kent relationship," Frazer said.

The mild-mannered Beale's Gold is a Munich helles by style; and at 4.8 percent ABV and 13 IBUs, it represents an alternative to some of the extreme brews common at craft breweries. "There are so many craft brews out there, and a lot of them are doing the same thing—tons of IPAs and high-ABV beers," McCormack observed. "The entire Beale's brand is meant to feel a little vintage, back when beer was really simple and fun."

That's not to rule out hoppy options. Beale's Red weighs in at 75 IBUs and 6.7 ABV—it's nobody's ninety-pound weakling and it has built its own following among Bedford beer aficionados. An oatmeal stout and a German-style brown lager offer chewy flavor profiles, and once again the ABV is below 5 percent.

Beale's taproom is filled with light from high ceilings and big windows, and there's a steady buzz from families at picnic tables and quaffers at an expansive bar. A dining area by the restaurant looks onto brewing barrels on one side; a wall-size map of the county marks local landmarks—the sister Peaks of Otter (Sharp Top and Flat Top), Suck Mountain, Goose Creek, and more. It does

Bedford County is home to the Peaks of Otter, the National D-Day Memorial, and a rural legend about the Beale Treasure, which inspired the Beale's brewery name.

not, however, indicate where you might find the gold that Thomas Jefferson Beale allegedly buried in the Montvale area after returning from a journey out West in the 1820s.

Bringing Beale's to life required years of planning and a $600,000 grant from the Virginia Department of Housing and Community Development. McCormack, who had opened loft apartments earlier in Bedford through his Waukeshaw Development company, was able to use historic tax credits on the $2.3 million project. Beale's Gold broke ground in another manner—by being the first Virginia-made beer packaged in an eight-pack. Distribution began in the immediate area and is targeted eventually to cover the state.

Full disclosure: I lived in Bedford from 1975 to 1981. Suffice it to say that my timing was off.

Try this: Go for the Gold, then the Red. I am a fan of the helles style, and Frazer does it right. It's also the right beer for a small town that's never had a craft brewery. That's not to say there aren't plenty of sophisticated beer lovers in Bedford. I've seen many a pint of Red go down with smiles on faces.

CHAPTER 12

a Corridor of Breweries in the Valley

Begin in Lexington, home of the voluminous Devils Back-bone's Outpost. Move north on Interstate 81, just enough to stop at Great Valley brewery by Natural Bridge. Then Staunton and Waynesboro will call you, with Basic City, Seven Arrows, Shenandoah Valley, Redbeard, and Bedlam breweries offering a smorgasbord of brews. If you have time, check out Stable Craft in the horse country outside Waynesboro. But leave plenty of time for Harrisonburg— Pale Fire, Brothers, Restless Moons, and Three Notch'd await you there. Woodstock offers a pit stop, and Win-chester can persuade you to park your vehicle and spend some time at Alesatian, Escutcheon, and Winchester Brew Works. One more stop awaits—Backroom Brewery, where Billie Clifton will pour her famous Lemon Basil Wheat Beer.

Great Valley Farm Brewery

When Thomas Jefferson first viewed the magnificent stone arch of Natural Bridge in Rockbridge County, he de-scribed it as the "most sublime of Nature's works." He'd made the trek in 1767 from his Poplar Forest retreat in Bedford County, a journey of some forty miles that re-quired crossing the Blue Ridge Mountains. Being an avid fan of the brewing arts, he might have smiled to think that two and half centuries later he would be able to quench his thirst at nearby Great Valley Farm Brewery.

You can't see Natural Bridge from Nathan and Irma

Bailey's taproom, though the hill it sits on affords views of pastures and glens swelling eastward to wooded ridges. It's a small section of the Great Valley, the fertile trough that stretches from Alabama to New England and encompasses the Shenandoah Valley. Oddly, you can get a taste of Belgium as much as Virginia's breadbasket in the Baileys' brews. The farmhouse tradition of Wallonia in particular appeals to Nathan; Great Valley's Lemongrass Basil Saison won first place in its category at the 2017 Virginia Craft Beer Cup. The same judges awarded a bronze medal for Great Valley's stout, showing Nathan's knack for British styles as well. "Being our small size, we'll be able to experiment a lot," he said.

The couple acquired the twenty-seven-acre site in 2008. Planting grapes followed in 2012, and now a four-acre vineyard serves to supply the raw ingredients for wines they plan to produce. Hops also figure into the agricultural mix, along with fruits and herbs, including the basil and lemongrass that went into the award-winning saison. "Our hops are not a big part of it. We have just a few hills that we will use for fresh-hopped beer," explained Nathan.

Belgian styles dominate the brewing because "that's what I like to drink and to make. Also, not a lot of people around here do Belgian beers as a niche. I'd say two-thirds of the beers we keep on tap are Belgians. It helps to differentiate us," he said. The Belgian Blonde (5.1 percent ABV) is the most popular, with the Hibiscus Wit coming in a close second. An IPA loaded with Centennial, Chinook, and Cascade hops (61 IBUs) anchored the hoppy side of the tap list in September 2017.

Tourists drawn to the area to marvel at Natural Bridge feed some of the business but not as much as the Baileys anticipated. "We've gotten more local traffic than we thought, which is really nice," Nathan observed.

He and Irma are originally from Illinois but bounced around to Kentucky and North Carolina following career paths. While living in Charlotte, North Carolina, they decided to wave goodbye to city life for a more rural setting. Nathan had started making batches of wine at home, which led to brewing beer. It made sense to pull the trigger on the brewery operation before making wine, and in the meantime they are selling grapes to other vineyards. Estimated beer production from the seven-barrel system is two hundred to two hundred and fifty barrels a year, and Nathan said Great Valley hopes to distribute to some local accounts in the near future.

Try this: I was impressed by the Belgian Tripel, which is aged for two months in red-wine barrels. It pours a slightly hazy gold. Noble Saaz hops combine with the Belgian yeast for a spicy, floral aroma; hints of clove and banana come through in the nose and flavor as well. A malty, round softness marks the mouthfeel, and the finish is dry and clean. The 9.2 percent ABV gives it the gravitas that a tripel deserves.

Basic City Beer Company

The ability to take what's old and make it new has been a major force of Virginia's craft brewing culture—in Richmond's Scott's Addition . . . in Harrisonburg's industrial pockets . . . in a previously vacant warehouse in Botetourt County . . . and in a dilapidated building in a part of Waynesboro that had withered from previous glory days.

A railroad and industrial center once provided the hustle and bustle for the southeastern edge of town, where the Basic City Mining, Manufacturing, and Land Company thrived in the late 1800s. The area was incorporated as Basic City, and it merged with Waynesboro in 1924, only to have voters later reject a hyphenated city name. Basic City faded into memory—until Chris, Bart, and Joe Lanman came along.

The brothers had a sad wake-up call when their father, who had introduced them to craft beer, died before retirement. That spurred discussions of a brewery, and the vacant Virginia Metalcrafters site off U.S. 250 drew their attention. "I'd driven by this thing a thousand times. I knew the building needed a lot of work, but this is a really cool spot," Bart said in January 2016 as we stood on a concrete floor amid puddles and broken windows.

Plans took shape for a sixteen-thousand-square-foot operation with a twenty-barrel system. The Lanmans tagged veteran Jacque Landry as head brewer; pilot batches helped define the offerings, and in October 2016 doors opened and taps flowed with Basic City beers. The debut showcased a tasting room blending old and new features. High ceilings and large windows invited light into the space, where brewing tanks posed beyond framed glass. Reclaimed wood had been fashioned into tables, and a hefty stretch of vintage pipe served to connect the taps behind the zinc bar. The initial eight offerings ranged from Advance DIPA, juicy and accessible at 7.6 percent ABV, to Oopsproch Lager, brewed in the German helles style.

Basic City Beer Company's grand opening in October 2016 drew scores of beer aficionados to the tasting room in Waynesboro.

By the following spring, Basic City cans of Sixth Lord IPA, distinctive for its Scottish yeast as well as its American hop aroma, and Waynesbeeroh, a 4.7 percent ABV lager, were finding space on retailers' shelves. Five other beers, including the Oopsproch Lager and Advance IPA, were also being distributed by Blue Ridge Beverage.

In addition to invigorating an industrial area, Basic City provides an easy point of entry in connecting breweries east of the mountains—particularly those along the Brew Ridge Trail—with destinations in the Shenandoah Valley. Basic City is a twelve-minute drive across Afton Mountain from Blue Mountain's Afton site in Nelson County. From Basic City, it's another twelve-minute hop to Seven Arrows on the other side of Waynesboro, with a slight detour north to Stable Craft, then to Staunton for Redbeard and other breweries, then north to Harrisonburg or south to Lexington.

Attracting tourist dollars through craft breweries is one reason many government officials offer infusions of money—a $600,000 grant, in Basic City's case—to boost entrepreneurial energy. People's appreciation for renovation reaches down to a more grassroots level, though, as expressed by several folks on opening day. One gent, sipping from a pint of Foggy Lager, said he grew up in the neighborhood and had worked for Virginia Metalcrafters for fifteen years. Another said, "It's great to see a business come in and take over a [former] business that's just sitting here."

Try this: Oopsproch Lager is the best-selling beer in Basic City's taproom. It could easily be dismissed as a gateway beer, but brewer Jacque Landry gives it nice depth with an heirloom malt from Weyermann (a malt specifically designed for traditional styles of beer) and Swiss lager yeast. The beer's name also has a traditional derivation: Bart Lanman says it comes from the phonetic pronunciation of "hopsproche," a word used to describe the

German settlement in the Shenandoah Valley. Basic City's Oopsproch is inspired by the Märzen style but given an American craft translation. Don't worry if you stumble over the name. "The more you drink it, the better the pronunciation becomes," Bart jokes.

Seven Arrows Brewing Company

When Virginia changed its law to allow breweries to sell their beers without messing with food, a huge "hip hip hooray" went out among not only those already in the business but also those who were considering going pro with their homebrewing passion. Melissa and Aaron Allen seized the opportunity and opened Seven Arrows Brewing Company in Fishersville on New Year's Eve 2014–15. Beers flowed, medals followed, people flocked to the taproom, distribution grew, and the arrows pointed to success. But something was missing—food.

In March 2017, the Allens partnered with Nobos Restaurant to lease space in the building for a separate business arrangement; in May, the brewery opened an event hall. "The partnership with Nobos allows us to offer more to our customer base while keeping our focus on the beer," Aaron noted. "We now are also able to offer on-site catering for folks looking to use our new event hall space."

One relatively new focus for Seven Arrows is wild fermentation. The beer menu during my most recent visit in September 2017 featured three lambics, a "native" version plus cherry and raspberry offerings. I tasted the cherry lambic, which used Virginia hops and was aged in Meritage and Chambourcin wine barrels from Pollak Vineyards west of Charlottesville. Lambics have a great, weird tradition in Belgium (rooftop yeast inoculation? breweries with spiderwebs?) and I found this offering to be appropriately funky and tart, with the cherry notes blending with the wine-barrel oakiness.

On the other side of the spectrum, Seven Arrows offers a medal-winning gateway beer in Skyline Lager. At 4.5 percent ABV and 12 IBUs, it is a light (not "lite") offering that gives non-craft drinkers easy access to a broader range of flavors.

The adventures in barrel-aging and wild fermentation don't betray Aaron's philosophy of brewing. "My thing is that I try to be true to style when I'm making beer," he concluded. "I'm not interested in the crazy, everything-under-the-sun, throw-it-in beer. You can create a huge range of flavors just through your malts and hops." That range includes a black pilsner, a Vienna lager, and, of course, a couple of IPAs (Equinox DIPA weighs in at only 45 IBUs, a low number for that style but there's considerable perceived bitterness).

The Vienna lager, a style that most Virginians associate with Devils Backbone, has taken off. "We recognize that Devils Backbone has come to define the style in the last several years, but our focus has been on and will continue to be on making great true-to-style beer with an emphasis on lager beer," explained Aaron. "We believe that the current market is so 'hop-centric' that making flavorful lager beer brings a bit of balance to Virginia craft beer."

Seven Arrows benefits from the Allens' complementary talents and backgrounds. An Illinois native, Aaron began homebrewing while a student at Michigan State University, where he studied chemical engineering. He met Melissa while he was living in Indiana—she had come to visit her sister, one of his coworkers at Eli Lilly and Company. A job at MillerCoors whetted Aaron's appetite for professional brewing, and in 2010 he earned a diploma in brewing through the Institute of Brewing and Distilling. Melissa, who had studied software engineering at Florida State, earned a master's degree in business administration at James Madison University primarily to take care of the business side of their enterprise.

Adding food to the mix makes sense to them on more

Aaron and Melissa Allen combined talents—his as a chemical engineer, hers as a business school graduate—to run Seven Arrows brewery just outside Waynesboro.

than one level. "It keeps people in the taproom longer and brings in new people," Aaron noted. "It's also more responsible to consume alcohol with food."

The brewery's name and logo borrow from Native American lore. A blessing refers to the creator, the earth, the four directions, and back to the creator. The brewery logo is an eight-point compass—north, east, south and west, plus barley, water, hops, and yeast. Their distribution compass points throughout Virginia, with the exception of a few counties, and into the D.C. area. Production on the fifteen-barrel system was targeted at twelve hundred to fifteen hundred barrels in 2017.

Try this: I confess that it's easy for me to overlook gateway beers. So for all of you newbies out there, ask for a taste of Skyline Lager. It's one small step away from mainstream pilsners. If you want to take another step, order Falls Ridge Vienna Lager, one of the core brands. This style is elegantly malty but with sufficient noble hops and carbonation to keep the palate frisky. The ABV is 5.3 percent; IBUs are 20.

Redbeard, Shenandoah Valley, and More in Staunton

When it comes to producing beverages with a buzz, Jonathan Wright might have the best pedigree in the state. Generations of family farmers going back to the 1670s have included distilled spirits as a byproduct of their agricultural endeavors. "My great-grandfather had a federal distiller's license and sold ethanol to the government as a solvent during World War I—as well as employing a 'one for them, one for me' production method," Wright recalled. "My grandfather picked up the skill but had more of an 'all for me' mind-set. He ran stills in Virginia and North Carolina during and after Prohibition."

Unfortunately, that ancestor fought the law and the law won. Other relatives continued the tradition periodically, but there was a lull until Wright opened **Redbeard Brewing Company** in 2013 in the Wharf District of downtown Staunton. Now the agricultural bent of Wright's business takes a slightly different angle by using local products in some of his brews. The Whipple Creek Harvest Ale, for example, uses freshly picked hops from Whipple Creek Farms in Brownsburg for an IPA with a definite taste of place.

Wright's relatively small 1.5-barrel system allows him to craft the brews himself from recipe development to final release. He keeps seven beers on tap at the Lewis Street site; distribution beyond the taproom is not in his immediate plans. In 2017, he took over ownership of the building, so eventual expansion to a larger system, possibly seven barrels, could figure into Redbeard's future.

His two bestsellers are 221B Brown Ale, a bronze medalist at the 2016 Virginia Craft Brewers Cup competition, and A.M.O.G. Stout, a milk stout aged on whole coffee beans. Wright's creative range extends to an "extra-pale pilsen ale" (not lager) called Two Moons, a fruity rye grisette called Horn of Plenty (celebrating the farmhouse harvest tradition), and a black IPA, also made with rye. The menu during my most recent visit in 2017 featured two other IPAs, including a DIPA named Hype Train dry-hopped with Citra, Mosaic, and Simcoe varietals. "My IPAs are actually kind of sleeper hits at the moment, very well received by the nouveau beer geek types," Wright noted.

As with many small breweries, Redbeard serves as a community center. During my visit, two dozen people in an art class sipped on glasses of beer while an instructor led them in re-creating an emerald-and-pink scene of a swing hanging from a blossoming tree. On Tuesdays, "Some Kind of Jam" open-mic night gives musicians a chance to strum and hum together. More live music, pet-related fund-raisers, and improvisational comedy nights also draw folks to the taproom.

Wright's original vision of his career path didn't include making beer. He had gone to Richmond to study theater at Virginia Commonwealth University, but after receiving his degree and directing two plays, he returned to Staunton in 2010 with his wife, Fara. While he was working at Baja Bean Company on Beverley Street during a previous stint in Staunton in the late 1990s, one of the managers had introduced him to craft brewing. Thus began the revival of the family interest in ardent spirits.

Less than a five-minute walk from Redbeard, you'll find **Shenandoah Valley Brewing Company** at 103 West Beverley Street. The business moved to that site in February 2017 after years on Middlebrook Avenue, starting in 2012 as a homebrew supply store and then adding a tasting room to spotlight the brews of Mike Chapple. The new 2,500-square-foot spot takes advantage of increased foot traffic and has allowed Chapple to expand brewing capacity from 1.5 barrels to a three-barrel system. One thing remains the same—Chapple and his wife, Mary, still emphasize providing "Beers for the People." The taproom features a dozen offerings; look for First Brigade Red IPA (62 IBUs), one of the original recipes developed by Mike ("Chappy" to those who know him). Live music and more keep the place jumping.

Staunton also is the home of **Queen City Brewing**, the city's first brewery since Prohibition and a brew-on-premises site, and **Bedlam Brewing** (see the preface).

Pale Fire Brewing Company

I was early for my meeting with Tim Brady at Pale Fire, so I started to browse. Not on my iPhone, but through the shelves of the library on one wall of the tasting room in Harrisonburg. The titles ranged from *The Rise and Fall of the Third Reich* to *The Lord of the Rings*—perhaps an invitation to read about Sauron while sipping a saison? Brady, founder of Pale Fire, started the library with surplus books from home, in conjunction with a group called Little Free Library (whose motto reads, "Take a book, return a book"). "People are crazy about the books," Brady said.

Same goes for the beers. Since opening in April 2015, Pale Fire has established a reputation for excellent beers, as evidenced by the Great American Beer Festival bronze medal draped atop the bookshelves—that one for Salad Days American Saison (it also won bronze at the 2016 World Beer Cup). A blend of ingredients both traditional (saison yeast) and innovative (malted rye and three American hop varieties) marks Pale Fire's approach to brewing.

"Attention to detail—that's not very glamorous, but that's what makes really good beer, the consistency," Brady explained. "I have a great respect for style and tradition and for the foundation that the rest of the industry is built on." That doesn't limit creativity, though. A collaboration with Adroit Theory in Purcellville took a different look at the Belgian farmhouse turf with a saison called To Hell With Good Intentions, using New Zealand hops, blueberries, Thai basil, and lemon peel.

A native of Arlington, Brady began brewing professionally in 2001 at Calhoun's, a former brewpub in downtown Harrisonburg. A stint on the distribution side with Specialty Beverage added to Brady's knowledge of the beer world, and in 2013 he took advantage of space in a renovated historic icehouse to start Pale Fire. Production in 2017 was about two thousand barrels annually, and the addition of a bottling line was expected to raise the mark to thirty-five hundred barrels with distribution throughout Virginia.

As with the nation in general, Harrisonburg beer lovers show a fondness for hoppy brews, and Brady is on the same wavelength. Pale Fire's Village Green Double IPA, a two-time winner at the Virginia Craft Beer Cup, packs an aromatic punch with six hop varieties; the 100 IBUs satisfy without puckering, thanks to balancing Maris Otter barley malt.

Pale Fire's tasting room—with its library, fireplace, attached deck, three-sided bar, and glass windows looking onto the brewing tanks—creates a space where university professors share pints with family farmers, and where you're just as likely to find middle-agers as millennials

Tim Brady, founder of Pale Fire Brewing Company, renovated a historic icehouse in downtown Harrisonburg for the brewery's site.

enjoying the brews. "I love the way that those factors play together," Brady concluded.

Try this: Brady says it's his favorite, and I give Salad Days a hearty recommendation as well. The rye gives a crispness to the mouthfeel, and the Amarillo, Simcoe, and Cascade hops contribute a grapefruit-peach aroma. Brady even gets a note of bubblegum from the house saison yeast. The farmhouse style in general has broad parameters, and Salad Days is not a lightweight in terms of alcohol content (7 percent ABV). Drinkability is excellent, thanks to the dry finish.

Brothers Craft Brewing

As if it's not enough to deal with the process of brewing flavorful beer, packaging it efficiently and attractively, making sure it gets to market properly, and keeping the taproom bustling and profitable—craft brewers also have nightmares of intellectual property rights tussles to keep them awake at night. Old Ox locked horns with Red Bull about bovine-related names. Strangeways found itself at odds with a homebrew supply store, Strange Brew, in Massachusetts. And Three Brothers in Harrisonburg learned after opening that having the same name as an out-of-state brewery could impact long-term growth.

A quick decision and positive thinking turned what might have been a lemon into more like a lemon radler. "What started as three brothers following a passion has become something far greater than we ever imagined," the brothers posted on Reddit.com in April 2015. "After the brewery opened its doors in December of 2012, we quickly realized that our staff, our customers, and our collaborators have all become family. So why limit the brotherhood to three?"

Brothers Craft Brewing became the new identity, but little else changed in the operation started by Adam, Jason, and Tyler Shifflett. In particular, the quality of the beer remained high. In its first foray into the Great American Beer Festival, Brothers won a bronze with its rum barrel–aged Belgian dubbel. That and six other medals hang in frames on the taproom wall in Harrisonburg.

The tap list on my most recent visit in September 2017 included the four flagships—Lil' Hellion Helles Lager, The Great Outdoors Pale Ale, Hoptimization IPA, and The Admiral on Pineapple IPA. Two collaborations also drew my interest. Long Distance Relationship was a dry-hopped Belgian wit beer made with blueberries, a joint effort with Starr Hill; Rye Hard, a rye IPA, was made with Stone in Richmond. I love the beers' names—Hardy Brothers, a farmhouse ale made with pear and ginger, refers to the Hardy Boys (books I avidly read as a kid); the full name is "The Mystery of the Farmhouse Ale." Rye Hard is "A Good Day to Rye Hard," a must for Bruce Willis fans.

The beer that really put Brothers on the beer aficionado map is Resolute, a Russian imperial stout aged in bourbon barrels. The release each autumn draws flocks of fans and rave reviews for the complexity of this huge beer (13.5 percent ABV). The grain bill, which uses oats with roasted and chocolate malts, blends with the vanillin in the oak barrels to yield oak, chocolate, and espresso notes as well as vanilla and coffee flavors. A review in *All About Beer* magazine by noted beer writer Roger Protz observed, "It's as black as Hades with a cappuccino-colored head and an aroma so complex you could write a book about it."

Producing such beers is the fruit of plans that grew from all three brothers' homebrewing hobby. "Everybody kind of had this idea when they were homebrewing: 'Wouldn't it be cool to do this full time?'" Adam recalled. While stationed in Hampton Roads in the navy, he volunteered at O'Connor Brewing Company in Norfolk and honed his brewing chops. The dream of going pro turned serious when he left the service, and the brothers, who grew up just outside Harrisonburg, assessed their skills. Tyler was a biology major specializing in microbiology; Jason was a business major with sales experience; and Adam was a submarine officer with a background in engineering.

They found a suitable building on North Main Street that once had housed a Coca-Cola bottling plant. The decor features a blend of rustic—repurposed wood panels and huge beams—and modern, with digital TV screens and a plush lounge area with overstuffed furniture. A fifteen-barrel brew house with thirty- and sixty-barrel fermenters allows them to produce about five thousand barrels a year. A recent upgrade to a GEA centrifuge enhances clarity, aroma, and flavor in their beers while increasing brewing yield.

Try this: Resolute is the obvious choice. The taproom offers cellared bottles for on-site consumption only. At the time of my visit, a bottle of Resolute 2016 vintage was going for $32. Coffee Resolute also was available for $35. Otherwise, keep your eyes peeled for the release date in the fall.

Backroom Brewery

As you walk around the jumble of greenhouses, garden plots, hop bines, and hanging plants at Backroom, it would be easy to fantasize that somewhere in the vicinity of Middletown an organic eruption spewed vegetation around the area. But the abundance of growing things is a measure of owner Billie Clifton's green thumb and exuberant spirit rather than a seismic event. The lushness reflects the business's roots as Sunflower Cottage, an herb farm begun in 2005 that continues to produce thousands of potted plants for area patrons and garden centers. Before there was beer flowing from Backroom's taps, Cascade hops were growing on bines that twirl upward in spirals, like leafy fingers reaching for the heavens.

"Our property had previously been a vineyard, and the owner, I guess, lost all the grapes and wanted to sell the property. The vineyard structure was still on the property when we bought it," recalled Clifton, who was CEO of an insurance company before switching careers. She had a eureka moment when the logic of growing another type of herb—hops, the herb of beer—rather than grapes clicked in her brain. The first crop in 2013 was bountiful, and Backroom now hosts an annual hop-picking festival in August that yields more than two hundred pounds of cones destined for the brew kettle. "The smell of the beer being brewed kind of wafts across the lawn. And everybody's invited back in two weeks to drink the beer that we brewed," added Clifton.

The reality of starting a farm brewery did not sprout as readily as Clifton's herbs. The process began before statewide legislation existed, so Clifton worked with Warren County officials to create an enabling ordinance, and Backroom became the state's first farm brewery—on paper—in 2013. (Lickinghole Creek Craft Brewery in Goochland County was brewing in 2013; commercial brewing started at Backroom in early 2014.)

Backroom immediately made an impression with its profuse array of flavors, thanks to Clifton's palate savvy and knowledge of herbs. Taps flowed with Hibiscus Saison, Rosemary Orange Amber Ale, Peppermint Oatmeal Stout, a Belgian singel made with nasturtium and arugula and others. "We've experimented with all kinds of things," Clifton noted.

The Lemon Basil Wheat Beer, however, proved the brewery's mettle, winning bronze in the Best in Show category at the 2016 Virginia Craft Beer Cup and gold in the Herb and Spice Beer category. (Backroom also won gold for The Ferminator, a wee heavy, and its Oatmeal Stout.) "Lemon Basil Wheat Beer was the first beer that we kind of just threw everything behind. This is it. This is the beer that has shown us we can do this," said Clifton. "And that was nothing more than me knowing what flavors go together well and hoping that we could translate that into a wheat beer."

Backroom's taproom has that "make yourself at home" feel, with exposed beam ceilings, comfy chairs, a blackboard showing a hand-scrawled list of eighteen beers on tap, and a menu offering options from chicken wings to bratwurst. A porch and pergola accommodate outdoor quaffing when Mother Nature cooperates, and a leisurely stroll around the grounds yields more than herbs—be sure to check out the mannequins, one of whom has a potted plant for a head. And if you need any more convincing about the endearingly quirky character of Backroom, just ask Clifton about the man who took advantage of the "pets allowed" status by bringing his alligator.

Try this: Lemon Basil Wheat Beer, of course. This takes refreshing to a new place. Clifton says the water at

Backroom is particularly suited to wheat beers, and here the crispness of that grain complements the tang of lemon zest and the spicy aroma of the "holy herb." Alcohol content is low at 4.25 percent ABV; hops add some citrus fragrance but little bitterness (32 IBUs).

Alesatian Brewing Company and More

I was on a mission—in search of Virginia's best IPAs. When the names of several medal-winning breweries were announced at the 2017 Virginia Craft Beer Cup awards ceremony in June, my buddy Jay Burnham and I looked at each other with puzzled expressions. "Ever heard of them?" "No. You?" Among them was Alesatian Brewing Company in Winchester, second-place winner in the competition's most contested category.

I was already familiar with the bronze medalist, Astrognomer IPA from South Street in Charlottesville. But Alesatian's Hop Sneeze and Barrel Oak Farm Taphouse's BOFT IPA were unknowns. So the following Saturday found me on the mall in historic Old Town Winchester, asking for directions to a brewery that drew puzzled expressions from even the locals. Finally, I was steered into Roma Old Town Wood Fired Pizzeria, through side doors, and up a flight of stairs. I had the feeling I was headed toward some speakeasy in Prohibition days.

The space was intimate; I'd read that the capacity was forty-eight people in a tasting room less than a thousand square feet. It felt cozy, thanks to the repurposed wood in the bar area and the cloud of chatter among the two dozen or so people gathered around tables and the bar. A pair of glass windows, etched with the brewery's name, showcased the brewing tanks. A colorful placard advertising Winchester's Hop Blossom Craft Beer Festival displayed a Rosie the Riveter type, sleeve rolled up showing a tattoo of a hop cone, saying, "We Can Do It—With Beer."

I struck up a conversation with Bryan Bowser, an assistant brewer who was helping behind the bar. I told him of my mission, and he cheerfully filled me in on details of Hop Sneeze. Centennial, Galaxy, and Mosaic hops go into the brew, both in the boil and in the dry-hopping process. Pils malt makes up the backbone of the grain bill, and West Coast ale yeast from Bright Labs handles fermentation. At 80 IBUs and 7 percent ABV, it is not a beer to take lightly (or sneeze at). Nor is it a chore to drink. The citrus aroma all but jumped out of the glass, giving notes of tropical fruit. The flavor was equally fruity and well-balanced by the malt with a dry finish that, to quote Bowser, "tiptoes off the palate like a summer breeze." The silver medal seemed well-deserved.

The recipe belongs to head brewer Paul Froeschle, but Alesatian is the child of Caleb Ritenour. He grew up in the restaurant business and managed the pizza place below before launching the brewpub. A graduate of the aerospace program at the University of Virginia, he developed a taste for flavorful beer while a member of UVA's Jefferson Brewing Society. "It was more of a hobby then, and then it became a business," he recalled.

The tap menu on my visit sported nine beers, ranging from 5th Dimension Red Raspberry Berliner Weisse to Loka Koko Stout (made with wood-fired toasted coconut). Alesatian also has done a couple of collaborations I wish had been available. Say Son of a Funk, made with Lost Rhino, is a saison that connects with the brewery's heritage of farmhouse brews in the Alsace-Lorraine region of France, the ancestral home of the Ritenour family.

If time had allowed, I would have explored other Winchester breweries, including Escutcheon Brewing Company and Winchester Brew Works. But I was on a mission. The search for Virginia's best IPA of 2017 took me to Barrel Oak Winery, a sprawling complex on a hill near Delaplane. Finding the taproom was almost as challenging as locating Alesatian; I searched through a warren of wine spaces before coming to the beer nook. A colorful collection of vintage cans lined the wall above the taps, and the BOFT IPA (60 IBUs, 6.8 percent ABV) was in a flight of four that included a milk stout, a dubbel, and a Belgian-style golden strong ale brewed with Sichuan peppercorns and lemongrass. I struck up a text conversation with Jay Bergantim, the brewer, to get details about the IPA. "I hopped this beer with mostly Columbus and Mosaic; I like less juicy fruit and more citrus," his message read. He used about a pound of hops per barrel for dry-hopping, and "at least a portion of the hops are homegrown in each batch." I told him I enjoyed the beer and congratulated him on winning gold at the Virginia Craft Beer Cup. "It was a shock to win in that category," he concluded.

Try this: Hop Sneeze and BOFT IPA. And Astrognomer. Enough said.

CHAPTER 13

Looking Around, Looking Ahead

I was visiting Old Trade Brewery, a farm brewery near Brandy Station, when I struck up a conversation with a couple sitting outside at a table. They were from Boulder, Colorado, and they were visiting a bunch of Virginia breweries. They liked what they'd tasted, but they asked, "Why do so many breweries have so many different beers? Why can't the breweries focus on one particular thing and have a niche, like making all-Belgian beers?"

It was an interesting comment, and one with a flip side. I've always felt Virginia's brewing strength is in its diversity—not only in the creative breadth as a whole but also in the very point that the Coloradans faulted. Nearly every brewery you visit in Virginia offers an interesting mix of styles and interpretations. It's not uncommon to find a Belgian-style saison next to a West Coast IPA next to an Irish stout next to a German lager, even in small operations. Old Trade itself offers on a given day a blackberry Berliner weisse, a saison, two types of porters, an American pale ale, and more.

So it is as we stand in the glow of craft's golden age—more breweries than ever, more creativity than ever, more diversity than ever. We've looked at the past and we've sampled the present. What lies ahead? Virginia's explosive growth over the past five years has yet to peak in terms of numbers, but the crystal ball flickers with hints of things to come.

Nationally, two trends have taken shape. First, beer is

losing market share to wine and spirits. Second, competition in the retail sector is tight. Securing a facing in a grocery store or a tap in a restaurant is no longer taken for granted. Particularly in the regional brewery sector, among breweries producing fifteen thousand barrels a year and more, growth is hard to come by. The Brewers Association notes in its statistics that microbreweries—the ones producing less than fifteen thousand barrels annually—have kept the tide rising in terms of numbers and creating local destinations for craft beer lovers. As I noted in the Mustang Sally profile in chapter 5, Bart Watson, chief economist for the association, concluded that "the average brewer is getting smaller, and growth is more diffuse within the craft category, with producers at the tail helping to drive growth for the overall segment."

Dave Gott, vice president of operations at Legend Brewing Company, echoed those thoughts: "The market, from a distribution point of view, is saturated. Small breweries focused on in-house sales will probably be the model that is most prominent over the next few years." Some brewery owners are addressing concerns about getting their beer to market by forming separate, small distribution companies. Reverie in Richmond is a companion operation to The Veil; Saint X in Bedford, to Beale's; and Central Virginia Distributing in Charlottesville, to Three Notch'd.

Most brewers I've talked with agree, though, that the state's growth is not at its peak. In 2016, Virginia's per capita number of breweries ranked twentieth in the nation at 2.7 breweries per 100,000 adults aged twenty-one and older (with 164 breweries that year). At number one, Vermont had 10.8 breweries per capita (with only 50 breweries); Colorado had 8.4 breweries per capita (with 334 breweries); Oregon had 8.1 breweries per capita (with 243 breweries); and Washington State had 6.3 breweries per capita (with 334 breweries).

"I believe that we are just at the beginning of the development of Virginia's craft beer industry," observed Bill Butcher, founder and owner of Port City Brewing Company. "Craft beer is still gaining momentum in Virginia, and when you look at other states that have more established craft beer cultures, it is evident that we have great potential to continue this momentum."

During his term in office, Governor Terry McAuliffe played a key role in growing the beer culture, and local officials are realizing the potential in nurturing small businesses that have a habit of turning old buildings and vacant warehouses into revenue-producing job centers. "This is something that we'd like to see grow in Fairfax County. . . . It's an industry that is popular," said county supervisor Sharon Bulova regarding a change in the zoning code to minimize red tape for breweries.

Not all arms are open. Clifton residents complained about the traffic that a proposed farm brewery called Loudmouth would bring, and the proposal cratered. B Chord, another proposed farm brewery in Loudoun County, ran into similar opposition and was initially denied a license by the Virginia ABC board; undeterred, they went to Plan B, a merger with Corcoran Brewing Company, and opened in fall 2017.

Some small brewers have felt the squeeze of increased competition. "There's no room to grow anymore," concluded Chris Burcher, cofounder of Wolf Hills Brewing Company in Abingdon. His perspective is shaped by being in a rural region without the traffic generated by an urban population core. Jake Endres of Crooked Run Brewing expressed similar concerns about non-taproom sales in suburban Loudoun County when he observed, "It's been extremely difficult to sell beer. I think a lot of people think that local beer will sell itself, but that really is not the case." On the other hand, it's easy to rattle off breweries that are currently undergoing or have just completed expansion projects: Smartmouth, Big Lick, Hardywood Park, Legend,

Three Notch'd, Lickinghole Creek, Port City, Steam Bell, Starr Hill, and more.

Virginia also has become ground zero for a debate, often heated, about the craft beer business. When Devils Backbone Brewing Company was acquired by Anheuser-Busch InBev in 2016, the deal put the Virginia brewery outside the Brewers Association's definition of what constitutes a craft brewery (see chapter 3). Craft brewers are by definition small, local, and independent; breweries under the wing of the mega-producers have advantages in distribution and access to raw materials. Neither the Virginia Craft Brewers Guild nor the Brewers Association counts Devils Backbone among its members (some implications of this omission are discussed in chapter 10).

It's easy to understand both Devils Backbone's decision to grow its business through acquisition and the loss that Virginia's craft beer–loving community feels for its largest homegrown brewery. Emotions revolve around the sense of local pride that small entrepreneurs in general and brewers in particular feel toward their home turf. If you look at the number of breweries using Virginia farm products, the number of collaborations among breweries, and the sense of community emanating from those in the beer business, it becomes clear that all involved feel there is something special about what's going on. Four major West Coast breweries have seen it and remarked about it.

"Virginia is gaining recognition nationally as a growing force in craft beer," Port City's Butcher commented. "If you look at the awards that Virginia's small and independent breweries are winning, it is evident that Virginia will be known as a quality leader in craft beer."

Awards can be a fickle measure of anything, however. At the 2017 Great American Beer Festival, only four Virginia breweries won medals (one each)—Wild Wolf, Ocelot, Studio Brew, and Benchtop. The previous year, Virginia won fourteen, matching its highest mark ever at the festival.

I like what Bill Spence of Hampton's St. George Brewing Company said about the bigger picture when we chatted at the 2017 Virginia Craft Beer Cup: "Look at where we've gone in the last ten years, particularly when you look at the West Coast [and] the number of major breweries that have made an East Coast base in North Carolina and Virginia. That's saying something for our two states that we are now becoming the nexus of beer on the East Coast."

Here's my take: The craft beer industry is evolving from an explosive sector to a maturing industry. National annual growth rates by volume have gone from 18 percent in 2014 to 13 percent in 2015 to 6 percent in 2016. Over the same period, market share by volume has gone from 11 percent to 12.3 percent. Some of the zip is tapering off, and some bumps, wrinkles, detours, and pains are inevitable. Green Flash's closing in Virginia Beach and Deschutes' pause in Roanoke in 2018 bear witness to that. I firmly believe, however, that we have undergone a cultural shift. Brewery tasting rooms have become community destinations with a broad demographic appeal and activities that go from bingo to yoga to running clubs to charity events to live music to burlesque to places where you can simply chill with friends and have a fresh, flavorful beer. And there's the real bottom line: The nation has a whole new taste for craft beer, and that's not going anywhere anytime soon. In Virginia, we can take pride in our beer history, our brewing diversity, and the spirit that infuses our common wealth.

APPENDIX A

Beyond the Brew House

The beer world extends beyond kettles, kegs, tanks, and taprooms, so here's a partial list of things to know, do, and share.

Virginia Beer FAQs

How many breweries are there in Virginia?

On August 19, 2017, Brett Vassey, head of the Virginia Manufacturers Association, announced that Virginia had 213 breweries in operation and 30 in planning, giving it the most breweries in the Southeast.

What is the economic impact of craft brewing on Virginia?

According to the Brewers Association, the economic impact on Virginia in 2016 (when the association counted 164 breweries in the state) totaled $1.37 billion. That included 10,260 full-time equivalent jobs. The average wage of someone working in craft brewing in the state was $47,373. Virginia ranked thirteenth in the country in the number of breweries and in breweries per capita (2.7 per 100,000 adults aged twenty-one and older).

When is Virginia Craft Beer Month?

The celebration usually is in August. A highlight of the month is the Virginia Craft Brewers Fest, which was held at IX Art Park in Charlottesville in 2017.

What is Virginia's largest homegrown craft brewery?

Starr Hill produced about twenty-eight thousand barrels in 2016, making it the state's top craft brewery. Devils Backbone was the state's craft leader until it was acquired by Anheuser-Busch InBev in 2016.

Why is Devils Backbone no longer considered a craft brewer?

A craft brewery, as defined by the Brewers Association in Colorado, must be less than 25 percent owned or controlled by an alcohol industry member that is not itself a craft brewer. Devils Backbone's acquisition by Anheuser-Busch InBev made it fall outside that definition.

*Why are the MillerCoors plant in Elkton
and the Anheuser-Busch facility in
Williamsburg not considered craft breweries?*

Another part of the Brewers Association's definition of what constitutes a craft brewery is that it cannot produce more than six million barrels annually. The Elkton facility alone can produce up to eight million barrels annually, according to the MillerCoors website.

What is the Virginia Craft Brewers Guild?

The guild, which is a subsidiary of the Virginia Manufacturers Association, defines itself as "a coalition of independent, small, commercial breweries dedicated to growing the craft beer industry in the Commonwealth." One of its major functions is to work with state officials and elected leaders on legislation to encourage craft beer's growth.

Beer Festivals and Events

Arctoberfest: held in Harrisonburg in September
    https://www.facebook.com/events/343537926103918/
Beer, Bourbon, & BBQ Leesburg; held in Leesburg usually in October
    http://www.beerandbourbon.com/leesburg/show-info
Blacksburg Brew Do; held in Blacksburg usually in October
    https://www.blacksburgbrewdo.com
Front Royal Brew & Blues Festival; held in Front Royal usually in
    September
    https://www.facebook.com/frontroyalbrewblues
Know Good Beer & Music Festival; held in Charlottesville twice
    annually (January and May previously)
    http://www.knowgoodbeer.com
Microfestivus; held in Roanoke usually in August
    https://microfestivus.squaresociety.org
Northern Virginia Brewfest; held in Centreville in October
    http://www.novabrewfest.com
Off the Rails Craft Beer Festival; held in Ashland usually in
    September
    http://hanoverarts.org/off-the-rails-craft-beer-festival/
Old Town Okoberfest; held in Winchester usually in October
    http://oldtownwinchesterva.com/events/major-events
    /oktoberfest/
Richmond Oktoberfest; held in Richmond usually in October
    http://www.richmondoktoberfestinc.com/ricoktober.shtml

Rockbridge Beer and Wine Festival; held in Lexington usually in
September
http://www.lexrockchamber.com/?page_id=39
757 Battle of the Beers; held in Virginia Beach in September
http://www.757battleofthebeers.com
Thomas Jefferson Craft Beer Tasting; held at Poplar Forest in Bedford
County in April
https://www.poplarforest.org/event/thomas-jefferson-craft-beer
-tasting-2017/
Virginia Beach Craft Beer Festival; held usually in October
https://www.beachstreetusa.com/festivals/virginia-beach-craft
-beer-festival
Virginia Beer Festival; held in Norfolk usually in May
http://festevents.org/events/2016-season-events/vabeerfest/
Virginia Beer and Wine Festival; held in Daleville usually in June
http://www.vabeerandwinefestival.com
Virginia Craft Brewers Fest; held in Charlottesville as part of Virginia
Craft Beer Month at IX Art Park in August
http://vacraftbrewersfest.com
Virginia Historical Society BrewHaHa; held in Richmond in August
https://www.virginiahistory.org/events
Whistle Belly; held in Williamsburg in August
http://www.whistlebelly.com/

Beer Trails

Some of these trails and their websites are in progress; a good general
reference is the Virginia Is For Lovers site, https://www.virginia.org
/beertrails/.

Beltway Beer Trail; twenty-five breweries in Fairfax, Manassas,
Alexandria, Falls Church, Arlington, and more
http://beltwaybeertrail.com
Blue Ridge Beerway; nine breweries in Roanoke, Salem, Vinton, and
beyond
https://www.visitroanokeva.com/things-to-do/breweries/beerway/
Brew Ridge Trail; six breweries in Charlottesville and neighboring
counties
http://brewridgetrail.com
Coastal Virginia Beer Trail; twenty-four breweries in Williamsburg,
Norfolk, Hampton, Virginia Beach, and neighboring areas
http://covabeertrail.com

Grapes and Grain Trail; five breweries plus wineries and a distillery in
the Fredericksburg area
https://www.grapesandgraintrail.com
Helltown Beer Trail; ten breweries around Front Royal
http://helltownbeertrail.com
Historic Hops Beer Trail; ten breweries in Fredericksburg and
Spotsylvania County
http://historichopsbeertrail.com
LoCo Ale Trail; twenty-one breweries in Loudoun County
https://www.visitloudoun.org/things-to-do/loco-ale-trail
/breweries/
Nelson 151 Trail; breweries along state Route 151 in Nelson County
http://nelson151.com
Red, White, and Brew Trail; breweries, cideries, and vineyards in
Nelson County
https://www.virginia.org/listings/SuggestedItinerary
/RedWhiteandBrewTrail/
Richmond Beer Trail; nearly thirty breweries in Richmond and
adjoining counties
https://www.visitrichmondva.com/drink/richmond-beer-trail/
Seminole Beer Trail; nine breweries along U.S. 29 between
Charlottesville and Northern Virginia
http://seminolebeertrail.com
Shenandoah Beerwerks Trail; thirteen breweries in Waynesboro,
Staunton, Harrisonburg, Lexington, and Natural Bridge
http://beerwerkstrail.com
Shenandoah Spirits Trail; nine breweries plus wineries and distilleries
in Harrisonburg, Winchester, Woodstock, and beyond
https://www.shenandoahspiritstrail.com
Southwest Virginia Mountain Brew Trail; nineteen breweries (some in
planning) in Bristol, Abingdon, Blacksburg, and beyond
https://mountainbrewtrail.com
Steins, Vines, and Moonshine Trail; thirteen breweries plus wineries
and distilleries in Manassas, Woodbridge, and Prince William
County
https://www.steinsvinesandmoonshine.com
Virginia Beer Trail; maps of regions around the state
www.vabeertrail.net
Virginia 58 Beer Trail; twelve breweries in Abingdon, Danville, Bristol,
and beyond
http://va58beertrail.com

Women's Beer Groups

Barley's Angels—Coastal Virginia Chapter; local chapter in Tidewater
of an international group
http://barleysangels.org/coastalvirginia/
Brew Betties; meetup group based in Charlottesville
https://www.meetup.com/BrewBetties/
River City Beer Betties; meetup group based in Richmond
https://www.facebook.com/rvabeerbetties/

Social Media Groups

Some of these groups are closed and require approval to join.

Arts & Craft Beer
https://www.facebook.com/Arts-Craft-Beer-1822767897968023/
Charlottesville Beer Elite
https://www.facebook.com/search/top/?q=charlottesville%20beer
%20elite
Fans of Virginia Craft Breweries
https://www.facebook.com/groups/FansofVACB/
Harrisonburg Beer Elite
https://www.facebook.com/groups/harrisonburgbeerelite/
Loudoun Craft Beer
https://www.facebook.com/LoudounCraftBeer/
Norfolk Loves Craft Beer
https://www.facebook.com/norfolklovescraftbeer/
Nova Beer Friends
https://www.facebook.com/groups/450900251688872/
Nova Beer Slobs
https://www.facebook.com/groups/569405676539942/about/
RBE Richmond Beer Elite
https://www.facebook.com/groups/richmond.beer.elite/
Richmond Beer Experience
https://www.facebook.com/groups/444851902294303/
Richmond Beer Lovers
https://www.facebook.com/RVABeerLovers/
Roanoke Craft Beer Drinkers
https://www.facebook.com/groups/RoanokeDrinkersOfCraftBeer/
SOVA Beer Elite
https://www.facebook.com/groups/578068079002552/
Virginia Craft Beer Society
https://www.facebook.com/VirginiaCraftBeerSociety/

Brewery Tour Services

Brew Ridge Tours; based in Lynchburg
   https://www.virginia.org/listings/Tours/BrewRidgeToursLLC/
Charlottesville Brew Tour; run by Blue Ridge Wine Excursions, serves
   the Brew Ridge Trail and beyond
   http://www.blueridgebrewexcursions.com/specialty-charlottesville
   -brew-tour-packages/
Cork and Keg Tours; based in Loudoun County
   https://www.corkandkegtours.com
Cville Hop On Tours; includes distilleries, cideries and vineyards in
   addition to area breweries
   http://cvillehopontours.com
Drink Richmond; includes distilleries and cideries
   https://drinkrichmond.com
FXBG Brewery Tours; based in Fredericksburg
   https://www.fxbgbrewerytours.com
Roanoke Craft Beer Tours; targets four local breweries per outing
   https://www.visitroanokeva.com/listings/roanoke-craft-beer-tours
   /7851/
Taste Virginia Tours; includes customized tours of Tidewater,
   Peninsula, Norfolk, and Virginia Beach breweries
   http://www.tastevirginia.com
Virginia Brewery Tours; based in Richmond, serving regions of the
   state.
   http://www.virginiabrewerytours.com

Homebrewers Groups

Blue Ridge Brewers Association; based in Luray
   http://blueridgebrewers.blogspot.com
Brewers United for Real Potables (BURP); based in the D.C. area
   https://www.burp.org
Charlottesville Area Masters of Real Ale (CAMRA)
   http://www.cvillebrewing.com
Colonial Ale Smiths & Keggers (CASK); based in Hampton Roads and
   Williamsburg
   http://www.colonialalesmiths.org
Culpeper Brewing Society
   https://www.facebook.com/groups/1693869477555629/about/
GRIST Homebrew Club; based in Arlington
   https://www.facebook.com/groups/GRISTHomebrewClub/

Hampton Roads Brewing & Tasting Society
    http://hrbts.org
Harrisonburg Homebrewers
    https://www.facebook.com/groups/HburgHomebrew/about/
Hill City Homebrewers; based in Lynchburg
    http://hillcityhomebrewers.weebly.com
Homebrewers of Western Loudoun (HOWL)
    http://www.howlbrew.org
James River Homebrewers Club; based in Richmond
    http://jamesriverhbc.org
Mentoring Advanced Standards of Homebrewing (M.A.S.H.); based in
    Chesterfield County
    https://www.mashrva.com
Overmountain Brewers; based in Abingdon
    https://www.facebook.com/Overmountain-Brewers
    -141046739330624/
Prince William Brewers Guild
    http://www.pwbg.org
Seven City Brewers Homebrew Club; based in Hampton Roads
    https://www.sevencitybrewers.com
Shenandoah Valley Homebrewers Guild; based in Winchester
    http://shenbrew.org
Smithfield Hop and Malt Society (HAMS) Brew Club
    http://smithfieldhams.wixsite.com/hams
Southern Virginia Brewers' Collective; based in Mecklenburg County
    http://sovabrewco.com/index.php
Stafford Brewers Club; based in Stafford County
    http://www.staffordbrewersclub.com
Star City Brewers Guild; based in Roanoke
    http://www.starcitybrewers.org
Train Wreck Brewers; based in Danville
    https://www.facebook.com/trainwreckbrewers/

Beer Groups, Sites, Events

Beeristoric Tour; bus tour of historic sites held in Richmond each fall
    https://www.facebook.com/Beeristoricrva/
Blue and Gray Show; attracts breweriana collectors from around the
    country, held in February
    http://bluegrayshow.com
Richbrau Chapter of the Brewery Collectibles Club of America; based in
    Richmond
    http://www.bcca.com/chapters/united-states-chapters/richbrau-79/

Virginia Beer Museum; in Front Royal, includes historical displays and
serves beer on tap
https://www.facebook.com/VABeerMuseum/

Virginia Beer Publications

Virginia Craft Beer magazine; publishes bimonthly
www.virginiacraftbeer.com
Virginia Craft Brews magazine; publishes quarterly
http://virginiacraftbrews.com
Mid-Atlantic Brewing News; publishes bimonthly
http://www.brewingnews.com/mid-atlantic/

Virginia Beer Distributors

Al Pugh Distributing Company; based in Warsaw. Carries Anheuser-
Busch InBev domestic brands, imported beer brands, ciders,
wines, and national and Virginia craft beer brands. https://www
.alpughdistributingco.com

Balearic Beverage Distributors; based in Lorton. U.S. importer for Hijos
de Rivera brands, including Estrella Galicia beers, Maeloc Hard
Cider, and Ponte Da Boga Wines. https://www.facebook.com/pages
/Balearic-Beverage-Distributors/122671614456865

Blue Ridge Beverage; based in Salem with five offices in Central,
Western, and Southwestern Virginia. Carries MillerCoors domestic
brands, imported beer brands, ciders, wines, and national and
Virginia craft beer brands. http://www.blueridgebeverage.com
/beverages/beers-and-ciders/

Brown Distributing; Virginia branch based in Richmond. Carries
Anheuser-Busch InBev domestic brands, imported beer brands,
ciders, wines, and national and Virginia craft beer brands. http://
www.brown.com/virginia

Carey Wholesale Distribution; based in Nelsonia. Carries MillerCoors
domestic brands, imported beer brands, ciders, and national and
Virginia craft beer brands. https://www.facebook.com/Carey
-Wholesale-Inc-1671195719811895/

Central Virginia Distributing; based in Charlottesville. Carries Three
Notch'd Brewing Company and Blue Toad Cider brands. https://
www.facebook.com/pages/Central-Virginia-Distributing-for-Three
-Notchd-Brewery/198660890334981

Chesbay Distributing Company; based in Chesapeake. Carries
MillerCoors domestic brands, imported beer brands, ciders,

and national and Virginia craft beer brands. http://www
.chesbaydistributing.com

Danville Distributing Company; based in Danville. Carries Anheuser-
Busch InBev domestic brands, imported beer brands, ciders, and
national and Virginia craft beer brands. https://www.facebook.com
/pages/Danville-Distributing-Company/127281920630410

Dixie Beverage Company; based in Winchester. Carries national
domestic beer brands, ciders, wines, and national and Virginia craft
beer brands. http://www.dixiebeverage.com

Ferment Nation; based in Fairfax. Carries Virginia and regional craft
beer brands, including Caboose, James River, Spencer Devon, and
Vanish beer brands. http://www.ferment-nation.com

Hoffman Beverage; based in Chesapeake. Carries Anheuser-
Busch InBev domestic brands, imported beer brands, ciders,
and national and Virginia craft beer brands. http://www
.hoffmanbeverage.com/

Hop and Wine Beverage; based in Sterling. Carries ciders, mead,
imported beer brands and Virginia, regional, and national craft beer
brands. http://www.hopandwine.com

J. F. Fick Inc.; based in Fredericksburg. Acquired by Virginia Eagle in
November 2017. Carries Anheuser-Busch InBev domestic brands,
imported brands, ciders, and national and Virginia craft beer
brands. http://www.vaeagle.com/news/virginia-eagle-expands
-distribution-footprint-with-acquisition-of-j-f-fick/

Lawrence Distributing Company; based in Danville. Carries imported
and domestic beer brands and craft beer brands. http://www
.lawrencedistributing.net

Loveland Distributing Company; based in Richmond. Carries
MillerCoors domestic brands, imported beer brands, ciders, and
national and Virginia craft beer brands. http://www.lovelandinc.com

Monarch Distribution; based in Round Hill. Carries local craft beer
brands including Adroit Theory, Aslin, and BadWolf brands. http://
www.monarchdistribution.com

M Price Distributing Company; based in Hampton. Carries Anheuser-
Busch InBev domestic brands and imported brands. http://www
.mpriceco.com/

P. A. Short Distributing Company; based in Hollins. Carries Anheuser-
Busch InBev domestic brands, imported brands, ciders, and
national and Virginia craft beer brands. http://www.pashort.com

Pecht Distributors; based in Lawrenceville. Carries Anheuser-Busch
InBev domestic brands, imported brands, ciders, and national and

Virginia craft beer brands. https://www.facebook.com/pages/Pecht
-Distributors/165457363480363

Premium Distributors of Virginia; based in Chantilly. Carries
MillerCoors domestic brands, imported beer brands,
and national and Virginia craft beer brands. http://www
.premiumdistributorsofva.com

Pretty Ugly Distribution; based in Chesapeake. Carries local craft
brands including from Big Ugly, MoMac, Oozlefinch, Benchtop, and
Rip Rap breweries. https://www.facebook.com/pg/prettyuglydistro
/about/

Republic National Distributing Company; Virginia branch based in
Ashland. Carries imported and domestic beer brands. http://www
.rndc-usa.com

Reverie; based in Richmond. Carries a selection of national and
Virginia craft beers, including from The Veil, Ocelot, The Answer,
and Commonwealth breweries. https://www.facebook.com
/reveriedistribution

Saint X Distribution; based in Bedford. Carries Beale's Beer brands
(other brands anticipated). https://www.saintxva.com

Specialty Beverage; based in Sandston. Carries ciders, imported beer
brands, and national and Virginia craft beer brands. https://www
.specialtybevva.com/

Tri-Cities Beverage Corporation; based in Newport News. Carries
national domestic and imported brands and national Virginia craft
beer brands. http://www.tricitiesbeverage.com

Valley Distributing Corporation; based in Salem. Carries MillerCoors
domestic brands, imported beer brands, ciders, and national and
Virginia craft beer brands. http://valleydist.net

Virginia Eagle; based in Lynchburg with six office locations around the
state. Carries Anheuser-Busch InBev domestic brands, imported
brands, cideries, and a range of Virginia and national craft
breweries. http://www.vaeagle.com/our-beverages/?brand=craft#

Virginia Imports Ltd.; based in Springfield. Carries imported and
national craft beer brands. http://virginiaimports.net

Walling Distributing Company; based in Bristol. Carries Anheuser-
Busch InBev domestic brands, imported brands, ciders, and national
and Virginia craft beer brands. http://wallingdistributing.com/

Wendell Distributing Company; based in Cape Charles. Carries
Anheuser-Busch InBev domestic brands, imported brands, ciders,
and national and Virginia craft beer brands. https://www.facebook
.com/WendellDistributing/

APPENDIX B

List of Virginia Breweries by Region

Inner Northern Virginia

Aslin Beer Company
Andrew Kelley, Kai Leszkowicz, and Richard Thompson, founders
257 Sunset Park Drive, Herndon, VA 20170 • (703) 787-5766
www.aslinbeer.com • @Aslin_BeerCo

BadWolf Brewing Company
Jeremy and Sarah Meyers, founders
9776 Center Street, Manassas, VA 20110 • (571) 208-1064
www.badwolfbrewingcompany.com • @BadWolfBrewingC

Caboose Brewing Company
Matt Greer and Tim McLaughlin, founders
520 Mill Street NE, Vienna, VA 22180 • (703) 865-8580
www.caboosebrewing.com • @CabooseBrewing

Fair Winds Brewing Company
Casey Jones and Charlie Buettner, founders
7000 Newington Road, Suites K&L, Lorton, VA 22079 • (703) 372-2001
www.fairwindsbrewing.com • @FairWindsBrew

Forge Brew Works
Kerri and Matt Rose, founders
8532 Terminal Road, Suite L, Lorton, VA 22079 • (703) 372-2979
www.forgebrewworks.com • @ForgeBrewWorks

Gordon Biersch Brewery Restaurant (McLean; international brewpub chain)
7861 Tysons Corner Center, McLean, VA 22102 • (703) 388-5454
http://gordonbiersch.com/locations/mclean?action=view • @Gordon
  _Biersch

Heritage Brewing Company

Ryan and Sean Arroyo, founders
9436 Center Point Lane, Manassas, VA 20110 • (571) 208-1355
Heritage Brewing Company Market Common Brewpub and Roastery
1300–1398 N. Fillmore Street, Arlington, VA 22201 • (571) 319-0024
www.heritagebrewing.com • @HeritageBrews

Honor Brewing Company

Allen Cage, Dave Keuhner, and Sean Meyer, founders
14004A Willard Road, Chantilly, VA 20151 • (703) 596-1567
www.honorbrewing.com • @HonorBeer

Hops Grill & Brewery (chain restaurant)

3625 Jefferson Davis Highway, Alexandria, VA 22305 • (703) 837-9107
www.hopsgrill.com

Lake Anne Brew House

Jason and Melissa Romano, founders
11424 Washington Plaza West, Reston, VA 20190 • (571) 758-2739
www.lakeannebrewhouse.com • @lakeannebrew

Mad Fox Brewing Company

Bill and Beth Madden, Rick Garvin, and Randy Barnette, founders
444 West Broad Street, Suite 1, Falls Church, VA 22046 • (703) 942-6840
www.madfoxbrewing.com • @MadFoxBrewing

Mustang Sally Brewing Company

Sean Hunt, founder
14140 Parke Long Court A–C, Chantilly, VA 20151 • (703) 378-7450
www.msbrewing.com • @msbrewing

New District Brewing Company

Mike Katrivanos and family, founders
2709 South Oakland Street, Arlington, VA 22206 • (703) 888-5820
www.newdistrictbrewing.com • @NewDistrictBrew

Ono Brewing Company

Cyndi and Scott Hoffman, founders
4520 Daly Drive, Suite 102, Chantilly, VA 20151 • (571) 409-6662
www.onobrewco.com • @OnoBrewCo

Port City Brewing Company
Bill and Karen Butcher, founders
3950 Wheeler Avenue, Alexandria, VA 22304 • (703) 797-2739
www.portcitybrewing.com • @PortCityBrew

Portner Brewhouse
Catherine and Margaret Portner, founders
5770 Dow Avenue, Alexandria, VA 22304 • (571) 312-0243
www.portnerbrewhouse.com • @PortnerBrew

Sweetwater Tavern (Centreville)
14250 Sweetwater Lane, Centreville, VA 20121 • (703) 449-1100
http://www.greatamericanrestaurants.com/sweetwater/centreville/
Sweetwater Tavern (Merrifield)
3066 Gate House Plaza, Falls Church, VA 22042 • (703) 645-8100
www.greatamericanrestaurants.com/sweetwater/merrifield/

2Silos Brewing Company
Villagio Hospitality Group
9925 Discovery Boulevard, Manassas, VA 20109 • (703) 420-2264
www.2silosbrewing.com • @2SilosBrewingCo

Loudoun County

Adroit Theory Brewing Company
Mark and Nina Osborne, founders
404 Browning Court, Unit C, Purcellville, VA 20132 • (703) 722-3144
www.adroit-theory.com • @AdroitTheory

Barnhouse Brewery
Roger and Christine Knoell, founders
43271 Spinks Ferry Road, Leesburg, VA 20176 • (703) 675-8480
www.barnhousebrewery.com • @BrnhouseBrewery

B Chord Brewing Company
Marty Dougherty, founder
34266 Williams Gap Road, Round Hill, VA 20142
www.facebook.com/bchordbrewing

Belly Love Brewing Company
Tolga and Katie Baki, founders
725 East Main Street, Purcellville, VA 20132 • (540) 441-3159
www.bellylovebrewing.com • @BellyLoveBeer

Beltway Brewing Company

Sten Sellier, founder

22620 Davis Drive, Suite 110, Sterling, VA 20164 • (571) 989-BREW

www.beltwaybrewco.com • @BeltwayBrewCo

Black Hoof Brewing Company

Bill and Nikki Haase, founders

11 South King Street, Leesburg, VA 20175 • (571) 707-8014

www.blackhoofbrewing.com • @BlackHoofBeer

Black Walnut Brewery

Patrick Wilt, founder

212 South King Street, Leesburg, VA 20175 • (703) 771-9474

www.facebook.com/blackwalnutbrewery • @BlackWalnutBrew

Crooked Run Brewing

Jake Endres and Lee Rogan, founders

205 Harrison Street SE, Leesburg, VA 20175 • (571) 918-4446

www.crookedrunbrewing.com • @CrookedRunBrew

Crooked Run Central: 22455 Davis Drive, Suite 120, Sterling, VA 20164 •
    (571) 375-2652

Dirt Farm Brewing

Janell and Bruce Zurschmeide, founders

18701 Foggy Bottom Road, Bluemont, VA 20135 • (540) 554-2337

www.dirtfarmbrewing.com • @DirtFarmBrewing

Dog Money Restaurant & Brewery

Dean Lake, founder

50 Catoctin Circle NE, Leesburg, VA 20176 • (703) 687-3852

www.dogmoneyllc.com

Jack's Run Brewing Company

Al Bosco and Eric Mathewsom, founders

108 North 21st Street, Purcellville, VA 20132 • (540) 441-3382

www.jacksrunbrewing.com • @JacksRunBrewing

Lost Rhino Brewing Company

Favio Garcia and Matt Hagerman, founders

21730 Red Rum Drive, Suite 142, Ashburn, VA 20147 • (571) 291-
    2083

www.lostrhino.com • @LostRhino

Lost Rhino Retreat: 22885 Brambleton Plaza, Suite 100, Ashburn, VA
20148 • (703) 327-0311
www.lostrhinoretreat.com

Loudoun Brewing Company
Patrick and Alanna Steffens, founders
310 East Market Street, Leesburg, VA 20176 • (571) 223-6097
www.loudounbrewing.com • @loudounbrewing

MacDowell's Brew Kitchen
Gordon MacDowell and Nils Schnibbe, founders
202-B Harrison Street SE, Leesburg, VA 20175 • (703) 777-2739
http://macdowellsbrewkitchen.com/ • @BrewKitchen

Ocelot Brewing Company
Adrien Widman, Sebastian Widman, and Erik Zaber, founders
23600 Overland Drive, No. 180, Dulles, VA 20166 • (703) 665-2146
www.ocelotbrewing.com • @OcelotBrewing

Old Ox Brewery
Chris, Kristin, Mary Ann, and Graham Burns, founders
44652 Guilford Drive, Unit 114, Ashburn, VA 20147 • (703) 729-8375
www.oldoxbrewery.com • @OldOxBrewery

Old 690 Brewing Company
Darren and Tammy Gryniuk, Mark and Rhonda Powell, and Bob
Lundberg, founders
15670 Ashbury Church Road, Purcellville, VA 20132 • (540) 668-7023
www.old690.com • @Old690

Quattro Goomba's Brewery
David Camden, Jay CeCianno, and Adam and Jessica Meyers, founders
22860 Monroe-Madison Memorial Highway, Aldie, VA 20105 • (703)
327-6052
www.goombabrewery.com • @QuattroGoombas

Solace Brewing Company
Jon Humerick, Drew Wiles, and Mike Arms, founders
42615 Trade West Drive, Suite 100, Dulles, VA 20166 • (703) 345-5630
www.solacebrewing.com • @SolaceBrewing

Sweetwater Tavern (Sterling)
45980 Waterview Plaza, Sterling, VA 20166 • (571) 434-6500
www.greatamericanrestaurants.com/sweetwater/sterling/

Twinpanzee Brewing Company
Antonio and Maha Maradiaga, founders
101-D Executive Drive, Sterling, VA 20166 • (703) 791-9363
www.twinpanzee.com • @Twinpanzee

Vanish Farmwoods Brewery
Jonathan Staples, founder
42245 Black Hops Lane, Leesburg, VA 20176 • (703) 779-7407
http://vanishbeer.com • @vanishbeer

Outer Northern Virginia

Adventure Brewing
Tim Bornholtz, John Viarella, and Stan Johnson, founders
North location: 33 Perchwood Drive, Unit 101, Fredericksburg, VA
    22405 • (540) 242-8876
South location: 3300 Dill Smith Drive, Fredericksburg, VA 22408 • (540)
    242-8876
www.adventurebrewing.com • @AdventureBrewCo

Barrel Oak Farm Taphouse
Brian Roeder, founder
3623 Grove Lane, Delaplane, VA 20144-2226 • (540) 364-6402
www.barreloak.com/new-barrel-oak-farm-taphouse • @BarrelOak

Battlefield Brewing Company
4187 Plank Road, Fredericksburg, VA 22407 • (540) 785-2164
https://battlefieldbrewingcompany.wordpress.com •
    @battlefieldbrewingcompany

Beer Hound Brewery
Kenny Thacker, founder
201 Waters Place, No. 102, Culpeper, VA 22701 • (540) 317-5327
www.beerhoundbrewery.com • @BeerHoundBrewer

Brew Republic Bierwerks
Jeff and Amy Frederick, founders
15201 Potomac Town Place, Woodbridge, VA 22191 • (703) 594-7950
https://brewrepublic.beer • @Brew_Republic

Colonial Beach Brewing
Mark Turner and Ted Saffos, founders
215C Washington Avenue, Colonial Beach, VA 22443 • (804) 453-8966
https://www.facebook.com/ColonialBeachBrewing/

Fär Göhn Brewing Company
Steve Gohn, founder
301 South East Street, Culpeper, VA 22701 • (540) 321-4578
www.fargohnbrewing.com • @FarGohnBrewery

The Farm Brewery at Broad Run
Bill and Michelle Dewitt, founders
16015 John Marshall Highway, Broad Run, VA 20137 • (703) 753-3548
www.thefarmbreweryatbroadrun.com • @TheFarmBrewery

Growling Bear Brewing Company
Mike Blivens, founder
14051 Crown Court, Woodbridge, VA 22193 • (571) 535-1965
www.growlingbearbrewing.com • @gbbbear

Highmark Brewery
Chuck Rau and Brandon Newton, founders
390 Kings Highway, Fredericksburg, VA 22405 • (763) 300-7575
www.highmarkbrewery.com • @highmarkbrewery

Hopkins Ordinary Ale House
Sherri Fickel, Kevin Kraditor, and David Litaker, founders
47 Main Street, Sperryville, VA 22740 • (540) 987-3383
www.hopkinsordinary.com

Maltese Brewing Company
Bobby Cook and Joseph Smith, founders
11047 Pierson Drive, Suite B, Fredericksburg, VA 22408 • (540) 642-4512
www.maltesebrewing.com • @Maltesebrewing

Montross Brewery & Beer Garden
John and Roxanne Warren, founders
15381 Kings Highway, Montross, VA 22520 • (804) 493-3033
www.montrossbrewery.com • @montrossbrewery

Old Bust Head Brewing Company
Julie and Ike Broaddus and Charles Kling, founders
7134 Farm Station Road, Vint Hill, VA 20187 • (540) 347-4777
www.oldbusthead.com • @oldbustheadbrew

Old Trade Brewery

Garrett and Sara Thayer, founders
13270 Alanthus Road, Brandy Station, VA 22714 • (774) 218-8645
www.oldtradebrewery.com

Pen Druid Brewing

Lain, Van, and Jennings Carney, founders
7 River Lane, Sperryville, VA 22740 • (540) 987-5064
www.pendruid.com • @pendruidbrewing

Powers Farm & Brewery

Kevin and Melody Powers, founders
9269 Redemption Way, Midland, VA 22728 • (540) 272-5060
www.powersfarmbrewery.com

Red Dragon Brewery

Tom Evans and Dan Baker, founders
1419 Princess Anne Street, Fredericksburg, VA 22401 • (540) 371-8100
www.reddragonbrewery.com • @reddragonbreweryllc

1781 Brewing Company

Brandon Pallen, Harry Pagan, and David Paga, founders
11109 Plank Road, Spotsylvania, VA 22553 • (540) 842-0199
www.1781brewing.com

6 Bears and a Goat Brewing Company

Seven founders
1140 International Parkway, Fredericksburg, VA 22406 • (540) 356-9056
www.6bgbrewingco.com • @6bgbrewingco

Spencer Devon Brewing

Shawn and Lisa Phillips, founders
106 George Street, Fredericksburg, VA 22401 • (540) 479-8381
www.spencerdevonbrewing.com • @SpencerDevonBrewing

Strangeways Brewing

Neil Burton, founder
350 Lansdowne Road, Fredericksburg, VA 22401 • (540) 371-1776
www.strangewaysbrewing.com • @StrangewaysBrewingFredericksburg

Tin Cannon Brewing

Aaron Ludwig and John Hilkert, founders
7679 Limestone Drive, No. 130, Gainesville, VA 20155 • (571) 248-0489
www.tincannonbrewing.com • @TinCannonBrewCo

Water's End Brewery

Josh Fournelle, Zach Mote, and Ryan Sharkey, founders
12425 Dillingham Square, Lake Ridge, VA 22192 • (571) 285-1997
www.watersendbrewery.com • @watersendbrew

Wild Run Brewing Company

Everett Lovell, founder
3071 Jefferson Davis Highway, Stafford, VA 22554 • (540) 659-3447
https://www.facebook.com/WildRunBrewing • @WildRunBrewing

Wort Hog Brewing Company

Matt Lutz, Louis Oliva, and Cris Bezdek, founders
50A South Third Street, Warrenton, VA 20186 • (540) 300-2739
www.facebook.com/whbcllc • @whbcllc

Richmond Region

Ammo Brewing

Terry Ammons and Ann Adams, founders
235 North Market Street, Petersburg, VA 23803 • (804) 722-1667
www.ammobrewing.com

The Answer Brewpub

An Bui, founder
6008 West Broad Street, Richmond, VA 23230 • (804) 282-1248
theanswerbrewpub.com • @TheAnswerBrew

Ardent Craft Ales

Tom Sullivan, Kevin O'Leary, and Paul Karns, founders
3200 West Leigh Street, Richmond, VA 23230 • (804) 359-1605
www.ardentcraftales.com • @ArdentCraftAles

Canon and Draw Brewing Company

Brad Cooper, founder
1529 West Main Street, Richmond, VA 23220
www.canonanddraw.beer

Castleburg Brewery and Taproom

Karl Homburg, founder
1626 Ownby Lane, Richmond, VA 23220 • (804) 353-1256
www.castleburgbrewery.com • @Castleburgbrew

Center of the Universe Brewing Company

Chris and Phil Ray, founders

Main location: 11293 Air Park Road, Ashland, VA 23005 • (804) 368-0299

www.cotubrewing.com • @COTUbrew

Origin Beer Lab: 106 South Railroad Avenue, Ashland, VA 23005 • (804) 299-2389

www.originbeerlab.com • @originbeerlab

Champion RVA

Hunter Smith, founder

401 East Grace Street, Richmond, VA 23219 • (804) 344-5108

www.championbrewingcompany.com • @championrva

Extra Billy's Smokehouse and Brewery

Robert and Judy Harr, founders

1110 Alverser Drive, Midlothian, VA 23113 • (804) 379-8727

www.extrabillys.com • @ExtraBillysBBQ

Final Gravity Brewing Company

Tony Ammendolia, founder

6118 Lakeside Avenue, Richmond, VA 23228 • (804) 264-4808

www.oggravity.com • @OGgravity

Fine Creek Brewing Company

Lisa and Mark Benusa, founders

2425 Robert E. Lee Road, Powhatan, VA 23139 • (804) 372-9786

www.finecreekbrewing.com • @finecreekbrew

Garden Grove Brewing and Urban Winery

Ryan Mitchell and Mike Brandt, founders

3445 West Cary Street, Richmond, VA 23221 • (804) 918-6158

www.gardengrovebrewing.com • @gardengrovebrew

Hardywood Park Craft Brewery

Eric McKay and Patrick Murtaugh, founders

2408–2410 Ownby Lane, Richmond, VA 23220 • (804) 420-2420

West Creek location: 820 Sanctuary Trail Drive, Richmond, VA 23238 • (804) 418-3548

www.hardywood.com • @Hardywood

Intermission Beer Company

Courtney and Justin White, founders

10089 Brook Road, Unit A, Glen Allen, VA 23059 • (804) 585-0405

www.intermissionbeer.com

Isley Brewing Company
Mike Isley, founder
1715 Summit Avenue, Richmond, VA 23230 • (804) 716-2132
www.isleybrewingcompany.com • @isleybrewing

Kindred Spirit Brewing
Jason and Joe Trottier, founders
12830 West Creek Parkway, Suite J, Goochland, VA 23238 • (804) 708-0309
www.kindredspiritbrewing.com • @ksbbeer

Legend Brewing Company
Tom Martin, founder
321 West Seventh Street, Richmond, VA 23224 • (804) 232-3446
www.legendbrewing.com • @LegendBrewingCo

Lickinghole Creek Craft Brewery
Sean-Thomas and Lisa Pumphrey and Farris Loutfi, founders
4100 Knolls Point Road, Goochland, VA 23063 • (804) 314-2093
www.lickingholecreek.com • @LCCB_FarmBrews

Midnight Brewery
Trae Cairns, founder
2410 Granite Ridge Road, Rockville, VA 23146 • (804) 719-9150
www.midnight-brewery.com • @midnightbrewery

Rock Bottom Restaurant and Brewery
Frank Day, founder (chain)
Short Pump Town Center, 11800 West Broad Street, Suite 2098, Richmond, VA 23233 • (804) 237-1684
www.rockbottom.com • @RockBottomRVA

Steam Bell Beer Works
Brad Cooper, founder
1717 Oak Lake Boulevard, Midlothian, VA 23112 • (804) 728-1876
www.steambell.beer • @Steambellbeer

Stone Brewing (based in Escondido, California)
Greg Koch and Steve Wagner, founders
4300 Williamsburg Road, Richmond, VA 23231 • (804) 489-5902
www.stonebrewing.com • @stonestorerva

Strangeways Brewing

Neil Burton, founder
2277A Dabney Road, Richmond, VA 23230 • (804) 303-4336
www.strangewaysbrewing.com • @StrangewaysRVA

Three Notch'd Brewing Company RVA Collab House

Scott Roth, George Kastendike, and Derek Naughton, founders
2930 West Broad Street, Richmond, VA 23230 • (804) 269-4857
https://threenotchdbrewing.com/richmond-rva-collab-house/ •
@threenotchdbrewingRVACollabHouse

Trapezium Brewing Company

Dave McCormack, founder
423 Third Street, Petersburg, VA 23803 • (804) 477-8703
www.trapeziumbrewing.com • @tpzm_beer

Triple Crossing Brewing Company

Scott Jones, Adam Worcester, and Jeremy Wirtes, founders
Downtown location: 113 South Foushee Street, Richmond, VA 23220 •
(804) 495-1955
Fulton location: 5203 Hatcher Street, Richmond, VA 23231 • (804) 495-
1955
www.triplecrossingbeer.com • @TripleCrossing

Väsen Brewing Company

Joey Darragh and Tony Giordano, founders
3331 Monroe Street, Richmond, VA 23230 • (804) 588-5678
www.vasenbrewing.com • @vasenbrewing

The Veil Brewing Company

Dustin Durrance, Dave Michelow, and Matt Tarpey, founders
1301 Roseneath Road, Richmond, VA 23230 • (804) 355-5515
www.theveilbrewing.com • @theveilbrewing

Eastern Virginia

Alewerks Brewing Company

Chuck Haines, founder
189-B Ewell Road, Williamsburg, VA 23188 • (757) 220-3670
www.alewerks.com • @Alewerks

Anheuser-Busch, Williamsburg

Adolphus Busch, founder

7801 Pocahontas Trail, Williamsburg, VA 23185 • (757) 253-3600

www.anheuser-busch.com • @AnheuserBusch

Back Bay Brewing Company

Josh Canada, Charlie Burroughs, and three others, founders

614 Norfolk Avenue, Virginia Beach, VA 23451 • (757) 531-7750

www.backbaybrewingco.com

Bearded Bird Brewing Company

727 Granby Street, Norfolk, VA 23510 • (757) 938-6685

http://beardedbirdbrewing.com • @birdedbirdbrw

Benchtop Brewing

Eric Tennant, founder

1129 Boissevain Avenue, Norfolk, VA 23507 • (757) 321-9482

http://benchtopbrewing.com • @Benchtopbrewing

Big Ugly Brewing

Jim Lantry, founder

1296 Battlefield Boulevard South, Chesapeake, VA 23322 • (757) 609-
2739

www.biguglybrewing.com/ • @BigUglyBrewing

Black Narrows Brewing Company

Jenna and Josh Chapman, founders

4522 Chicken City Road, Chincoteague Island, VA 23336

https://blacknarrowsbrewing.com • @BlackNarrows

The Bold Mariner Brewing Company

Michael and Kerrie Stacks, founders

2409 Bowdens Ferry Road, Norfolk, VA 23508 • (757) 952-6533

www.boldmariner.com • @TheBoldMariner

Brass Cannon Brewing Company

Phil Norfolk, Scott Kennedy, and Tony Artrip, founders

5476 Mooretown Road, Williamsburg, VA 23188 • (757) 566-0001

www.brasscannonbrewing.com • @BrassCannonBrew

Bull Island Brewing Company

Doug Reier, founder

758 Settlers Landing Road, Hampton, VA 23669 • (757) 884-8884

www.bullislandbrewing.com • @BullIslandBrew

Cape Charles Brewing Company

Chris and Mark Marshall and Robert Wilson, founders
2198 Stone Road, Cape Charles, VA 23310 • (757) 695-3909
http://capecharlesbrewing.com

Coelacanth Brewing

Kevin Erskine, founder
760A West 22nd Street, Norfolk, VA 23517 • (757) 383-6438
www.coelacanth.com • @CoelacanthBrew

Commonwealth Brewing Company

Jeramy Biggie, founder
2444 Pleasure House Road, Virginia Beach, VA 23455 • (757) 305-9652
www.commonwealthbrewingcompany.com • @CWBrewCo

Deadline Brewing Project

Jason Marks, Erica Greenway, Darrell Cuenca, founders
2272 West Great Neck Road, Suite 2268, Virginia Beach, VA 23451 • (757) 502-4980
www.deadlinebrewing.com • @deadlinebrewing

Hilton Tavern Brewing Company

Lorain Cosgrave and Cory Cole, founders
10184 Warwick Boulevard, Newport News, VA 23601 • (757) 873-2337
https://www.facebook.com/HiltonTavernBC/ • @HiltonTavernBC

Home Republic Brewpub

Joe Curtis, founder
328 Laskin Road, Virginia Beach, VA 23451 • (757) 226-9593
www.homerepublicvabeach.com

Legend Brewing Depot

Tom Martin, founder
1 High Street, North Landing # B, Portsmouth, VA 23704 • (757) 998-6733
http://www.legendbrewing.com/portsmouth.asp • @LegendBrewingCo

MoMac Brewing Company

Five founders
3228 Academy Avenue, Portsmouth, VA 23703 • (757) 383-9572
www.momacbrewing.com

O'Connor Brewing Company

Kevin O'Connor, founder
211 West 24th Street, Norfolk, VA 23517 • (757) 623-2337
http://oconnorbrewing.com • @OconnorBrewing

The Oozlefinch Craft Brewery

Russ Tinsley, founder
81 Patch Road, Fort Monroe, VA 23651 • (757) 224-7042
www.oozlefinchbeers.com • @OzzlefinchBeers

Pleasure House Brewing

Tim O'Brien, Kevin Loos, and Drew and Alex Stephenson, founders
3025 Shore Drive, Virginia Beach, VA 23451 • (757) 496-0916
www.pleasurehousebrewing.com • @pleasurehousebr

Reaver Beach Brewing Company

Justin and Kristin MacDonald, founders
1505 Taylor Farm Road, Virginia Beach, VA 23453 • (757) 563-2337
www.reaverbeach.com • @ReaverBeach

Rip Rap Brewing Company

Liam Bell and Ben McElroy, founders
116 East 25th Street, Norfolk, VA 23517 • (757) 632-0159
www.riprapbrewing.com • @RipRapBrewing

St. George Brewing Company

Bill Spence, founder
204 Challenger Way, Hampton, VA 23666 • (757) 865-7781
www.stgbeer.com • @StGeorgeBrewery

Smartmouth Brewing Company

Porter Hardy and Chris and Chris Neikirk, founders
1309 Raleigh Avenue, Norfolk, VA 23507 • (757) 624-3939
Smartmouth Pilot House: 313 32nd Street, Virginia Beach, VA 23451 •
(757) 624-3939
www.smartmouthbrewing.com • @smartmouthbeer

Tradition Brewing Company

Dan Powell and four others, founders
700 Thimble Shoals Boulevard, Suite 103, Newport News, VA 23606 •
(757) 592-9393
http://traditionbrewing.com • @TraditionBrewCo

Virginia Beer Company
Robby Willey and Chris Smith, founders
401 Second Street, Williamsburg, VA 23185 • (757) 378-2903
www.virginiabeerco.com • @VirginiaBeerCo

Wasserhund Brewing Company
Aaron and Christine Holley, founders
1805 Laskin Road, Suite 102, Virginia Beach, VA 23454 • (757) 351-
  1326
www.wasserhundbrewing.com • @wasserhundbrew

Wharf Hill Brewing Company
Lee Duncan, founder
25 Main Street, Smithfield, VA 23430 • (757) 357-7100
www.wharfhillbrewing.com • @WharfHillBrew

Young Veterans Brewery Company
Thomas Wilder and Neil McCanon, founders
2505 Horse Pasture Road, Virginia Beach, VA 23453 • (757) 689-4021
yvbc.com • @YoungVetsBrew

Central Virginia

Antioch Brewing Company
Raymond and Chrystan Bunch, founders
PO Box 599, Palmyra, VA 22963 • (434) 249-6727
www.antiochbrews.com

Apocalypse Ale Works
Doug and Lee John, founders
1257 Burnbridge Road, Forest, VA 24551 • (434) 258-8761
www.endofbadbeer.com • @endofbadbeer

Bald Top Brewing Company
Dave Fulton and Julie Haines, founders
1830 Thrift Road, Madison, VA 22727 • (540) 999-1830
www.baldtopbrewing.com • @baldtopbrewing

Blue Mountain
Taylor and Mandi Smack, founders
Barrel House: 495 Cooperative Way, Arrington, VA 22922 • (434) 263-
  4002
Brewery: 9519 Critzers Shop Road, Afton, VA 22920 • (540) 456-8020
www.bluemountainbrewery.com • @BlueMtnBrewery

Brasserie Saison
Hunter Smith and Wilson Richey, founders
111 East Main Street, Charlottesville, VA 22902 • (434) 202-7027
www.brasseriesaison.net

Brewing Tree Beer Company
Mark Thompson, founder
9278 Rockfish Valley Highway, Afton VA 22920 • (540) 381-0990
https://www.facebook.com/BrewingTreeBeer/ • @BrewingTreeBC

Champion Brewing Company
Hunter Smith, founder
324 Sixth Street Southeast, Charlottesville, VA 22902 • (434) 295-2739
www.championbrewingcompany.com • @championbeer

Devils Backbone Brewing Company
Steve and Heidi Crandall, founders
Basecamp Brewpub & Meadows: 200 Mosbys Run, Roseland, VA 22967 • (540) 602-6018
http://dbbrewingcompany.com/locations/basecamp/ • @dbbrewingco

Hardywood Park Craft Brewery
Eric McKay and Patrick Murtaugh, founders
1000 West Main Street, Charlottesville, VA 22903 • (434) 234-3386
https://hardywood.com/visit-us/charlottesville/ • @Hardywood

James River Brewery
Founded by a group of investors
561 Valley Street, Scottsville, VA 24590 • (434) 286-7837
www.jrbrewery.com • @JamesRiverBrew

Loose Shoe Brewing Company
Derin and Kitty Foor, founders
198 Ambriar Plaza, Amherst, VA 24521 • (434) 946-BEER
www.looseshoebrewing.com

Pro Re Nata Farm Brewery
John Schoeb, founder
6135 Rockfish Gap Turnpike, Crozet, VA 22932 • (434) 823-4878
www.prnbrewery.com • @PRNBrewery

Random Row Brewing Company

Bradley Kipp, Kevin McElroy, and Bob Thiele, founders

608 Preston Avenue, Charlottesville, VA 22903 • (434) 284-8466

www.randomrow.com • @RandomRowBeer

Reason Beer

J. Patrick Adair, Jeff Raileanu, and Mark Fulton, founders

1180 Seminole Trail, Suite 290, Charlottesville, VA 22901 • (434) 260-
0145

www.reasonbeer.com

South Street Brewery

Fred Greenewalt and Duffy Papas, founders

106 South Street West, Charlottesville, VA 22902 • (434) 293-6550

www.southstreetbrewery.com • @SouthStBrewery

Starr Hill Brewery

Mark Thompson, founder

5391 Three Notched Road, Crozet, VA 22932 • (434) 823-5671

www.starrhill.com • @StarrHill

Third Street Brewing Company

John Dudley and Mark Kernohan, founders

312 West Third Street, Farmville, VA 23901 • (434) 315-0471

https://www.thirdstbrewing.com • @thirdstbrewing

Three Notch'd Brewing Company

Scott Roth, George Kastendike, and Derek Naughton, founders

Three Notch'd Craft Kitchen & Brewery: 520 Second Street SE,
Charlottesville, VA 22902 • (434) 956-3141

www.threenotchdbrewing.com • @ThreeNotchdBeer

Wild Wolf Brewing Company

Mary and Danny Wolf, founders

2461 Rockfish Valley Highway, Nellysford, VA 22958 • (434) 361-0088

www.wildwolfbeer.com • @WildWolfBeer

Wood Ridge Farm Brewery

Barry Wood, founder

165 Old Ridge Road, Lovingston, VA 22949 • (434) 422-6225

www.facebook.com/WoodRidgeFarmBrewery •
@WoodRidgeFarmBrewery

Roanoke, Southwestern, and Southern Virginia

Ballad Brewing
Ross Fickensher and Garrett Shifflett, founders
600 Craghead Street, Danville, VA 24541 • (434) 799-4677
www.balladbrewing.com • @BalladBrewing

Ballast Point Brewing Company
Jack White, founder
555 International Parkway, Daleville, VA 24083 • (540) 591-3059
https://www.facebook.com/ballastpointvirginia/ •
   @ballastpointvirginia

Barrel Chest Wine and Beer
Martin Keck, founder
4035 Electric Road, Suite B, Roanoke, VA 24018 • (540) 206-3475
www.barrelchestwineandbeer.com

Beale's Beer
Dave McCormack, founder
510 Grove Street, Bedford, VA 24523 • (540) 583-5113
www.bealesbeer.com • @bealesbeer

Big Lick Brewing Company
Bryan Summerson and Chuck Garst, founders
409 Salem Avenue, SW, Roanoke, VA 24016 • (540) 562-8383
www.biglickbrewingco.com • @biglickbrewing

Bristol Station Brews & Taproom
Ken Monyak, founder
41 Piedmont Avenue, Bristol, VA 24201 • (276) 608-1220
www.bristolbrew.com • @bristolbrew

Buggs Island Brewing Company
Michael Elliot and Richard Castle, founders
110 College Street, Clarksville, VA 23927 • (434) 265-3343
www.facebook.com/buggsislandbrewing/

Bull & Bones Brewhaus & Grill
Mark Shrader and Jon and Peggy Coburn, founders
1470 South Main Street, Blacksburg, VA 24060 • (540) 953-2855
www.bullandbones.com • @bullandbones

Chaos Mountain Brewing Company
Joe and Wendy Hallock, founders
3135 Dillons Mill Road, Callaway, VA 24067 • (540) 334-1600
www.chaosmountainbrewing.com • @ChaosMtnBrewing

Creek Bottom Brewing Company
John and Brandy Ayers and Tonya Reavis, founders
307 North Meadow Street, Galax, VA 24333 • (276) 236-2337
www.cbbrews.com • @CreekBottomBrew

Damascus Brewery
Adam Woodson, founder
32173 Government Road, Damascus, VA 24236 • (276) 469-1069
www.thedamascusbrewery.com

Deschutes Brewery
Gary Fish, founder
Deschutes Brewery Tasting Room: 315 Market Street SE, Roanoke, VA
    24011 • (540) 259-5204
Deschutes Brewery East Coast site: Mason Mill Road NE, Roanoke, VA
    23011
www.deschutesbrewery.com/roanoke • @DeschutesBeer

Flying Mouse Brewery
Frank Moeller, founder
221 Precast Way, Troutville, VA 24175 • (540) 992-1288
www.flyingmousebrewery.com • @flyingmousebrew

Hammer & Forge Brewing Company
Caleb Williamson, founder
70 Main Street, Boones Mill, VA 24065 • (540) 909-3200
www.hammerandforgebrewing.com

Mountain Valley Brewing
Peggy Donivan and Herb Atwell, founders
4220 Mountain Valley Road, Axton, VA 24054 • (276) 833-2171
www.mountainvalleybrewing.com

Olde Salem Brewing Company
Sean Turk, founder
21 East Main Street, Salem, VA 24153 • (540) 404-4399
www.oldesalembrewing.com • @OldeSalemBrew

Parkway Brewing Company
Mike "Keno" and Lezlie Snyder, founders
739 Kessler Mill Road, Salem, VA 24153 • (540) 404-9810
http://parkwaybrewing.com • @ParkwayBrewing

Right Mind Brewing (in Lefty's Main Street Grille)
Frank Perkovich, founder
1410 South Main Street, Blacksburg, VA 24060 • (540) 552-7000
www.rightmindbrewing.com • @rightmindbrew

Rising Silo Brewery
Greg and Jess Zielske, founders
2351 Glade Road, Blacksburg, VA 24060 • (540) 750-0796
www.risingsilobrewery.com • @RisingSiloBrew

The River Company Restaurant and Brewery
Mark Hall, founder
6633 Viscoe Road, Radford, VA 24141 • (540) 633-3940
https://www.facebook.com/pg/The-River-Company-Brewery
-72765483602/posts/

Soaring Ridge Craft Brewers
Nathan Hungate, Mike Barnes, and Sean Osborne, founders
523 Shenandoah Avenue NW, Roanoke, VA 24016 • (540) 339-
9776
www.soaringridge.com • @soaringridge

Starr Hill Pilot Brewery and Side Stage
Mark Thompson, founder
6 Old Whitmore Avenue, Roanoke, VA 24016 • (540) 685-2012
https://starrhill.com/tap-room-locations/roanoke-pilot-brewery-side
-stage/ • @StarrHill

Staunton River Brewing Company
Paul and Cameron Anctil, founders
1571 Mount Calvary Road, Brookneal, VA 24528 • (434) 376-9463
www.stauntonriverbrewing.com

Studio Brew
Erich and Pamela Allen, founders
221 Moore Street, Bristol, VA 24201 • (423) 360-3258
www.studiobrew.beer • @StudioBrew

Sugar Hill Brewing Company
Greg and Jennifer Bailey, founders
16622 Broad Street, Saint Paul, VA 24283 • (276) 738-1088
www.sugarhillbrewing.com • @sugarhillbrewin

Sunken City Brewing Company
Jerome Parnell III, founder
40 Brewery Drive, Hardy, VA 24101 • (540) 420-0476
http://sunkencitybeer.com • @SunkenCityBeer

Twin Creeks Brewing Company
Andy and Jason Bishop and Barry Robertson, founders
111 South Pollard Street, Vinton, VA 24179 • (540) 400-0882
www.twincreeksbrewing.com

2Witches Winery and Brewing Company
Ethan and Julie Brown, founders
209 Trade Street, Danville, VA 24541 • (434) 549-BREW
www.2witcheswinebrew.com • @2witchesbrew

Wolf Hills Brewing Company
Chris Burcher, Rich Buddington, Matt Bundy, and Cameron Bell,
    founders
350 Park Street SE, Abingdon, VA 24210 • (276) 477-1953
www.wolfhillsbrewing.com • @wolfhills

Shenandoah Valley

Alesatian Brewing Company
Caleb Ritenour, founder
21–23 North Loudoun Street, Winchester, VA 22601 • (540) 667-2743
www.alesatianbrewing.com • @Alesatian

Backroom Brewery
Billie Clifton, founder
150 Ridgemont Road, Middletown, VA 22645 • (540) 869-8482
www.backroombreweryva.com • @Backroombrews

Basic City Beer Company
Chris, Joe, and Bart Lanman, founders
1010 East Main Street, Waynesboro, VA 22980 • (540) 943-1010
www.basiccitybeer.com

Bedlam Brewing
Mike McMackin, founder
2303 North Augusta Street, Staunton, VA 24401 • (540) 416-4634
www.bedlambrewing.com

Brothers Craft Brewing
Adam, Jason, and Tyler Shifflett, founders
800 North Main Street, Harrisonburg, VA 22802 • (540) 421-6599
www.brotherscraftbrewing.com • @broscraftbrew

Devils Backbone Brewing Company
Steve and Heidi Crandall, founders
Outpost Brewery & Taproom: 50 Northwind Lane, Lexington, VA 24450
 • (540) 817-6071
http://dbbrewingcompany.com/locations/outpost/ • @dbbrewingco

Escutcheon Brewing Company
John Hovermale and Art Major, founders
142 West Commercial Street, Winchester, VA 22601 • (540) 773-3042
www.escutcheonbrewing.com/home.html • @EscutcheonBrew

The Friendly Fermenter
Shawn Gatesman, founder
20 South Mason Street, Harrisonburg, VA 22801 • (540) 217-2614
www.friendlyfermenter.com

Great Valley Farm Brewery
Nathan and Irma Bailey, founders
60 Great Valley Lane, Natural Bridge, VA 24578 • (540) 521-6163
www.greatvalleyfarmbrewery.com

Hawksbill Brewing Company
Jim Turner, Kevin Crisler, and David Sours, founders
22 Zerkel Street, Luray, VA 22835 • (540) 860-5608
www.hawksbillbrewing.com • @HawksbillBrewingCompany

MillerCoors Shenandoah Brewery
Adolph Coors, founder
5135 South East Side Highway, Elkton, VA 22827 • (540) 289-8000
http://millercoors.com • @MillerCoorsShenandoah

Pale Fire Brewing Company
Tim Brady, founder
217 South Liberty Street, No. 105, Harrisonburg, VA 22801 • (540) 217-5452
www.palefirebrewing.com • @palefirebrewing

Queen City Brewing
Greg Ridenour, founder
834 Springhill Road, Staunton, VA 24401 • (540) 213-8014
www.qcbrewing.com • @qcbrewing

Redbeard Brewing Company
Jonathan Wright, founder
120 South Lewis Street, Staunton, VA 24401 • (540) 430-3532
www.redbeardbrews.com • @Redbeard.Brewing

Restless Moons Brewing Company
Josh Canada, George Powell, Leo Cook, and Alex Wolcott, founders
120 West Wolfe Street, Harrisonburg, VA 22802 • (540) 217-2726
www.restlessmoons.com

Seven Arrows Brewing Company
Aaron and Melissa Allen, founders
2508 Jefferson Highway, Waynesboro, VA 22980 • (540) 221-6968
www.sevenarrowsbrewing.com • @sevenarrowsbrew

Shenandoah Valley Brewing Company
Mary and Mike Chapple, founders
103 West Beverley Street, Staunton, VA 24401 • (540) 887-2337
www.shenvalbrew.com • @shenvalbrew

Stable Craft Brewing
Craig Nargi, founder
375 Madrid Road, Waynesboro, VA 22980 • (540) 490-2609
www.stablecraftbrewing.com • @stablecraft

Swover Creek Farms Brewery
Lynn and Dave St. Clair, founders
4176 Swover Creek Road, Edinburg, VA 22824 • (540) 984-8973
www.swovercreekfarms.com • @swovercreekbrewery

Three Notch'd Valley Collab House

Scott Roth, George Kastendike, and Derek Naughton, founders
241 East Market Street, Harrisonburg, VA 22801 • (540) 217-5939
https://threenotchdbrewing.com/harrisonburg-valley-collab-house/ •
   @3NBhburg

Winchester Brew Works

Bonnie Landy and Holly Redding, founders
320 North Cameron Street, Winchester, VA 22601 • (540) 692-9242
www.winchesterbrewworks.com

Woodstock Brewhouse

Karl Rouston and seven others, founders
123 East Court Street, Woodstock, VA 22664 • (540) 459-2739
www.woodstockbrewhouse.com • @Wdstkbrewhouse

APPENDIX C

Glossary of Selected Beer and Brewing Terms

ABV Alcohol by volume, measured in percentages.

ale Beer made with yeast that sits atop the brew and operates at a relatively higher temperature (55 to 75 degrees Fahrenheit) than lager yeast. Most beers are ales or lagers; ales are the oldest of brews.

alternating proprietorship An arrangement where a brewer or brewing entity arranges to lease or otherwise temporarily take over a portion of an existing brewery from the host brewer. The tenant brewer holds title to the beer. *See also* contract brewing

barley Traditionally, the main grain used to make beer. Kernels from the plant are used to make malt.

barrel As a unit of measure, one barrel of beer equals thirty-one U.S. gallons.

beer engine A piston-operated hand pump, located at the bar, that draws cask-conditioned beer from the container without being artificially pressurized or carbonated.

bottle-conditioned When a small portion of yeast is left in the bottle to advance conditioning and fermentation. Tastes vary as to including the yeast in the pour or avoiding it.

brew on premises (or BOP) Breweries where patrons pay to brew various batches of beer using equipment on the brewery premises. Customers experience the brewing process without the muss and fuss of owning, cleaning, and storing equipment.

cask-conditioned Beer that goes through secondary fermentation in a cask. Rather than being carbonated through forced carbon dioxide, the beer relies on this secondary fermentation for its carbonation. The term "real ale" refers to beers that have been carbonated naturally through this or a similar process. A special apparatus called a beer engine is required to serve this delicate beverage.

contract brewing Where a brewer contracts with an independent brewery to make the beers according to the brewer's specifications. The contract brewer, not the brewery, holds title to the beer. *See also* alternating proprietorship

craft brewery *See "What Is a Craft Brewer?" on page 63.*

fermentation The process by which yeast produces enzymes to break down sugar molecules in the wort, producing mainly alcohol and carbon dioxide.

foeder A large wooden barrel or vat set on end to enable long periods of fermentation. Often used for producing sour beers.

growler A glass or metal container that can be purchased and/or filled at a brewery with fresh beer for a patron to consume off-premises. Crowlers are similar to growlers but are metal and sealed like cans to prolong freshness and stability.

hops *Humulus lupulus,* a vining perennial plant that produces cones used to add bitterness to beer. A member of the *Cannabaceae* family, hops also serve as a preservative.

IBUs International Bitterness Units. Used to measure the hop bitterness in beer. The greater the value, the more bitterness you can expect to perceive. For example, American pale ales generally range in bitterness from 30 to 45 IBUs; India pale ales, from 40 to 70 IBUs; imperial IPAs, up to 120 IBUs.

kettle souring A process generally where bacteria, usually *Lactobacillus,* is introduced into a batch of beer to acidify the wort and produce tartness. A common procedure in brewing Berliner weisse, gose, and other tart styles.

lager Beer made with yeast that ferments at lower temperatures (48 to 58 degrees Fahrenheit) than ale and is often called "bottom fermented" because the yeast settles to the bottom.

lupulin powder A powder that is created by a proprietary process involving freezing hop cones and separating out the lupulin glands that contain the acids and resins that give beer bitterness, flavor, and aroma. The resulting powder retains the hops' qualities yet increases yield for brewers.

Maillard reaction A non-enzymatic browning (pronounced "my-YARD"), such as charring, that adds flavor and color to food and beer. Different from caramelization, which is a thermal decomposition of sugars.

malt The cereal grain that is allowed to germinate, usually after soaking in water, then dried with hot air to arrest germination. The malting process helps develop enzymes needed to convert the grain's starches to sugars and to break down proteins.

mash The porridge-like mixture of ground barley malt and hot water that is strained to make wort. Mashing precedes the boiling phase, where hops are added.

specific gravity The density of beer or wort at standard temperature and pressure, relative to a standard reference (water, generally). Original gravity refers to the measured density when beer is ready for fermentation; final gravity, when beer is ready to be served or packaged.

Standard Reference Method (SRM) One system used to gauge the color density of beer, using a numerical range from one (light straw) to forty (black).

steam beer A beer style originating in California during the Gold Rush of the 1800s that uses lager yeast to ferment at ale temperatures. The term was trademarked by Anchor Brewing Company, so the style now is called California Common (or Virginia Common in the Old Dominion). The "steam" reference comes from the steam rising from hot liquid in open fermentation vessels or from carbon dioxide escaping from kegs as they were tapped.

terroir "The combination of factors including soil, climate, and sunlight that gives wine grapes their distinctive character" (pronounced "tayr-WAHR"), according to *Merriam Webster.* Substitute "beer" for "wine" and the same principle applies. From the French word for "land" but with Latin roots.

wort The unfermented mixture of water and sugars from grains (commonly malted barley) and hops.

yeast Single-celled fungi found widely in nature. In beer, yeast converts sugars into alcohol, carbon dioxide, and various byproducts. Yeast's role in brewing was not entirely understood until the nineteenth century. Two prominent yeast strains are *Saccharomyces cerevisiae* for ales and *Saccharomyces pastorianus* for lagers. A wild yeast strain called *Brettanomyces,* traditionally used in styles such as Belgian lambics, has become popular among brewers looking to add a funky tartness to brews, though flavor profiles can range widely.

Notes

Virginia Beer: A Guide from Colonial Days to Craft's Golden Age
is based on a variety of resources, from historical first-person
accounts to personal interviews with various individuals, particularly brewers, and brewery owners. These interviews span a
period from 1996, when I began writing about beer in a weekly
column for the *Richmond Times-Dispatch,* through two earlier
books focusing on the Richmond and Charlottesville areas to
the current effort for this volume. As noted in the preface, today's craft brewing scene is a shifting landscape with openings,
closings, staff realignments, expansions, and other changes occurring weekly.

Chapter 1 relies most heavily on historical documents, newspaper accounts, books of the period, and information from
family members and other personal resources. In particular, the
Library of Congress's *Chronicling America* site has proved invaluable over the years for newspaper accounts and advertisements.
A lot of beer background information comes from *The Oxford
Companion to Beer* and other books. Some sources I have cited in
the text of the narrative; a more detailed accounting and elabo-
ration on some points follows (see the bibliography for complete
references).

1. An Ancient Beverage Endures

5 There are numerous sources for the role of beer in ancient history,
but one I liked is Joshua Mark's "Beer in the Ancient World."

7 *Tiswin* is described in Stan Hieronymus's *Brewing Local:
American-Grown Beer.* The corn-based drink was brewed by Apache
women and "would keep about a day and a half before it was too
sour to drink, so it was usually brewed for a party or dance (29).

7 Thomas Hariot's account is in the 1588 work, *A briefe and true
report of the new found land of Virginia.*

8 Gabriel Archer, one of the Englishmen who made the 1607 trip up
the James River, chronicled the encounter in his journal. Virginius
Dabney also describes it in *Richmond: The Story of a City.*

8 Details about small beer, the difference between ale and beer, and some other general information about colonial brewing come from several sources, including Garrett (ed.), *The Oxford Companion to Beer; Baron, Brewed in America;* and Smith, *Beer in America: The Early Years (1587–1840)*. Frank Clark, master of historic foodways for Colonial Williamsburg Foundation, questions the rationale that bad water was a predominant reason folks drank beer. "People drank beer because they liked beer," he said at a conference on beer history.

8 This quote about Duppe's beer and many other details about Jamestown brewing are from the National Park Service's Historic Jamestowne website, *Brewing in the Seventeenth Century* (https://www.nps.gov/jame/learn/historyculture/brewing-in-the -seventeenth-century.htm).

9 Captain John Smith's quote is from volume 2 of *The Generall Historie of Virginia, New England & the Summer Isles: Together with The True Travels, Adventures and Observations, and a Sea Grammar* (Glasgow: J. MacLehose, 1907).

9 These insights are from Philip Alexander Bruce's *Economic History of Virginia in the Seventeenth Century.*

10 Details about beer and the slave community at Mount Vernon are described in an article, *"Better . . . Fed Than Negroes Generally Are:" Diet of Mount Vernon Slaves,* by Mary V. Thompson, research historian with the Fred W. Smith National Library for the Study of George Washington.

11 The brewing misadventures of John Mercer make for fascinating and somewhat disheartening reading. Mercer's tale is told in C. Malcolm Watkins's *The Cultural History of Marlborough, Virginia.* Garrett Peck extends the story by following the footsteps of Marlborough's primary brewer in "Alexander Wales: Alexandria's First Brewer." In addition, the Adventure Brewing Company website gives a good account (https://adventurebrewing.com/marlborough -brewery).

15 Thomas Jefferson made this oft-quoted statement in a letter to Charles Yancey dated January 6, 1816 (see http://rotunda.upress .virginia.edu/founders/TSJN-03-09-02-0209). The missive includes an appeal for information about a petition before the General Assembly concerning Captain Joseph Miller. Jefferson knew Miller's background in brewing—"in which art I think him as skilful a man as has ever come to America"—and seized the opportunity for Miller to teach Peter Hemings.

16 A primary source for much of the information about brewing at Monticello comes from the Thomas Jefferson Foundation's materials and website. Research by Mary Thompson concerning Mount Vernon, Lucia Stanton regarding Monticello, and the faculty at the College of William and Mary via The Lemon Project is invaluable in documenting the involvement of the slave community in growing hops and brewing beer.

17 Resources on the German influence include *The Virginia Germans* by Klaus Wust, Andrea Mehrlander's *The Germans of Charleston, Richmond and New Orleans during the Civil War Period, 1850–1870*, and Herrmann Schuricht's *The History of the German Element in Virginia*.

18 Samuel Mordecai's *Virginia, Especially Richmond, in By-Gone Days*, is a lively and engaging read filled with humor and eye-winking insights.

18 Carol C. Green's *Chimborazo: The Confederacy's Largest Hospital* provided many details for this section.

19 Three sources are helpful for tracking Portner's enterprise: Timothy J. Dennée's *Robert Portner and His Brewing Company;* Garrett Peck's *Capital Beer: A Heady History of Brewing in Washington, D.C.;* and Mike Williams's blog *Robert Portner and Alexandria's Pre-Prohibition Brewing History* (https://blogs.weta.org /boundarystones/2016/01/27/robert-portner-and-alexandrias-pre -prohibition-brewing-history).

20 Sources for the tale of James River Steam Brewery come from Mark Moon's *Yuengling: A History of America's Oldest Brewery,* newspaper ads and articles, and the National Register of Historic Places' nomination document that led to the cellars being designated a state and national landmark in 2014 (http:// www.dhr.virginia.gov/registers/Counties/Henrico/043-5313 _JamesRiverSteamBreweryCellars_2013_NRHP_FINAL.pdf).

23 Much of the information about the Virginia Brewing Company in Roanoke is from the Rusty Cans website (www.rustycans.com /COM/month0606.html).

23 Danny Morris's *Richmond Beers* tracks the rise of these two figures—Alfred von Nickisch Rosenegk and Peter Stumpf—in great detail. However, one of the juiciest episodes, involving the dispute and eventual court case regarding the award for best lager at the 1892 State Exposition, surfaced while I was trolling through the Library of Congress's *Chronicling America* website (https:// chroniclingamerica.loc.gov/lccn/sn85038614/1892-10-26/ed-1/seq

-1/#date1=1892&index=4&rows=20&words=Stumpf&searchType
=basic&sequence=0&state=Virginia&date2=1892&proxtext
=Stumpf&y=18&x=13&dateFilterType=yearRange&page=1).

24 The 4,131 figure from 1873 comes from the Brewers Association.

25 Sources for information about Virginia's Prohibition era include
the Library of Virginia's *"How Dry I Am!"* analysis of the Virginia
Prohibition Commission records; Rustycans.com; Breweryhistory
.com; Shaffer Library of Drug Policy; and numerous newspaper
articles accessed through *Chronicling America*. In particular, the
scenes painted by Richmond journalists evoke colorful images
of Halloween 1916, when midnight tolled the change from "wet"
to "dry."

26 Morris's *Richmond Beers* and newspaper accounts tell the story of
Rosenegk's death and Home Brewing Company's transition.

28 Potato skins? That's according to http://www.rustycans.com/COM
/month0606.html.

28 The ad that ran in the *Richmond Times-Dispatch* on January 27,
1935, gives wonderful details on the historic release of Krueger's
Cream Ale. Look at the instructions for using the "Quick & Easy"
opener, aka church key.

30 Charlie Papazian has been gracious in granting me interviews over
the years, particularly for an in-depth account in my book *Charlottesville Beer.*

32 Much of the material for the microbrewing era of the 1990s and
the information leading to the current golden age come from my
interviews, research, and travels while writing for the *Richmond
Times-Dispatch,* magazines, and my two previous books.

2. Making the Most of "Taste of Place"

36 Information about events leading to and including adoption of the
Reinheitsgebot came from a variety of sources, online and print—
primarily *Prost! The Story of German Beer* by Horst D. Dornbusch.

37 The official Brewers Association guidelines concerning ingredients
can be found at www.brewersassociation.org.

37 The Polish-style Piwo Grodziskie, which I was fortunate enough to
taste, was brewed by the Virginia Beer Company in Williamsburg.

37 The reference to "perfect" water was from Mary Wolf of Wild Wolf
Brewing Company (see chapter 4).

37 Details about Lost Rhino's Native Son come from interviews with
cofounders Favio Garcia and Matt Hagerman over the course of
several years, most recently in 2017. I sampled the beer for the first
time at the Virginia Craft Brewers Fest in 2014.

38 Details about Lickinghole Creek came from various visits and interviews with cofounders Sean-Thomas and Lisa Brotherton Pumphrey.

38 Information about the formation of the Old Dominion Hops Cooperative comes from interviews with Stan Driver (the initial chairman), Laura Siegle (agricultural and natural resources agent for Virginia Cooperative Extension), and other sources.

39 The records of hops transactions regarding slaves come from primary sources, including Thomas Jefferson's *Memorandum Book* and the accounts kept by Martha Jefferson.

39 Landon Carter's essay on hops can be found at the Albert and Shirley Small Special Collections Library at the University of Virginia, where I was able to read the document personally.

42 The U.S. Department of Agriculture was formed in 1862, and the annual reports then and onward provided bounteous information about hops production in Virginia and elsewhere.

43 The information about Ike's Fresh Hops Smash comes from an April 9, 2017, article titled "Farm to Glass Movement Drives Brewers to Find Local Ingredients," by Tiffany Holland in the *Roanoke Times* (http://www.roanoke.com/business/news/farm-to -glass-movement-drives-brewers-to-find-local-ingredients/article _7e2118df-b9b1-5bb4-ae3e-f66f0dfce263).

43 I visited Black Hops Farm and talked with Jonathan Staples on a tour of Loudoun County breweries in 2017.

44 Thomas Jefferson made numerous efforts to procure Joseph Coppinger's *American Brewer,* which contained information about brewing with corn.

45 I interviewed Wade Thomason, professor and Extension grains specialist at Virginia Tech, in early 2017.

48 Dave Michelow, cofounder of The Veil, was kind enough to show me the coolship operation in 2016.

49 Ami Riscassi of the University of Virginia was interviewed in early 2016 as part of my research for the *Charlottesville Beer* book.

49 Much of the information about the water quality and sustainability at Stone and other breweries comes from an April 13, 2015, article titled "A Look at Stone Brewing's Sustainability Issues" by Sara Harper in *Craft Brewing Business* (www.craftbrewingbusiness.com /featured/a-look-at-stone-brewings-sustainability-initiatives) and a March 27, 2017, article titled "San Diego Breweries Experiment with Recycled Water" by Jason Daley in *Smithsonian* magazine (www.smithsonianmag.com/smart-news/san-diego-breweries -experiment-recycled-water-180962681).

55 Stan Driver's quote is from an interview for the *Charlottesville Beer* book.

3. Making It, Tasting It

56 The quote "beer is the most complex beverage" comes from *Water: A Comprehensive Guide for Brewers* by John Palmer and Colin Kaminski (Boulder, CO: Brewers Publications, 2013).

56 The $108 billion total ($107.6, specifically) comes from the Brewers Association "State of the Industry" figures for 2016, and includes all breweries in the U.S., craft and non-craft.

57 The description of the brewing process comes from my own experience as a homebrewer, from reading numerous sources ranging from Charlie Papazian's *The New Complete Joy of Homebrewing* (New York: Avon Books, 1991) to *The Oxford Companion to Beer,* and from hanging out in breweries and talking with brewers.

61 Details about Charlie Papazian's introduction to homebrewing come from several personal interviews; the quotes are from a 2016 phone interview.

62 Details about Chesapeake Bay Brewing Company come from interviews and coverage in the *Richmond Times-Dispatch,* particularly "After a Batch of Brew Comes the Brewery," September 5, 1982.

64 I interviewed Dan Mouer for my *Richmond Beer* book.

64 Information about BURP comes from the group's website, which includes archived newsletters (www.burp.org/the-origins-of-burp -the-first-meetings).

64 Details about Charlottesville Area Masters of Real Ale and Jamey Barlow come from an interview for the *Charlottesville Beer* book. Information about BARF and the other clubs came from online sources (see appendix A).

65 Mark Williams provided details of his winning recipe via email.

4. Pairing Flavors, Exploring Styles

67 I attended the 2016 Top of the Hops festival, and the quotes are from my notes taken at the event.

67 Tasting details are taken from the *CraftBeer.com Beer & Food Course, Professional Course* (https://www.craftbeer.com/food/beer-and -food-course).

67 Margaret Bradshaw of Truckle Cheesemongers provided notes and quotes in an email.

69 Starr Hill routinely provides food-pairing information for its beer releases.

69 I attended the Brothers Craft Brewing Company dinner; notes are taken from the official menu.

72 The hops guidebook mentioned is from the Barth-Haas group, a prominent supplier of hops products.

73 The description of Blue Ridge Mountains water as perfect came from a 2016 interview with Mary Wolf, owner of Wild Wolf Brewing Company in Nellysford.

73 The Beer Judge Certification Program guidelines are available online at www.bjcp.org or via an app. Make sure you access the current edition.

76 Ardent's persimmon ale was presented in December 2014 at a Virginia Historical Society program. An Associated Press story about the beer by Michael Felberbaum ("Virginia Brewery Taps 300-Year_old Beer Recipe") was picked up by numerous media in the United States and abroad (http://www.burlingtonfreepress .com/story/life/food/2014/12/04/virginia-brewery-taps-year-old -beer-recipe/19899077/).

82 I was fortunate enough to tour The Veil and see its rooftop fermentation setup in 2016.

83 Statistics on the popularity of IPAs and seasonal beers were part of a "State of the Industry" presentation made by members of the Brewers Association at the 2017 Craft Brewers Conference in Washington, D.C.

84 Details about Devils Backbone's Vienna Lager come from interviews with head brewer Jason Oliver and others that I conducted for magazine articles and the *Charlottesville Beer* book.

84 Information about Bill Madden and his kölsch ales comes from personal interviews ranging from 2000 to 2017 and from other sources, including an article in *Northern Virginia Magazine*, by Whitney Pipkin, January 12, 2016 ("A Decade of Drinking in Northern Virginia." https://www.northernvirginiamag.com/food /drinks/2016/01/12/decadeofdrinking/) and *Beer Lovers' Virginia: Best Breweries, Brewpubs and Beer Bars* by Tanya Birch. The quote from *Virginia Craft Beer* magazine comes from an article by Jeff Maisey, June 6, 2014, entitled "Crafty Like a Mad Fox" (http:// virginiacraftbeer.com/crafty-like-a-mad-fox-.

5. History and Innovation in Northern Virginia

88 I've known Bill Butcher for years and interviewed him several times, but a lengthy conversation we had in June 2017 provided the bulk of information for the Port City profile. Additional details

about Port City's expansion come from a September 7, 2016, article, "Port City Brewing Company to Expand," by Chris Teale in *Alexandria Times* (http://alextimes.com/2016/09/port-city-brewing-company-to-expand/) and an August 31, 2016, article, "Port City Brewing C. Will Stay in Alexandria with Help from Virginia Governor," by Rebecca Cooper in *Washington Business Journal* (https://www.bizjournals.com/washington/news/2016/08/31/port-city-brewing-co-will-stay-in-alexandria-with.html).

91 Information comes from a visit to the Portner Brewhouse in March 2017; an interview with Catherine Portner; an October 19, 2015, article titled "The Portner Brewhouse Finds a Home" by Jefferson Evans and Chuck Triplett in *Virginia Craft Beer* magazine (http://virginiacraftbeer.com/the-portner-brewhouse-finds-a-home/); and an article, "Portner Brewhouse: Reviving a Brewery and its Brews," by Evans in the October/November 2013 issue of *Mid-Atlantic Brewing News* (http://archive.brewingnews.com/publication/index.php?i=178168&m=&l=&p=25&pre=&ver=html5#{"page":16,"issue_id":178168}).

94 I've interviewed Bill Madden several times over the years, most recently at Mad Fox's Falls Church location in June 2017. Additional details come from a journal entry Madden wrote on September 16, 2003, for *Realbeer.com* (http://www.realbeer.com/edu/gabf/diaries/madden02.php).

96 Much of this information comes from conversations with Jason and Melissa Romano on several occasions, including a visit to the Lake Anne Brew House in August 2017. Additional information and quotes come primarily from two articles—an April 21, 2015, piece, "Arriving Soon: Brews with Views at Lake Anne Brew House," by Mary Ann Barton in *Reston Patch* (https://patch.com/virginia/reston/arriving-soon-brews-views-lake-anne-brew-house-0) and an April 11, 2016, story, "Sneak Peek: Lake Anne Brew House," by Karen Goff in *Reston Now* (https://www.restonnow.com/2016/04/11/sneak-peek-lake-anne-brew-house/).

99 Information for the Fair Winds profile comes primarily from an interview with Casey Jones and a visit to the taproom in September 2017. Additional details come from the brewery's website; a March 30, 2014, article titled "8 Things to Know about Fair Winds Brewing Company" by Natalie Manitius in *Northern Virginia* magazine (https://www.northernvirginiamag.com/food/food-news/2014/03/30/8-things-to-know-about-fair-winds-brewing-company/); and a June 7, 2017, article titled "Craft Breweries Are Booming—and Winning Awards—in Northern Virginia"

by Andrea Cwieka in *Washington Business Journal* (https://www
.bizjournals.com/washington/news/2017/06/07/craft-breweries
-are-booming-and-winning-awards-in.html).

101 Most of this information comes from visits to the BadWolf sites
and interviews with Sarah Meyers at the original site and via
phone in January 2016. Tasting notes for "Try This" come from
my own experience, the website, and online reviews. The final
quote from Jeremy is from a 2013 article by Paul Keily, "Bad Wolf
Brewing Company: Craft Beer Comes to Manassas," in *Prince
William Living* magazine (https://princewilliamliving.com/2013
/10/badwolf-brewing-company-2/). The announcement to cease
operations at the Kao Circle facility and accompanying quote come
from the brewery's website and an April 29, 2018, posting on the
Cheers Virginia website (https://www.cheersva.org/events/events
-breweries/last-day-of-business-big-badwolf-kao-circle/).

103 A visit to Mustang Sally in August 2017 provided some details
for the profile. Additional information comes from a May 25,
2016, article titled "Chantilly: Mustang Sally Brewing Company
Holds Grand Opening" by Ryan Dunn in *The Connection* (http://
www.connectionnewspapers.com/news/2016/may/25/chantilly
-mustang-sally-brewing-company-holds-gran/); a May 25, 2016,
piece titled "Mustang Sally Brewing Opens in Chantilly" by Jeff
Clabaugh for WTOP-TV (http://wtop.com/business-finance/2016
/05/mustang-sally-brewing-opens-in-chantilly/slide/1/); and a
December 23, 2015, article titled "Former Tech Startup Lawyer
to Open Fairfax County's Newest Brewery" by Rebecca Cooper
in *Washington Business Journal* (https://www.bizjournals.com
/washington/blog/top-shelf/2015/12/former-tech-startup-lawyer
-opening-fairfax-county.html). Bart Watson's quote and statistics
come from a presentation at the 2017 Craft Brewers Conference in
Washington, D.C., and also are posted on the Brewers Association
website (https://www.brewersassociation.org/press-releases/2016
-growth-small-independent-brewers/).

6. Loudoun Experiences a Growth Spurt

108 Information about Dirt Farm comes from conversations with
Janell Zurschmeide, including during a visit to the farm in June
2017, and media sources, including a September 1, 2016, article by
Jefferson Evans and Chuck Triplett in *Virginia Craft Beer* magazine
entitled "Views and Brews High Above Bluemont at Dirt Farm
Brewery" (http://virginiacraftbeer.com/views-and-brews-high
-above-bluemont-at-dirt-farm-brewing).

110 Details for the Corcoran and B Chord brewery profile come from several visits to the sites and a March 17, 2014, article entitled "Corcoran Brewing Set to Open in Purcellville March 29" by Karen Graham in the *Loudoun Times-Mirror* (http://www.loudountimes .com/news/article/corcoran_brewing_set_to_open_in_purcellville _march_29).

112 Information about Adroit Theory comes from two visits, one in 2015 and the other in 2017, interviews with Mark Osborne, and the brewery's website.

115 Two visits to the tasting room, an interview with Tolga and Katie Baki, and perusals of the website provided much of the information for the Belly Love profile. Added details come from a June 2, 2014, article entitled "Belly Love Brewing Coming to Purcellville" by Karen Graham in the *Loudoun Times-Mirror* (https:// www.loudountimes.com/news/belly-love-brewing-coming-to -purcellville/article_acf5cec3-8524-5fdd-b8ee-9e01256fd50e.html) and an August 17, 2015, *YouTube* video introducing the brewery produced by the Bakis (https://www.youtube.com/watch?v =JW6p8AWK4GQ).

117 Visits to both of the Crooked Run taprooms, an interview with Jake Endres in September 2017, and information on the brewery's website provide much of the details for the profile. Additional information comes from an August 30, 2016, press release entitled "Crooked Run Brewing to Open Second Location" posted in *BrewBound* (https://www.brewbound.com/news/crooked-run -brewing-open-second-location); a May 10, 2016, article entitled "Leesburg's Crooked Run Wins Gold Medal at World Beer Cup, Plans New Brewery," by Fritz Hahn in the *Washington Post* (https:// www.washingtonpost.com/news/going-out-guide/wp/2016/05/10 /leesburgs-crooked-run-wins-gold-medal-at-world-beer-cup-plans -new-brewery/?utm_term=.c783fa4d18e8); an August 24, 2016, article entitled "Nanobrewery Crooked Run Expands to Sterling" by Danielle Nadler in *Loudoun Now* (http://loudounnow.com/2016 /08/24/nanobrewery-crooked-run-expands-to-sterling/); and a January 23, 2017, article entitled "Crooked Run Brewing, Senor Ramon Taqueria Partner Up for Sterling Expansion" by Chantelle Edmunds in the *Loudoun Times-Mirror* (http://www.loudountimes .com/news/article/crooked_run_brewing_senor_ramon_taqueria _partner_up_for_sterling432).

119 Most of the information for the Loudoun Brewing Company profile comes from an interview with Phil Fust and Shannon Burnett during a visit in September 2017. Patrick Steffens's quote comes from a September 19, 2016, article entitled "Loudoun Brewing Co. Throws Anniversary Party" by Danielle Nadler in *Loudoun Now* (http://loudounnow.com/2016/09/19/loudoun-brewing-co-throws-anniversary-party/).

121 The bulk of this information comes from two visits to Old Ox, in 2016 and 2017, and talking with Chris Burns. I gleaned details of the Red Bull dispute from several sources, notably a February 9, 2015, article in the *Washington Post* by Fritz Hahn entitled "Red Bull Wants to Rename an Ashburn Brewery, Because an Ox Looks Like a Bull" (www.washingtonpost.com/news/going-out-guide /wp/2015/02/09/red-bull-wants-to-rename-an-ashburn-brewery -because-an-ox-looks-like-a-bull/). Another article that proved helpful was "Family-Owned Old Ox Brewery Will Open in Ashburn on Memorial Day Weekend" by Evan Milberg, appearing May 1, 2014, in *Northern Virginia* magazine (www.northernvirginiamag .com/food/food-news/2014/05/01/family-owned-old-ox-brewery -will-open-in-ashburn-by-memorial-day-weekend).

123 Most of this information comes from an extensive interview with Matt Hagerman in March 2017, numerous visits to Lost Rhino's taproom, and one visit to Lost Rhino Retreat. Additional details and quotes come from a May 5, 2011, YouTube interview with Hagerman (https://www.youtube.com/watch?v=LLG1UnrQs6U). Background on Kenny Lefkowitz comes a personal interview at the Great American Beer Festival and from Lefkowitz's website (http://newriverbrewingcompany.com/story.html).

127 Several visits to Ocelot's taproom, conversations, a formal interview with Adrien Widman, and my being in the front row at the 2016 Great American Beer Festival provided the details for this profile. Additional information comes from a December 9, 2015, article entitled "Ocelot Brewing Doesn't Have to Repeat Itself to Sell Beer" by Michael Stein in *DC Beer* (http://www.dcbeer.com /news/ocelot-brewing-doesn't-have-repeat-itself-sell-beer) and an article titled "Prance with the Beasts at Ocelot" by Jefferson Evans and Chuck Triplett in the June 2015 issue of *Virginia Craft Beer* magazine (www.virginiacraftbeer.com).

7. The Outer Reaches of Northern Virginia

131 Head brewer Bryan Link provided information for the Adventure profile, plus I visited both taprooms, interviewed Tim Bornholtz, and gleaned details from the brewery's website. Additional information comes from an April 2015 article entitled "Adventure Brewery: Stafford County Community Embraces Their First Brewery in

247 Years" by Steve Deason in *Virginia Craft Beer* magazine (www .virginiacraftbeer.com); a July 7, 2017, article entitled "Adventure Brewing Company in Mid-Stafford Keeps the Beer Flowing" by Alex Korna in *Inside NOVA* (https://www.insidenova.com/news /adventure-brewing-company-in-mid-stafford-keeps-the-beer -flowing/article_f4916cda-6322-11e7-930f-43d9dadfbf33.html); and a January 15, 2016, article entitled "Adventure Brewing Purchases Blue & Gray Brewing" by Robyn Sidersky in the *Fredericksburg Free Lance-Star* (http://www.fredericksburg.com/business /local_business/adventure-brewing-purchases-blue-gray-brewing /article_93213054-bbba-11e5-961d-9b19be6b9e13.html).

134 Information comes largely from my visit to Red Dragon in June 2017, speaking with then-manager Hilary Kanter and interviewing co-owner Tom Evans, as well as the brewery's website and media sources, including a July 29, 2016, article by Lindley Estes in the *Richmond Times-Dispatch* entitled "Red Dragon Brewery Opening in Fredericksburg in August" (http://www.richmond.com/food-drink /red-dragon-brewery-opening-in-fredericksburg-in-august/article _6d6fc96d-b8db-5336-99af-be3f39208b9e.html).

136 I visited Maltese Brewing Company on September 3, 2017, and had an extended conversation with Michael Cooper, the taproom manager. Additional information comes from a March 8, 2015, article entitled "Maltese Brewing Moves Closer to Brewing, Opening" by Robyn Sidersky in the *Fredericksburg Free Lance-Star* (http://www .fredericksburg.com/business/local_business/maltese-brewing -moves-closer-to-brewing-opening/article_42cbcf2c-c5b8-11e4 -89bf-1b148c1f80d7.html) and a March 5, 2017, article entitled "Building a Sense of Community: Maltese Brewing Company" by James Bernard in *Virginia Craft Brews* magazine (http:// virginiacraftbrews.com/blog-1/2017/3/5/building-a-sense-of -community-maltese-brewing-company).

138 Visits to Beer Hound in 2016 and 2017 provided most of the details. Additional information comes from the brewery's website and from a video accompanying a June 12, 2015, article entitled "How an Unemployed Construction Worker Became a Craft Beer Entrepreneur" by Kerry Hannon in *Money* magazine (http://time .com/money/3919129/beer-hound-brewery-kenny-thacker/).

141 Information comes from talking with Steve Gohn during my initial visit, from the brewery website, and from media sources, including a September 13, 2015, article entitled "Big Changes Coming to Far Gohn Brewing Company" in the *Culpeper Star-Exponent* by Vincent Vallia (http://www.starexponent.com/uncategorized/big

-changes-coming-to-far-gohn-brewing-company/article_eac39b77
-e91f-5518-b7a7-d65aee059103.html). I visited the brewery
again in September 2017 and was tickled to see Steve wearing
a felt hat displaying the name of the world's oldest brewery,
Weihenstephaner—a fitting bit of apparel for Culpeper's second
annual Hoptoberfest.

143 Several visits to the Vint Hill taproom, information provided by
Ike and Julie Broaddus, and details from the brewery's website
form the basis of the Old Bust Head profile. Additional information comes from an August 15, 2014, article entitled "Old Bust
Head Brewing Co. puts Fauquier Beer on the Map" by Lawrence
Emerson in *Fauquier Now* (http://www.fauquiernow.com/index
.php/fauquier_news/article/fauquier-old-bust-head-brewing
-puts-fauquier-beer-on-map-2014); an October 16, 2014, article
entitled "What's Brewing in Northern Virginia: Old Bust Head,
Heritage Brewing, and BadWolf Brewing" by Fritz Hahn and John
Taylor in the *Washington Post* (https://www.washingtonpost.com
/goingoutguide/whats-brewing-in-northern-virginia-old-bust-head
-heritage-brewing-and-badwolf-brewing/2014/10/16/0ab8d752
-52e4-11e4-809b-8cc0a295c773_story.html?noredirect=on&utm
_term=.d37cdb54d453); and an August 15, 2014, video entitled
"Old Bust Head Brewing Co. Comes to Life in 2014" on YouTube
(https://www.youtube.com/watch?v=4QEv_04E934).

146 A visit to Pen Druid on August 26, 2017, provided the details for
the brewery's profile. Information also was gleaned from an August 26, 2015, article by Steve Deason entitled "Pen Druid Brewing:
Members of Psych-Rock Band Pontiak Launch Brewery in Sperryville" in *Virginia Craft Beer* magazine (http://virginiacraftbeer
.com/pen-druid-brewing-members-of-psych-rock-band-pontiak
-launch-brewery-in-sperryville/) and from the brewery's website.
Information about Hopkins Ordinary Bed & Breakfast and Copper
Fox Distillery come from visits on the same day and from the
operations' websites.

8. Breweries Change the Face of Richmond

151 I've interviewed Tom Martin, Dave Gott, John Wampler, and
others at Legend numerous times for articles in the *Richmond
Times-Dispatch* and *Virginia Craft Beer* magazine as well as for my
Richmond Beer book and for this book. I also visited the Legend
Depot in Portsmouth in September 2017.

154 The bulk of this information comes from numerous interviews,
conversations, and visits to Hardywood Park over the years.

Quotes from Kate Lee come from an interview that aired on RVA Beer Show, WRIR FM 97.3, on August 14, 2017. Some details about Hardywood Gingerbread Stout are from the brewery's website, and some information about the West Creek project comes from a November 13, 2015, article entitled "Hardywood Park Craft Brewery to Start Work on Expansion" by John Reid Blackwell in the *Richmond Times-Dispatch* (http://www.richmond.com/business /local/hardywood-park-craft-brewery-to-start-work-on-expansion /article_9fc64cba-86e0-5ce2-9edb-d58358606d1e.html).

158 Numerous conversations and interviews with An Bui and Brandon Tolbert over the years provide the bulk of information for The Answer profile. Bui's quote in *The Washington Post* comes from an April 13, 2017, article entitled "The Veil, Triple Crossing, and The Answer are Putting Richmond on the Craft Beer Map" by Rudi Greenberg (https://www.washingtonpost.com/express/wp /2017/04/13/the-veil-triple-crossing-and-the-answer-are-putting -richmond-on-the-craft-beer-map/?utm_term=.a19be4349994).

160 Much of this information comes from numerous interviews, conversations, visits, and hanging out with folks at Ardent. Additional information comes from a June 28, 2017, article entitled "Culmination of Experimentation for Ardent Craft Ales" by Annie Tobey in *Boomer* magazine (https://www.boomermagazine.com /ardents-inaugural-sour-ales/); from an April 22, 2015, article by Robey Martin entitled "No Gluten? No Problem: Ardent Craft Ales Launches Gluten-Free Pilot Series" in *Richmond Magazine* (http:// richmondmagazine.com/restaurants-in-richmond/food-news /gluten-free-beer-ardent-craft-ales-launches-its-gluten-free-pilot -series/); and from Ardent's website.

163 Conversations and interviews over the years with Scott Jones, Adam Worcester, and Jeremy Wirtes, plus multiple visits to both the Foushee Street and Fulton locations, provide much of the detail for the Triple Crossing profile. Additional information comes from the brewery's website, media releases, a December 19, 2016, article entitled "Triple Crossing Brewing Opens New Taproom, Production Facility" by J. Elias O'Neal in *Richmond BizSense* (https:// richmondbizsense.com/2016/12/19/triple-crossing-brewing-opens -new-taproom-production-facility/), and a December 13, 2016, article entitled "Triple Crossing Brewing Co. to Open in Fulton on Friday" by Brandon Fox in *Style Weekly* (https://www.styleweekly .com/ShortOrderBlog/archives/2016/12/13/triple-crossing -brewing-co-to-open-in-fulton-on-friday).

166 Much of the information comes from numerous conversations and interviews with Greg Koch, Steve Wagner, and other Stone officials and employees. Members of the Richmond brewing community also expressed opinions that I have woven into this profile. I also have been a frequent visitor to Stone's taproom and brewery in Richmond and have visited the mother ship in Escondido, California. In addition, details about the incentives and business aspects of Stone's coming to Richmond come from numerous articles in the *Richmond Times-Dispatch* and *Richmond BizSense*.

169 Much of this information comes from visits to the Richmond and Fredericksburg Strangeways locations and numerous interviews with Neil Burton and Mike Hiller. Additional information comes from the brewery's website and from news articles, primarily a November 7, 2016, article entitled "Keeping it Strange: Q&A with Strangeways Brewing's Neil Burton" by J. Elias O'Neal in *Richmond BizSense* (http://richmondbizsense.com/2016/11/07/keeping -it-strange-qa-with-strangeways-brewings-neil-burton/) and a September 29, 2016, article entitled "Strangeways Brewing to Open Location in Fredericksburg" by Cathy Jett in the *Fredericksburg Free Lance-Star* (http://www.fredericksburg.com/business /local_business/strangeways-brewing-to-open-location-in -fredericksburg/article_1e71c8df-16e1-5598-8dfa-0d63f368b60f .html).

172 Most details about Steam Bell come from my on-site interview with Brad and his family in June 2016. I also attended the bill signing in May 2017. Some information about Canon and Draw, including the quote from Brittany Cooper, came from a May 4, 2017, article entitled "Double Vision: Chesterfield Craft Brewery to Open Second Spot in City" by Alix Bryan for WTVR-TV (http://wtvr.com /2017/05/04/canon-and-draw-opening-near-vcu-1/).

174 Information comes from numerous interviews and conversations with Trae Cairns over the years as well as visits to Midnight Brewery.

176 Conversations and interviews with the Pumphreys, particularly for my *Richmond Beer* book, as well as visits over the years provided the bulk of information for the Lickinghole Creek profile. Details about the brewery's expansion come from a media release and from articles entitled "Lickinghole Creek Craft Brewery Planning a $14 Million Expansion in Goochland and Lynchburg" (http://www .richmond.com/business/local/lickinghole-creek-craft-brewery -planning-a-million-expansion-in-goochland/article_f7896ccb -a8a4-5e18-ba45-673e3e5d5460.html) on May 26, 2017, and "Lick- inghole Creek Craft Brewery Opens Shockoe Bottom Location;

Lynchburg Brewery on Hold," (http://www.richmond.com
/business/local/lickinghole-creek-craft-brewery-opens-shockoe
-bottom-location-lynchburg-brewery/article_bc01ff47-20b2-51e0
-ad5b-4a1f1bfc79f3.html) on August 29, 2017, both by John Reid
Blackwell in the *Richmond Times-Dispatch*.

9. Diverse Pockets Mark Tidewater

180 Visits to Alewerks and conversations/interviews with Frank
Clark and Geoff Logan provide details for this profile. Additional
information comes from the brewery's website; a June 8, 2017,
article entitled "Alewerks Brewing to Open Williamsburg Premium
Outlets Store" by Tara Bozick in the *Daily Press* (http://www
.dailypress.com/business/tidewater/dp-alewerks-brewing-to-open
-williamsburg-premium-outlets-store-20170608-story.html); a
December 4, 2016, article entitled "Once a Guitarist in Nashville,
Geoff Logan Hits High Note as Local Brewmaster" by Brandy
Centolanza in *Williamsburg Yorktown Daily* (http://wydaily.com
/2016/12/04/once-a-guitarist-in-nashville-geoff-logan-hits-high
-note-as-local-brewmaster/); and an April 10, 2014, article entitled
"Alewerks Brewing Company Claims Three Titles at U.S. Beer Tasting Championships" by Brittany Voll, also in *Williamsburg Yorktown
Daily* (http://wydaily.com/2014/04/10/alewerks-brewing-company
-claims-three-titles-at-u-s-beer-tasting-championships/).

183 I've visited the Virginia Beer Company several times and had
numerous conversations with Robby Willey, Chris Smith, and
Jonathan Newman. I also used information from three articles in
Williamsburg Yorktown Daily: a November 11, 2014, story entitled
"New Craft Brewery Plans to Open in York County by Summer
2015" by Marie Albiges (http://wydaily.com/2014/11/11/new-craft
-brewery-plans-to-open-in-york-county-by-summer-2015/); a
July 28, 2015, article entitled "Local Craft Breweries Partner for
Specialty Beer" by Ian Brickey (http://wydaily.com/2015/07/28
/local-news-local-craft-breweries-partner-for-specialty-beer/); and
a February 3, 2016, piece entitled "Two Breweries in One: Virginia
Beer Co. Begins Brewing, Readies for Spring Opening" by Nicole
Trifone (http://wydaily.com/2016/02/03/local-news-neighbors
-two-breweries-in-one-virginia-beer-co-starts-first-brew-readies
-for-spring-opening/).

186 Visits to St. George's Hampton brewery, an interview with Bill
Spence, notes from Andy Rathmann, and the brewery's website
provided information for this profile. I also interviewed Rathmann
and Legend brewer John Wampler about Teach's Oyster Stout

when it was released. Additional details come from a January 16, 2014, article entitled "Family Business: St. George Brewing Makes It Work" by John-Henry Doucette in the *Virginian-Pilot* (https://pilotonline.com/life/flavor/alcohol/article_737d5eb5-6253-58e0-a60e-10fe356bb218.html) and a January 8, 2001, article entitled "In Spite of Fire, Brewery President Remains Positive" by Yoon K. Om in the *Daily Press* (http://articles.dailypress.com/2001-01-08/business/0101060078_1_brewing-beer-porter-ale).

189 The details about the Green Flash grand opening are from my visit that day. The quote about Virginia being in the "no" binder is from an October 14, 2014, *Virginian-Pilot* article entitled "Craft Brewing Locally, Statewide Shows Heady Growth" by Sarah Kleiner (https://pilotonline.com/business/article_ee5b27c7-088c-5cc2-bdb1-1fb87ed5de40.html). The quotes by Chris Ross come from an October 13, 2016, article entitled "Green Flash Opens in Virginia Beach" by Jeff Maisey in *Veer* magazine (http://veermag.com/2016/10/green-flash-opens-in-virginia-beach/).

190 A visit to Wasserhund in early September 2017 provided details for this profile. I also relied on information and quotes in two articles by Stacy Parker in the *Virginian-Pilot,* the first on August 8, 2015, entitled "Wasserhund Brewery Brings German Lagers to Virginia Beach" (https://pilotonline.com/business/consumer/article_d0c5ebbf-51cc-5360-9c8e-6ce3f008beaf.html), and another on July 22, 2016, "Wasserhund Brewing Co. in Virginia Beach Expands its Brewing Capacity" (https://pilotonline.com/business/consumer/article_3b5d97d6-3cd8-58d5-a0b5-b03057c8fb40.html).

192 Most of the information for the O'Connor profile comes from an in-depth interview with Kevin O'Connor on November 14, 2016, visits to the taproom, and the brewery's website. Additional details come from a May 16, 2016, article entitled "Norfolk's O'Connor Brewing Wins World Beer Cup Medal" on the *Beer Up* blog (http://www.beerup.beer/blog/norfolks-oconnor-brewing-wins-world-beer-cup-medal).

196 Several interviews and conversations with Porter Hardy IV over the years plus two visits to Smartmouth's taproom in Norfolk provided information for this profile. Additional details come from the brewery's website; a media release; a December 20, 2016, article entitled "Smartmouth Brewing Plans to Turn Old Post Office into New Brewery at Virginia Beach Oceanfront" by Robyn Sidersky and Mary Beth Gahan in the *Virginian-Pilot* (https://pilotonline.com/life/flavor/alcohol/article_00143dde-a933-5b51-b73c

-3ce79690ec6f.html); and a July 13, 2013, article entitled "Smart-mouth Set to Tickle Local Tastebuds" by Burl Rolett in *Richmond BizSense* (https://richmondbizsense.com/2013/07/11/smartmouth -set-to-tickle-local-tastebuds/).

198 My visit to Benchtop Brewing in September 2017 provided details for the taproom and tastings (I also referred to the brewery's web-site). Additional details come from a May 21, 2016, article entitled "Norfolk Craft Beer Scene Grows Stout," by Elisha Sauers in the *Virginian-Pilot* (https://pilotonline.com/inside-business/article _a96467e9-db2e-5168-b841-9a65c26044a2.html); a Decem-ber 11, 2016, article entitled "New Norfolk Brewer Uses Virginia Ocean Water in Resurrected Beer Style," also by Sauers (https:// pilotonline.com/life/flavor/alcohol/article_0dfd1a4a-eda9-55d5 -9f55-49349be07682.html); and a January 13, 2016, article en-titled "Chelsea Loves its Beer: Benchtop Brewing Company on the Way," by Mark Harris in *AltDaily.com* (http://altdaily.com/chelsea -loves-its-beer-Benchtop-brewing-company-on-the-way/).

10. Charlottesville Builds on Early Success

203 Numerous conversations, lengthy interviews with Taylor and Mandi Smack in 2015 and 2017, an interview with Mitch Hamil-ton, and repeat visits to South Street provide much of the infor-mation. Additional details come from the brewpub's website and media releases as well as a June 25, 2015, story entitled "Married with a Blue Mountain View: An Interview with Taylor and Mandi Smack" by Jeff Maisey in *Virginia Craft Beer* magazine (http:// virginiacraftbeer.com/tag/blue-mountain-brewery) and a July 2, 2014, story entitled "South Street Brewery Sold, Holds Last Night" by Ruth Martin on *Newsplex.com* (http://www.newsplex.com /home/headlines/South-Street-Brewery-Sold—265646611.html).

205 Information for this profile comes from numerous interviews and talks with Dave Warwick and others, beginning with interviews for my *Charlottesville Beer* book. Warwick's and George Kastendike's quotes are from a 2016 personal interview. Details on the IX Art Park location came through several visits and my attendance at the 2017 Virginia Craft Brewers Fest.

208 Conversations and interviews with Hunter Smith provide the bulk of information for the Champion profile. Additional details come from a June 12, 2017, article entitled "Champion Brewing Co. Con-siders Historic Church Along the Hague for Norfolk Microbrewery" by Elisha Sauers in the *Virginian-Pilot* (https://pilotonline.com/life /flavor/alcohol/article_02a857a7-7f16-5e4b-bece-5e8feadee5f3

.html) and a December 26, 2016, article entitled "As Champion Expands, Owner Relies on Team, Culture to Sustain Success" by Aaron Richardson in *Charlottesville Tomorrow* (http://www.cvilletomorrow.org/news/article/25890-as-champion-expands-owner-relies-on-team-culture-t/).

210 Numerous visits to Random Row and several interviews with Kevin McElroy, most recently in September 2017, provided the information for this profile. Details about the King Lumber Company come from a July 2, 2016, article entitled "Businesses Enjoying Renovated King Lumber Site" by Aaron Richardson for *Charlottesville Tomorrow* (http://www.cvilletomorrow.org/news/article/24336-businesses-enjoying-renovated-king-lumber-site/).

213 Most of the information comes from talking with all three Reason cofounders during the release at Beer Run on July 20, 2017, and from an interview at their facility the following Monday. I also referred to a June 14, 2017, article entitled "New Brewery Wants to Tap Into Under-Served Market" by Jackson Landers in *C-Ville Weekly* (www.c-ville.com/new-brewery-wants-tap-served-market/#.WXDsEsaZPq0) and a March 11, 2017, article entitled "First Brewery in Albemarle's Urban Ring Set to Open in June" by Allison Wrabel in the *Daily Progress* (http://www.dailyprogress.com/news/local/first-brewery-in-albemarle-s-urban-ring-set-to-open/article_610acdd0-06c0-11e7-9679-4f02640f3c60.html).

216 Interviews with several key Starr Hill employees and with Mark Thompson provide the bulk of information for the brewery profile. Additional details come from a January 31, 2017, article entitled "Starr Hill Brewery to Open a Roanoke Location" in the *Roanoke Times* (http://www.richmond.com/news/virginia/starr-hill-brewery-to-open-a-roanoke-location/article_50ba0166-8a9b-53bc-9305-4c5643c73a59.html) and a May 2, 2017, article entitled "Instead of a Brewhouse, Starr Hill Will Open a Beer Bar at Waterside" by Robyn Sidersky in the *Virginian-Pilot* (https://pilotonline.com/life/flavor/alcohol/article_74b3cb82-644a-5b55-847b-aae5754dd05a.html).

218 Numerous conversations, lengthy interviews with Taylor and Mandi Smack in 2015 and 2017, and repeat visits to the Afton and Arrington sites provide much of the information. Additional details come from the Blue Mountain website and the aforementioned June 25, 2015, article by Jeff Maisey in *Virginia Craft Beer* magazine (http://virginiacraftbeer.com/tag/blue-mountain-brewery).

222 Information for the Wild Wolf profile comes from numerous

interviews and conversations over the years, most recently in September 2017. Additional details come from the brewery's website.

225 I've had numerous interviews and conversations with Steve and Heidi Crandall and with Jason Oliver, particularly in connection with the *Charlottesville Beer* book, and I've visited both the Basecamp and the Outpost many times. Additional information comes from a September 7, 2017, article entitled "Anheuser-Busch InBev Slashes Workforce, Hundreds of High End Employees Impacted" by Justin Kendall (https://www.brewbound.com/news/anheuser-busch-inbev-slashes-workforce-hundreds-high-end-employees-impacted).

11. Roanoke Comes of Age

231 A visit on September 19, 2017, to the taproom in downtown Roanoke provided some details for the Deschutes profile. Additional information comes from the brewery's website; an April 17, 2017, article entitled "Deschutes Brewery to Open Tasting Room in Downtown Roanoke" by Tiffany Holland in the *Roanoke Times* (http://www.roanoke.com/business/news/roanoke/deschutes-brewery-to-open-tasting-room-in-downtown-roanoke/article_7ec4b6d3-c966-5c23-8a7c-e147de232138.html); a January 10, 2017, article entitled "Deschutes Founder Says Brewery Felt Sense of Belonging in Roanoke" by Duncan Adams in the *Roanoke Times* (http://www.roanoke.com/business/news/deschutes-founder-says-brewery-felt-sense-of-belonging-in-roanoke/article_845b9577-1bf3-517b-ab27-0ae6f4324ebf.html); a May 1, 2016, article entitled "Deschutes 2 Roanoke: Anatomy of a Deal," also by Duncan Adams in the *Roanoke Times* (http://www.roanoke.com/business/news/deschutes-roanoke-anatomy-of-a-deal/article_ce2ed89f-362e-59d4-a107-fa2c5f556a88.html); and an August 31, 2017, article entitled "Hundreds Attended Deschutes Roanoke Pub Opening" by Joseph Ditzler in the Bend, Oregon, *Bulletin* (http://www.bendbulletin.com/home/5557368-151/hundreds-attended-deschutes-roanoke-pub-opening).

233 A visit to Big Lick on January 6, 2017, provided some details for the brewery profile. Information also comes from the brewery's website; a September 20, 2016, article entitled "Big Lick Brewing to Open Larger Brewery in Downtown Roanoke" by Tiffany Holland in the *Roanoke Times* (http://www.roanoke.com/business/news/roanoke/big-lick-brewing-to-open-larger-brewery-in-downtown-roanoke/article_2044e1f0-a231-5109-9db1-4adcc1fef9a4.html); and a June 5, 2017, story titled "Big Lick Brewing Moves Equip-

ment to New Location" by Alison Wickline for WSLS-TV Channel 10 (https://www.wsls.com/news/virginia/roanoke/big-lick-brewing-moves-equipment-to-new-location).

234 A visit to Soaring Ridge in January 2017 provided details for the brewery profile. Additional information comes from the Soaring Ridge website, Tad Dickens of the *Roanoke Times*—one on February 4, 2014 entitled "Big Daddy's Brewing Co. Brewmaster to Reopen Downtown as Soaring Ridge Craft Brewers" (http://www.roanoke.com/business/news/roanoke/big-daddy-s-brewing-co-brewmaster-to-reopen-downtown-as/article_1d4f4f96-8e17-11e3-aa2b-001a4bcf6878.html) and the other on January 19, 2014 entitled "New Downtown Roanoke Brewery Taps Some Known Talent" (http://www.roanoke.com/life/food/new-downtown-roanoke-brewery-taps-some-known-talent/article_d24c73cc-7fb4-11e3-a80f-0019bb30f31a.html).

236 My visit to Ballast Point in Daleville provided some information for this profile. Additional details come from the brewery's website, Ballast Point representatives, and several news articles: a May 24, 2016, story entitled "San Diego's Ballast Point Marks Virginia's Fourth Craft Brewery Score" by Tara Nurin of *Forbes* magazine (https://www.forbes.com/sites/taranurin/2016/05/24/san-diegos-ballast-point-to-build-new-brewery-in-virginia/#6cd4815139b9); a May 24, 2016, article entitled "Ballast Point to Build $48 Million Brewery in Virginia" by Chris Furnari for the *Brewbound* news site (https://www.brewbound.com/news/ballast-point-build-48-million-brewery-virginia); a November 16, 2015, article entitled "Constellation Brands to Buy Craft Brewer Ballast Point" by John Kell for *Fortune* magazine (http://fortune.com/2015/11/16/constellation-brands-ballast-point/); and a June 29, 2017, article entitled "Constellation Brands Reports 8 Percent Increase in Beer Sales" by Justin Kendall for *Brewbound* (https://www.brewbound.com/news/constellation-brands-reports-8-percent-increase-beer-sales).

239 Interviews with Keno Snyder and visits to Parkway provided details for the brewery profile. Additional information comes from a July 7, 2014, article entitled "CornerShot: Salem Brewery Celebrates Beth Macy's Book with Factory Girl Beer" by Ralph Berrier Jr. in the *Roanoke Times* (http://www.roanoke.com/life/cornershot/cornershot-salem-brewery-celebrates-beth-macy-s-book-with-factory/article_5a5e0ad2-9a4b-586c-88dc-a309fe328b97.html).

241 I've had several conversations with Wendy and Joe Hallock, who made time in their day to give me a tour of the brewery on my visit

in August 2017. Additional information comes from the brewery's website; a November 25, 2014, article entitled "Surviving the Chaos" by Jack Crowder in *22807* magazine (http://22807mag.com /2014/11/25/surviving-the-chaos/); a December 16, 2015, article entitled "Chaos Mountain Brewing Expanding in Franklin County" by Tiffany Holland in the *Roanoke Times* (http://www.roanoke .com/business/news/franklin_county/chaos-mountain-brewing -expanding-in-franklin-county/article_97295f8d-619e-5a46 -b51b-073f90267beb.html); and a September 18, 2014, article entitled "Success Shines on Virginia's Chaos Mountain Brewing" by Karl H. Kazaks in *Wine and Craft Beverage* magazine (http:// wineandcraftbeveragenews.com/success-shines-on-virginias-chaos -mountain-brewing/).

243 An interview with then-brewer Alex Werny during my visit in December 2016 and an interview with Chris Burcher in September 2017 provided information for the Wolf Hills profile. Additional details come from a June 8, 2010, "Brewer Profiles" feature on the Brewers Association website (https://www.brewersassociation.org /profile/chris-burcher/) and two Q&A interviews in 2010 on the *Lug Wrench Brewing* website (http://www.lugwrenchbrewing.com /2010/07/nanobrewery-interviews-wolf-hills.html).

246 Information and quotes concerning Bristol Station Brews & Tap-room come from a visit to the site in December 2016. Details about Studio Brew come from a visit, also in December 2016, and from a July 22, 2014, article entitled "Studio Brew Expands into Bristol, VA" by Erich Allen on *CraftBeer.com*. (https://www.craftbeer.com /news/brewery-news/studio-brew-expands-bristol-va). Menu notes come from the brewpub's online menu in June 2017.

247 Numerous conversations with James Frazer and Dave McCor-mack, repeated visits to the taproom, and an intimate knowledge of the community inform the Beale's Beer profile. Additional information comes from a June 17, 2017, article entitled "Large Brewery, Restaurant to Open in Bedford" by Tiffany Holland in the *Roanoke Times* (http://www.roanoke.com/business/large-brewery -restaurant-to-open-in-bedford/article_22e2252f-7a3e-5cbb-b289 -678f763e885f.html); a June 14, 2017, article entitled "Beale's Brewery Opening Soon in Bedford" by Irisha Jones for WSLS-TV Channel 10 (https://www.wsls.com/news/virginia/bedford/beales -brewery-opening-soon-in-bedford); and a June 12, 2017, article entitled "Town of Bedford's First Brewery Opens June 24th" by Megan Irvin for *Craftbeer.com* (https://www.craftbeer.com/news /brewery-news/beales-open-bedford).

12. A Corridor of Breweries in the Valley

251 A visit to the taproom in July 2017, an interview with Nathan Bailey, and the brewery's website provided much of the information for the Great Valley Farm Brewery profile. Additional details come from an August 9, 2016, staff report entitled "New Brewery to Open in Natural Bridge" on the WDBJ-TV website (http://www.wdbj7.com/content/news/New-brewery-to-open-in-Natural-Bridge-389685222.html); an August 14, 2016, article titled "Business Intel: New Brewery Headed to Natural Bridge" by Tiffany Holland in the *Roanoke Times* (http://www.roanoke.com/business/business-intel-new-brewery-headed-to-natural-bridge/article_9cac9a01-9bea-5754-97fb-dae3a48159e7.html); and an August 10, 2016, article entitled "New Brewery to be Added Along Valley Trail" by Laura Peters in Staunton's *News Leader* (http://www.newsleader.com/story/news/local/2016/08/10/new-brewery-added-along-valley-trail/88509268/).

253 Information about Basic City comes from several interviews with the Lanman brothers and Jacque Landry, plus attending the brewery's debut in October 2016. Quotes from opening day attendees were taken from a YouTube video posted by Anubis ElBey of Kruel World Entertainment (www.youtube.com/watch?v=5zGJQvSKljk). The $600,000 figure for the government grant was taken from a March 11, 2015, article entitled "Brothers Hope to Brew Craft Beer at Metalcrafters Site" by Laura Peters in Waynesboro's *The News Leader* (http://www.newsleader.com/story/news/local/2015/03/11/metalcrafters-building-gets-government-funding-for-renovations/70145276/).

256 Details for the Seven Arrows profile come from interviews with and information provided by Aaron and Melissa Allen, visits to the taproom, and the brewery's website. Additional information comes from a March 1, 2017, article entitled "Kitchen Latest Thing Brewing at Seven Arrows" by Michelle L. Mitchell in the *News Virginian* (http://www.dailyprogress.com/newsvirginian/news/local/kitchen-latest-thing-brewing-at-seven-arrows/article_6b7dc036-fede-11e6-8ef6-53f50dcfa322.html).

259 Details about Redbeard come from several visits to the taproom, information provided by Jonathan Wright, and the brewery's website. I've also visited Shenandoah Valley Brewing several times, including the new location, and interviewed Mary Chapple. Some details about its new location come from a February 8, 2017, article entitled "Staunton Brewery Expands; Doughnut Shop Coming"

by Laura Peters in the *News Leader* (http://www.newsleader
.com/story/news/local/2017/02/08/staunton-brewery-expands
-doughnut-shop-coming/97634814/).

261 Details of the Pale Fire profile come from personal interviews over
the years, including most recently an interview with Tim Brady in
June 2017. Some of the tasting notes come from Pale Fire's website. Other details come from an April 3, 2014, article entitled "Pale
Fire Brewing Company Coming Soon to an Ice House Near You" on
the *Old South High* website (http://www.oldsouthhigh.com/2014
/04/03/pale-fire-brewing-company-coming-soon-to-an-ice-house
-near-you/) and a November 29, 2016, article entitled "A Calling
to Brew" by Nolan Stout in the *Shenandoah Valley Business Journal*
(https://issuu.com/dailynews-record/docs/shenandoah_valley
_business_journal_5185fce01e2607/6).

263 Several interviews and conversations with Adam Shifflett plus
several visits to the Brothers Harrisonburg taproom (including
for a beer dinner—see chapter 4) provide details for this profile.
In addition, information comes from the brewery's website and
the 2015 post on Reddit.com (https://www.reddit.com/r/beer
/comments/31qvz6/three_brothers_brewing_in_va_changes
_name_to). Roger Protz's comment is from a March 27, 2014,
article in *All About Beer* magazine (http://allaboutbeer.com/review
/resolute/).

266 Some of this information comes from interviewing Billie Clifton
and from a visit to Backroom Brewery in May 2017. Additional
information and quotes come from Michael Moeller's "Building
Breweries" podcast program, June 9, 2016, (https://soundcloud
.com/building-breweries/backroom-brewery-three-floyds) and a
July 25, 2017, interview by Janet Michael on WZRV "The River,"
95.3 (http://theriver953.com/podcast/backroom-brewery/).

268 Visits to all three breweries, conversations with the brewers, and
material on their websites provided information for this profile.
Additional details, including Caleb Ritenour's quote, come from a
June 2, 2017, article entitled "Local Craft Breweries Enjoy Increasing Numbers" by Tom Crosby in *The Northern Virginia Daily* (http://
www.nvdaily.com/life/lifestyle/2017/06/hold-local-craft-breweries
-enjoy-increasing-numbers/).

13. Looking Around, Looking Ahead

271 Statistics come from the Brewers Association website (https://
www.brewersassociation.org/statistics/by-state/) and notes taken
at the Craft Brewers conferences I have attended. Quotes from

Dave Gott and Bill Butcher come directly from email exchanges. Sharon Bulova's quote comes from an October 21, 2016, article entitled "This Wealthy County Is Hoping Beer Can Help Heal its Budget Hangover" by Antonio Olivo in the *Washington Post* (https://www.washingtonpost.com/local/virginia-politics/this -wealthy-county-is-hoping-beer-can-help-heal-its-budget-hangover /2016/10/18/1999dc30-8f28-11e6-a6a3-d50061aa9fae_story.html ?utm_term=.676cd1bea9c7).

Bibliography

Note: This book makes use of numerous magazine, newspaper, and online articles written by the author, including those published by the *Richmond Times-Dispatch*, *Richmond BizSense*, *Virginia Business* magazine, *Virginia Craft Beer* magazine, and *Virginia Golfer* magazine. Additional article citations can be found in the endnotes.

Books

Acitelli, Tom. *The Audacity of Hops: The History of America's Craft Beer Revolution*. Chicago: Review Press, 2013.

Alexander, James. *Early Charlottesville: Recollections of James Alexander, 1828–1874*. Reprinted from the Jeffersonian Republican by the Albemarle County Historical Society. Charlottesville, VA: The Michie Company, Printers, 1942.

Baron, Stanley. *Brewed in America: A History of Beer and Ale in the United States*. Boston, MA: Little, Brown and Company, 1962.

Birch, Tanya. *Beer Lover's Virginia: Best Breweries, Brewpubs & Beer Bars*. Guilford, CT: Globe Pequot, 2015.

Blanton, Wyndham Bolling. *Medicine in Virginia in the Seventeenth Century*. New York: Arno Press, 1972.

Bruce, Philip Alexander. *Economic History of Virginia in the Seventeenth Century: An Inquiry into the Material Condition of the People, Based upon Original and Contemporaneous Records*. New York: McMillan Company, 1935.

Child, Samuel. *Every Man His Own Brewer: Or, a Compendium of the English Brewery*. London, 1798. Reprint edition. Arlington, TX: Colonial Printer & Bookbindery, 2015.

Combrune, Michael. *The Theory and Practice of Brewing*. 1762. London: Vernor and Hood, 1804.

Craughwell, Thomas J. *Thomas Jefferson's Crème Brûlée: How a Founding Father and His Slave James Hemings Introduced French Cuisine to America*. Philadelphia, PA: Quirk Books, 2012.

Dabney, Virginius. *Richmond: The Story of a City*. Garden City, NY: Doubleday & Company, 1976.

Dornbusch, Horst D. *Prost! The Story of German Beer*. Boulder, CO: Brewers Publications, 1997.

Ellis, William. *The London and Country Brewer.* London: J & J Fox, 1735.

Gordon-Reed, Annette. *The Hemingses of Monticello: An American Family.* New York: W. W. Norton & Company, 2008.

Green, Carol C. *Chimborazo: The Confederacy's Largest Hospital.* Knoxville, TN: University of Tennessee Press, 2004.

Hatch, Peter J. *A Rich Spot of Earth: Thomas Jefferson's Revolutionary Garden at Monticello.* New Haven, CT: Yale University Press, 2012.

Hieronymus, Stan. *Brewing Local: American-Grown Beer.* Boulder, CO: Brewers Publications, 2016.

———. *For the Love of Hops: The Practical Guide to Aroma, Bitterness, and the Culture of Hops.* Boulder, CO: Brewers Publications, 2012.

Jackson, Michael. *Ultimate Beer.* London: DK Publishing, Inc., 1998.

———. *The World Guide to Beer.* Upper Saddle River, NJ: Prentice-Hall, Inc., 1977.

Little, John P. *History of Richmond.* Petersburg, VA: Dietz Press, 1933.

Meacham, Sarah Hand. *Every Home a Distillery: Alcohol, Gender, and Technology in the Colonial Chesapeake.* Baltimore, MD: Johns Hopkins University Press, 2009.

Mehrlander, Andrea. *The Germans of Charleston, Richmond, and New Orleans during the Civil War Period, 1850–1870.* Berlin: De Gruyter, 2011.

Moon, Mark A. *Yuengling: A History of America's Oldest Brewery.* Jefferson, NC: McFarland & Company, 1958.

Mordecai, Samuel. *Virginia, Especially Richmond, in By-Gone Days.* Richmond, VA: West & Johnson, 1860.

Morris, Danny. *Richmond Beers: A Directory of the Breweries and Bottlers of Richmond, Virginia.* Richmond, VA: Book Printers, 1990. Second edition, with Jeff Johnson. Hong Kong: Colorprint International Ltd., 2000.

Ogle, Maureen. *Ambitious Brew: The Story of American Beer.* New York: Harcourt, Inc., 2006.

Oliver, Garrett. *The Brewmaster's Table: Discovering the Real Pleasures of Real Beer with Real Food.* New York: HarperCollins, 2003.

———, ed., *The Oxford Companion to Beer.* Oxford: Oxford University Press, 2012.

Peck, Garrett. *Capital Beer: A Heady History of Brewing in Washington, D.C.* Charleston, SC: History Press, 2014.

Schuricht, Herrmann. *The History of the German Element in Virginia.* Baltimore, MD: Genealogical Publishing Company, 1977.

Smith, Gregg. *Beer in America: The Early Years (1587–1840).* Boulder, CO: Siris Books, 1998.

Stanton, Lucia. *Free Some Day: The African-American Families of Monticello.* Charlottesville, VA: The Thomas Jefferson Foundation Inc., 2000.

———. *"Those Who Labor for My Happiness": Slavery at Thomas Jefferson's Monticello.* Charlottesville, VA: University of Virginia Press in association with the Thomas Jefferson Foundation, 2012.

Stanton, Lucia, and James Bear, ed. *Jefferson's Memorandum Books: Accounts, with Legal Records and Miscellany, 1767–1826.* Princeton, NJ: Princeton University Press, 1997.

Steele, Mitch. *IPA: Brewing Techniques, Recipes, and the Evolution of India Pale Ale.* Boulder, CO: Brewers Publications, 2012.

Ward, Harry M., and Harold E. Greer Jr. *Richmond During the Revolution, 1775–83.* Charlottesville: University Press of Virginia, 1978.

Watkins, Malcolm C. *The Cultural History of Marlborough, Virginia.* Washington, D.C.: Smithsonian Institution Press, 1968.

Wust, Klaus. *The Virginia Germans.* Charlottesville: University Press of Virginia, 1969.

Articles

Benbow, Mark. "The Old Dominion Goes Dry: Prohibition in Virginia." *Brewery History: The Journal of the Brewery History Society Online* 138. http://www.breweryhistory.com/journal/archive/138/index.html.

Charlottesville Area Real Estate Weekly. "Business is Brewing." November 27–December 3, 1995.

Crozet Gazette. "Blue Mountain Brewery Launches Big Expansion." June 2, 2011.

———. "Re-beer-th: South Street Joins the Big Leagues with Striking Renovation, New Beer List." November 19, 2014.

———. "Starr Gazing: Longest Tenured Local Brewery Makes Big Change at the Top." March 5, 2015.

Daily Progress [Charlottesville]. "Albemarle Board OKs Much Smaller Growth Area Expansion." October 2015.

———. "Better Beer: Microbrewery Strives for Quality." June 5, 1988.

———. "Big Victory Celebrated." November 1, 1916.

———. "Virginia Dry Midnight Tonight." October 31, 1916.

Library of Virginia. "Out of the Box," *How Dry I Am—The Virginia Prohibition Commission Records.* http://ead.lib.virginia.edu/vivaxtf/view?docId=lva/vi01055.xml.

Mark, Joshua J. "Beer in the Ancient World." *Ancient History Encyclopedia.* West Sussex, UK, March 2, 2011. www.ancient.eu/article/223.

Mariners' Museum. "Colonial Period: Gabriel Archer." *Chesapeake Bay: Our History and Our Future.* 2002. www.marinersmuseum.org/sites/micro/cbhf/colonial/col008.html.

Mid-Atlantic Brewing News. "What's Brewing in Virginia." June/July 2015.

NBC29 [Charlottesville]. "Blue Mountain Brewery Purchases South Street Brewery." July 3, 2014.

Newsplex.com [Charlottesville]. "South Street Brewery Sold, Holds Last Night." July 3, 2014.

Peck, Garrett. "Alexander Wales: Alexandria's First Brewer." *The Alexandria Chronicle* (published by the Alexandria Historical Society), Alexandria, VA. Spring 2015.

Williams, Mike. "Robert Portner and Alexandria's Pre-Prohibition Brewing History." *WETA's Local History Blog, "Boundary Stones."* January 27, 2016. https://blogs.weta.org/boundarystones/2016/01/27/robert-portner-and-alexandrias-pre-prohibition-brewing-history.

Other Online Sources

Dennée, Timothy J. *Robert Portner and His Brewing Company.* https://www.alexandriava.gov/uploadedFiles/historic/info/archaeology/SiteReportDenneePortnerBreweryHistoryAX196.pdf.

Ingram, David Lee. "History of the Fairfax Line." www.surveyhistory.org/the_fairfax_line1.htm.

Massachusetts Historical Society's Thomas Jefferson Papers. "Farm Book, [manuscript], 1774–1824." http://www.masshist.org/thomasjeffersonpapers/farm/.

——. "Garden Book, [manuscript], 1766–1824." http://www.masshist.org/thomasjeffersonpapers/garden/.

RustyCans.com. "Krueger Ale." www.rustycans.com/COM/month0406.html.

Thomas Jefferson Papers at the Library of Congress. "Volume 1: Household Accounts and Notes of Virginia Court Legal Cases." https://www.loc.gov/item/mtjbib026553/.

Thomas Jefferson's Monticello. "African-American Gardens at Monticello." https://www.monticello.org/site/house-and-gardens/african-american-gardens-monticello.

——. "Beer." https://www.monticello.org/site/research-and-collections/beer.

——. "Humulus lupulus—Hops." https://www.monticello.org/site/plantation-and-slavery/humulus-lupulus-hops.

——. "Jefferson Quotes and Family Letters." http://tjrs.monticello.org.

———. "Joseph Miller." https://www.monticello.org/site/research-and
-collections/joseph-miller.

Waynesboro Historical Commission. "The Founding of Basic City, Virginia to its merger with Waynesboro, Virginia 1890–1923." http://
www.visitwaynesboro.net/DocumentCenter/View/79.

Zacek, N. *A briefe and true report of the new found land of Virginia*
(1588). (2012, January 18). In *Encyclopedia Virginia.* http://www
.EncyclopediaVirginia.org/A_briefe_and_true_report_of_the_new
_found_land_of_Virginia_by_Thomas_Hariot_1588.

Index

Amelia County, 43

American Brewers Guild, 182

American Can Company, 28

American Homebrewers Association, 62, 66, 168

Ammo Brewing (Petersburg), 295

Anchor Brewing (San Francisco, California), 24, 154, 174

Andatu (Sumatran rhino), 124

Anheuser-Busch, 22, 23, 30, 32, 84, 154, 157; Bevo, 26; Bud Light, 76; Williamsburg facility, 30, 299

Anheuser-Busch InBev (Leuven, Belgium), 84, 218, 225, 274; High End division, 226

Answer Brewpub, The (Richmond), 65, 151, 158–60, 196, 295; Andall, 159; Citra Secret double IPA, 160; Guava Mangito Gose, 159; Larceny IPA, 159, 160

Antioch Brewing Company (Palmyra), 302

Anti-Saloon League, 25

Apocalypse Ale Works (Forest), 82, 302; Lustful Maiden, 82

Aquavitae (brandy), 8

Archer, Gabriel, 315

Ardent Craft Ales (Richmond), 54, 76, 150, 160–63, *161*, 167, 168, 295; Berliner Weisse, 78; Defenestrator Doppelbock, 70; gluten-free beers, 163; historic persimmon beer, 76, 162, 321; Honey Ginger Ale, 162; IPA series, 162; Robust Porter, 162; Roggenbier, 162; rye kölsch, 163; Saison, 162; Virginia Common, 162

Arnold, Benedict, 14, 15

Ashburn, 107, *125*, 125

Ashby, Charlie, 144

Asheville (North Carolina), ix, 232

Ashwell, Quinlan, 149

Aslin Beer Company (Herndon), 287, *CG7*

Babylonians, and brewing, 6

Back Bay Brewing Company (Virginia Beach), 195, 299

Backroom Brewery (Middletown), 38, *39*, 82, 251, 266–68, 308; Belgian singel, 267; The Ferminator, 267;

Hibiscus Saison, 267; Lemon Basil Wheat Beer, 267, 268; Peppermint Oatmeal Stout, 267; Rosemary Orange Amber Ale, 267

BadWolf Brewing Company (Manassas), 101–3, *102*, 287; Kao Circle location, 101. Beers: Aces High American Pale Ale, 103; Blackreach Stout, 81; Cygnus X1, 103; Jalapeno IPA, 103; Jesse's Girl American Amber Ale, 103; Justin's Pilsner, 70; Kaiju IPA, 103; Mother Pucker Witbier, 103; Virginia Hooligan IPA, 103; You Will Not Like This IPA, 101

Bailey, Irma, 251–52

Bailey, Jerry, 32, 123

Bailey, Nathan, 251–52

Bailey, William, 12, 13

Baker, Dan, 134

Baki, Katie, 115–16

Baki, Tolga, 115–16

Bald Top Brewing Company (Madison), 302

Ballad Brewing (Danville), 305

Ballast Point Brewing Company (Daleville location), 34, 45, 54, 87, 189, 230, 232, 236–39, *238*, 305; CA2VA IPA, 237; Grapefruit Sculpin, 237; Habanero Sculpin, 237; Padre Dam Pilsner, 54; Pineapple Sculpin, 237; Sculpin IPA, 236, 237, 239

Barchet, Ron, 32

Bardo Rodeo brewpub, 33, 123

barley, 6, 9, 17, 20, 36, 44–45, 46–47, 55, 72, 109, 163, 200, 212, 243, 259; characteristics of, 45, 46–47; as grist, 57; historic cultivation of, 9, 14, 15, 44; malting process, 46, 47, *47*, 57, 149; modern cultivation in Virginia, 37, 44, 45, 54. Varieties: Maris Otter, 120, 262; six-row, 38, 45, 73, 149; Thoroughbred, 45, 178; two-row, 46, 73, 120, 146, 149, 189

barleywine, 71, 112, 114, 168, 217, 241

Barlow, Jamey, 64

Barnhouse Brewery (Leesburg), 289

barrel aging, 51, 96, 103, 118, 119, 129, 162, 165, 179, 182, 195, 198,

218, *219*, 221, 222, 257; vanillin, 265

Barrel Chest Wine and Beer (Roanoke), 305

Barrel Oak Farm Taphouse (Delaplane), 268, 269–70, 292, *CG1;* Belgian-style golden strong ale, 270; BOFT IPA, 268, 270; dubbel, 270; milk stout, 270

Basic City Beer Company (Waynesboro), ix, 203, 251, 253–56, *254,* 308; Advance DIPA, 254, 255; Brazen Pan Bock, 70; Foggy Lager, 255; N&W Porter, 67; Oopsproch Lager, 254, 255; Sixth Lord IPA, 255; Waynesbeeroh, 255

Basic City Mining, Manufacturing and Land Company, 253

Battlefield Brewing Company (Fredericksburg), 292

B Chord Brewing Company (Round Hill), 107, 110–12, 115, 273, 289, *CG2;* Helles lager, 112; IPA, 111; scotch ale, 112; stout, 111

Beale, Thomas Jefferson, 250

Beale's Beer (Bedford), 230, 247–50, *249,* 305; Beale's Gold, 248, 250; Beale's Red, 249; German-style brown lager, 249; oatmeal stout, 249

Bearded Bird Brewing Company (Norfolk), 299

Bearer Farms (Oilville), 54

Beaufont Company, 27

Bedford, 203, 230, 247, 248, 249, *249,* 250

Bedlam Brewing (Staunton), ix, x, 251, 261, 309; Farmhouse Ale, x

beer: ale versus beer, 10; ale versus lager, 17, 57, 60; bad, 11, 13; complexity of, 56, 60, 67, 72–73; first canned, 157; four ingredients of traditional, 54, 56, 63 (*see also* barley; hops; water; yeast); gluten-free/reduced, 129, 163, 164; industry, 5, 56, 63, 145, 180, 190, 239, 271–75; as nutritious beverage, 5, 7, 25, 26; pairing with cheese, 67, 69, 70–71; pairing with food in general, 5, 67–75, 72, *75;* refrigeration of, 17, 21, 23, 24;

styles in Virginia, 76–86; tasting, 56, 58–59. *See also specific styles of beer by name*

BeerAdvocate magazine, 156, 160, 181

Beer and Ale Research Foundation, The, 64

Beer Hound Brewery (Culpeper), 131, 138–41, *140,* 292; Kujo Imperial IPA, 139, 140; Oktoberfest, 138, 139; Olde Yella Pale Wheat Ale, 140; Skrappy Dew, 139; Teddy Cream Ale, 139, 140; Teufelhunde Belgian tripel, 139

Beeristoric Tour, 150

Beer Judge Certification Program, 59, 73, 105

Belgian-style dubbel: style, 82; varieties, 71, 82, 93, 210, 264, 270

Belgian-style tripel, 117, 140; style, 82; varieties, 82, 115, 118, 132, 139, 140, 208, 253

Belgium, x, 37, 51, 77, 82, 83, 242, 252, 256

Bell, Cameron, 245

Belle Grove, 143

Bell's Brewery (Comstock, Michigan), 32; Bell's Two Hearted Ale, 224

Belly Love Brewing Company (Purcellville), 82, 107, 115–17, 289; Duchess Belgian tripel, 115; Duke Belgian Tripel, 82; Eye of Jupiter oatmeal stout, 115; 50 Shades of Gold Belgian golden strong ale, 115, 116; Flying Unicorn Crotch Kick IPA, 115; Narcissist lager, 115

Beltway Beer Trail, 88

Beltway Brewing Company (Sterling), 88, 108, 111, 290

Benchtop Brewing (Norfolk), 180, 198–201, 299, *CG8;* Chelsea-Tidewater Grisette, 201; Hazing Face Pale Ale, 200; Juicy Thoughts DIPA, 199; Mermaid's Scorn Gose, 200; Proven Theory IPA, 199, 200, 201; Quick Pickle Carrot Cucumber Gose, 199; Trial of Dmitri, 199

Bergantim, Jay, 270

Berliner weisse: style, 78; varieties, 78, 118, 182, 209, 217, 269, 271

Betz, John Frederick, 20

foot Blonde Ale, 246–47; Bearded Goat Bock, 246; BFW, 246; Bristol Helle Raiser, 246; Double Loco Imperial IPA, 246; Vanilla Porter, 246

Britain, 30, 37

Broaddus, Ike, 143–45

Broaddus, Julie, 143–45

Brothers Craft Brewing (Harrisonburg), 54, 69, 72, 251, 263–66, 309; The Admiral on Pineapple IPA, 264; Belgian dubbel, 264; Brown Out brown ale, 69; Five Pound Fall Ale, 54; Great Outdoors Pale Ale, 264; Hardy Brothers, 264; Hoptimization IPA, 264; Lil' Hellion Helles Lager, 70, 264; Long Distance Relationship, 264; Resolute Russian imperial stout, 70, 264, 265; Rye Hard, 264; Scarlet Empire imperial red ale, 69

brown ale, 69, 70, 73, 182; style, 80; varieties, 32, 33, 37, 69, 70, 71, 73, 80, 110, 120, 124, 125, 151, 169, 175, 181, 182, 188, 207, 208, 233, 236, 248, 260

Buettner, Charlie, 100

Buggs Island Brewing Company (Clarksville), 305

Bui, An, 151, 158, 160

Bull & Bones Brewhaus & Grill (Blacksburg), 305

Bull Island Brewing Company (Hampton), 299

Bulova, Sharon, 273

Burcher, Chris, 245–46, 273

Burnett, Shannon, 119, 120

Burns, Chris, 107, 121, 122

Burns, Graham, 121

Burns, Kristen, 122

Burns, Mary Ann, 122

Burton, Neil, 169–72

Burton-on-Trent (England), 52, 73

Butcher, Bill, 88–90, 91, 273, 274

Caboose Brewing Company (Vienna), 287; Crossroads Vienna Lager, 80

Cahas Mountain, 241, 243

Cairns, Trae, 174–76

Camacho, Johnny, 231

Cannon, James, Jr., 25

Canon and Draw Brewing Company (Richmond), 173, 174, 295

Cape Charles Brewing Company (Cape Charles), 300

Capitol City Brewing Company, 32, 84, 85, 94, 95; kölsch, 84–85

Carney, Jennings, 146

Carney, Lain, 146

Carney, Van, 146–47

Carter, Jimmy, 30, 61

Carter, Landon, 39

Carter, Robert "King," 39

Casey, Dan, 234

Casselmonte Farm (Powhatan), 54

Castleburg Brewery and Taproom (Richmond), 295

Center of the Universe Brewing Company (Ashland), 65, 65, 184, 296

Central Virginia Distributing, 272

Century brewery, 27

Champion Brewing Company (Charlottesville), 83, 84, 203, 208–10, 303; Brasserie Saison, 83, 209, 303; Missile Factory, 209; Richmond location, 209, 296. Beers: Berliner Weisse, 209; Face Eater Gose, 209, 210; Missile IPA, 208, 210; Positive Jam, 210; Shower Beer, 70, 210; Stickin' in My IPA, 210

Chaos Mountain Brewing Company (Callaway), 230, 232, 241–43, 306; Agents of Chaos, 242, 243; Cocoborealis, 243; 4 Mad Chefs Belgian Quadrupel, 242; Shine Runner Pils, 241–42, 243; Squatch Ale, 242, 243; Theory of Chaos, 242

Chapple, Mary, 261

Chapple, Mike, 261

Charleston (South Carolina), 232

Charlottesville, ix, xiii, 10, 21, 30, 31, 33, 61, 64, 67, 83, 139, 155, 165, 202–18, 206, 211, 220, 221, 256, 268, 272, CG2; region, 202–29

Charlottesville Area Masters of Real Ale, 64

Chastain, John Wesley "Wes," 245

Chesapeake Bay Brewing Company, 30, 31, 62; Chesbay Amber beer, 31; Chesbay Superior Lager, 31

Mechanic IPA, 175; Rockville Red, 175; Vernal Elixir, 176; Virginia Midway, 176

Miller, Captain Joseph, 15, 316

MillerCoors Shenandoah Brewery (Elkton), *53*, 257, 309

Mink, Eric, xiii

Mobjack Bay Brewing Company, 33

Mohawk brewery, 27

molasses, 19; as brewing ingredient, 10, 11, 76, 138, 184, *184*

MoMac Brewing Company (Portsmouth), 300

Monticello, xiii, xiv, 15, 16, 127

Monticello Brewing Company (Charlottesville), 33, 203

Montross Brewery & Beer Garden (Montross), 293

Monyak, Ken, 246

Mordecai, Samuel, 18

Morris, Danny, 317

Morven, 143

Mosher, Randy, 59, 183

Mouer, Dan, 64

Mountain Brewing Company, 29

Mountain Valley Brewing (Axton), 306

Mount Vernon, 14, 39; brewing at, 10, 16; hops sold at, 16

mouthfeel, 56, 59, 71, 73, 81, 86, 117, 118, 134, 213, 239, 243, 253, 263

Moyer, Alan, 139

mulberries, as brewing ingredient, 10

Mullin, Rob, 32

Munich (Germany), 36, 52, 80, 156, 170, 191, 192, 217

Murtaugh, Patrick, 155, 156, 175

Mustang Sally Brewing Company (Chantilly), 32, 88, 103–6, 272, 288; amber lager, 104; Dortmunder Lager, 104, 105; East Coast IPA, 104; Irish red ale, 104; kölsch, 104; porter, 104

Nargi, Craig, *CG6*

Natale, Cody, 134, 136

National Homebrew Competition, 64

National Homebrewers Conference, 66

Native Americans, 7; and brewing, 7

Natural Bridge, 251, 252

Naughton, Derek, 207

Neikirk, Chris, 197

Nelson County, 33, 38, 44, 49, 54, 159, 202, 218, 221, 225, 227, 255, *CG5*

New Belgium Brewing Company (North Carolina location), ix

New District Brewing Company (Arlington), 288

Newman, Jonathan, 183, *184*, 185

Newman, Paige, xiv, *184*

New Market Hotel (Richmond), 18

New Mexico, 7

Newport, Christopher, 8, 163

New Realm Brewing (Virginia Beach location), 190

Ninkasi (Sumerian goddess), 6

Nobos Restaurant (Waynesboro), 256

Norfolk, 15, 26, 27, 33, 77, 80, 175, 178, 182, 193, 194, 195, 196, 198, 200, 209, 218, 265

North Carolina, ix, 7, 29, 116, 182, 187, 188, 193, 199, 217, 232, 239, 252, 253, 259, 275

North Carolina State University, 38

Northeastern University, 210

Northern Neck, 37, 44, 125

Northern Virginia, 38, 64, 88–106, 116, 119, 121, 128, 153, 170, 191, 207, 224; outer reaches of, 131–49

Notes on the State of Virginia (T. Jefferson), 39

"Nottoway Negroes," 16

Nucci, Matt, 221

Nürnberg (Germany), 36

Oak Hill, 143

O'Cain, Robbie, 216–17

Ocelot Brewing Company (Dulles), 71, 83, 107, 127–30, *128*, 274, 291; Baltic porter, 127; Break My Balls IPA, 129; Capsized, 129; From the Bottom, 129; From the Top, 129; The Gallows, 129; Hangman, 129; Hearts & Thoughts, 129; Honey Pie Farmhouse Ale, 83; Lemon Yellow Sun Imperial Hoppy Wheat Ale, 129; My Only Friend Russian Imperial Stout, 129; Sunnyside Dweller, 127, 130; Tangerine Trees IPA, 129; Time After Time IPA, 129

rye, 38, 178, 199; used in brewing, 36, 47, 83, 123, 162, 163, 183, 185, 201, 210, 260, 262, 263, 264

sack (wine), 8
Sage Hill Farms (Leesburg), 37
St. George Brewing Company (Hampton), 33, 180, *186*, 186–89, 275, 301; bock, 187; English IPA, 187; golden ale, 187; Imperial Amber Bock, 186, 188, 189; Imperial Stout, 186, 188; Märzen, 187; Nut Brown Ale, 73, 188; pilsner, 187; porter, 187; Summer Ale, 187, 188; Teach's Oyster Stout, 188; Vienna-style lager, 187; Winter Scotch Ale, 188
Saint X distribution company, 272
saison, 37, 68, 72, *72*, 83, 271; style, 77; varieties, x, 54, 69, 74, 77, 83, 88, 96, 99, 101, 114, 117, 118, 123, 129, 137, 149, 160, 162, 163, 172, 176, 183, 193, 196, 210, 212, 214, 232, 241, 252, 261, 262, 267, 269, 271
Salem, 78, 230, 240, *CG3*
sassafras, as brewing ingredient, 10
SAVOR, 74–75, *75*
Schneider Aventinus (wheat doppelbock), 170
Schoeb, Wes, 108
Scholz, Louis A., 23, 28
Schopp, John, 242
Schuetzen Park (Richmond), 20
Scottish whiskies, 45
Scott's Addition (Richmond), *48*, 69, 76, 150, 151, 160, 161, 253
Sebago Brewing Company (Portland, Maine), 214
Second Baptist Church (Richmond), 25
Second Virginia Charter of 1609, 8
Sedona Taphouse (Midlothian), 165
Senate Bill 604 (Virginia), 5, 34, 103, 155, 175
Senor Ramon Taqueria restaurant (Leesburg), 118
Sessoms, Will, Jr., 189
Seven Arrows Brewing Company (Waynesboro), 251, 255, 256–59, *258*, 310; Bear Mountain Barleywine, 71; black pilsner, 257; Equinox DIPA, 257; Falls Ridge Vienna Lager, 257; fruited lambics, 256; Hermenator Doppelbock, 80; Native Lambic, 70; Skyline Lager, 257, 259
Seven City Brewers, 64
1781 Brewing Company (Spotsylvania), 294
Shenandoah Brewing Company, 33
Shenandoah Valley, 17, 251–70
Shenandoah Valley Brewing Company (Staunton), 261, 310; First Brigade Red IPA, 261
Shenandoah Valley Homebrewers Guild, 64
Shifflett, Adam, 264, 265
Shifflett, Jason, 264
Shifflett, Tyler, 264
Shockoe Bottom (Richmond), 178
Shockoe Slip (Richmond), 32, 111, 152
Shooter's Hill Brewery, 17, 19
Shuter's Hill Brewery, 17
Siebel Institute of Technology (Chicago), 109, 156, 175, 217, 220–21, 224
Siegle, Laura, 43
Sierra Nevada Brewing Company (North Carolina location), ix, 51, 123, 154; Sierra Nevada Pale Ale, 100
Sitterding, Frederick, III, 29
Sitterding, Fritz, 26–27
6 Bears and a Goat Brewing Company (Fredericksburg), 294
Smack, Mandi, 202, 204, 220–22
Smack, Taylor, 38, 49, 202, *203*, 204, 218–22, *219*
small beer, 8, 10, 316
Smartmouth Brewing Company (Norfolk), 83, 180, 187, 196–98, *197*, 273, 301; Pilot House location, 198, 301. *Beers:* Alter Ego Saison, 196; Cargo Schwarzbier, 198; Cowcatcher Milk Stout, 198; Farmer's Tan Hoppy Saison, 83, 149; Golden Standard Golden Ale, 198; Notch 9 Double IPA, 71, 196, 198; Safety Dance Pilsner, 77, 180, 187, 196, 197
Smith, Captain John, 8, 150, 163
Smith, Chris, 183
Smith, Hunter, 84, 208–10

d Ridge Farm Brewery (Loving-
   ston), 38, 203, 304
Woodstock Brewhouse, 311
Woodville, 146
Worcester, Adam, 164, 165, *CG8*
World Beer Cup, 84, 117, 217, 221,
   228, 229, 237, 262
World Guide to Beer, The (Jackson), 30
wort, 48, 50, 51, 57, 60, 62, 65, *65*,
   73, 82
Wort Hog Brewing Company (Warren-
   ton), 295
Wright, Jonathan, 259, 260
Wust, Klaus, 25
Wyatt, Sir Francis, 8

Yakima Valley (Washington state), 128
Yancey, Charles, 316
yeast, 5, 6, 11, 17, 36, 37, 48, *50*, 56,
   57, 58, 60, 72, 77, 82, 123, 147,
   175, 214, 220, 241, 255, 259; ale
   versus lager, 17, 51, 60, 73, 129;
   characteristics of, 48, 50–51;
   converting fermentable sugars to
   alcohol and carbon dioxide, 50,

57, 60; scientific description of,
50, 51. *Varieties:* Belgian, 60, 99,
101, 117, 119, 140, 198, 163, 246,
253; *Brettanomyces*, 51, 114, 118,
124, 129, 147, 162, 171, 172, 183;
Saccharomyces cerevisiae, 51; *Saccharomyces pastorianus*, 51; saison,
73, 74, 83, 262, 263; West Coast
Chico, 51, 73, 222, 269; wild, xi,
16, 48, *48, 50*, 51, 60, 73, 82, 110,
114, 118, 123, 124, 125, 131, 162,
164, 195, 233, 256
York County, 181, 183
Young, Allen, 31
Young Veterans Brewery Company
   (Virginia Beach), 302
Yuengling, D. G., Jr., 20, 21; James
   River Steam Brewery, *21*

Zeisler, Joseph, 242
Zurschmeide, Bruce, 108, 109, *109*
Zurschmeide, Jannell, 108, 109, *109*
Zurschmeide, Nick, 108
Zymurgy magazine, 168, 224

OCT - - 2018